Short of War
Major USAF Contingency Operations
1947–1997

A. TIMOTHY WARNOCK, Editor
Air Force Historical Research Agency

Air Force History and Museums Program
in association with
Air University Press

2000

Disclaimer

Opinions, conclusions, and recommendations expressed or implied within are solely those of the authors and do not necessarily represent the views of the Air Force Historical Research Agency, the United States Air Force, the Department of Defense, or any other U.S. government agency. Cleared for public release: distribution unlimited.

Contents

	Page
FOREWORD	ix
PREFACE	xi
ACKNOWLEDGEMENTS	xv
INTRODUCTION: From Cold War to Global Engagement	xvii
Berlin Airlift: Operation VITTLES	1
Daniel L. Haulman	
Lebanon Crisis: Operation BLUE BAT	11
David A. Byrd	
Crisis in the Congo: Operation NEW TAPE	23
Daniel L. Haulman	
Cuban Missile Crisis	33
Edward T. Russell	
Indo-Chinese Conflict: Operation LONG SKIP	43
William J. Allen	
Rebellion in the Congo: Operation DRAGON ROUGE	53
Daniel L. Haulman	
Dominican Crisis: Operation POWER PACK	63
A. Timothy Warnock	
Military Airlift to Israel: Operation NICKEL GRASS	75
Edward T. Russell	
Vietnam Evacuation: Operation FREQUENT WIND	83
Daniel L. Haulman	
Cambodian Airlift and Evacuation: Operation EAGLE PULL	95
Daniel L. Haulman	
Crisis in Southeast Asia: Mayaguez Rescue	105
Daniel L. Haulman	
Crisis in Tropical Africa: Operations ZAIRE I and II	115
Daniel L. Haulman	
Crisis in Iran: Operation EAGLE CLAW	125
Edward T. Russell	

	Page
Crisis in Grenada: Operation URGENT FURY	135
Daniel L. Haulman	
Raid on Libya: Operation ELDORADO CANYON	145
Judy G. Endicott	
Persian Gulf Crisis: Operation EARNEST WILL	157
William J. Allen	
Intervention in Panama: Operation JUST CAUSE	167
William J. Allen	
Crisis in Iraq: Operation PROVIDE COMFORT	179
Daniel L. Haulman	
Crisis in Southern Iraq:	
Operation SOUTHERN WATCH	189
William J. Allen	
Crisis in Bosnia: Operation PROVIDE PROMISE	197
Frederick J. Shaw Jr.	
Crisis in Somalia: Operations PROVIDE RELIEF	
and RESTORE HOPE	209
Daniel L. Haulman	
Resolution of Bosnian Crisis:	
Operation DENY FLIGHT	219
Daniel L. Haulman	
Crisis in Haiti: Operation UPHOLD DEMOCRACY	229
William J. Allen	
GLOSSARY	237
BIBLIOGRAPHY	243
CONTRIBUTORS	249
INDEX	253

Maps

Germany during Berlin Airlift	
Inset: Berlin during Operation VITTLES	3
BLUE BAT Area of USAF Operations	12
Operation NEW TAPE Routes	
Inset: Democratic Republic of the Congo	26
Area of USAF Operations in Cuban Missile Crisis	35

CONTENTS

	Page
Area of USAF Operations for LONG SKIP	46
Democratic Republic of the Congo	54
Area of USAF Operations during Dominican Crisis	64
USAF Flight Route during Operation NICKEL GRASS	76
Southeast Asia during the Vietnam Evacuation Inset: Saigon during Operation FREQUENT WIND	84
Area of USAF Operations during Cambodian Airlift and Evacuation	97
Area of USAF Operations during Mayaguez Crisis	106
Area of USAF Operations during ZAIRE I and II	116
Iran and Persian Gulf during Hostage Rescue Attempt	130
Area of USAF Operations during URGENT FURY Inset: Areas of Operational Responsibilities on Grenada	137
USAF Strike Force Route for ELDORADO CANYON Inset: Operation ELDORADO CANYON Targets	147
Persian Gulf Region during Operation EARNEST WILL	158
Panama Canal Zone during Operation JUST CAUSE	169
No-Fly Zones in Iraq during Operation PROVIDE COMFORT	183
No-Fly Zones in Iraq during Operation SOUTHERN WATCH	190
Europe during Operation PROVIDE PROMISE Inset: Bosnia-Herzegovina	199
USAF Area of Operations during the Crisis in Somalia	211
USAF Area of Operations in DENY FLIGHT	221
Haiti, Site of Operation UPHOLD DEMOCRACY	231

Photographs

Maj. Gen. William H. Tunner	5
Moving Coal to a C–54	9
USAF Troop Carrier C–54	14
First RB–66	16
KB–50 Tanker Refueling F–100, F–101, and RB–66	18

	Page
C–130s at Wheelus AB	28
USAF Crew Members Dine on a Congo Airstrip	29
Ground-to-Ground Missile Base in Cuba	36
Missile Site in Cuba	40
Loading a C–124	48
C–124 in Flight	48
C–130 Lands at Paulis	59
Paratroopers Prepare to Board C–130	60
Tents at San Isidro AB	68
Members of 82d Airborne Division Return to Pope AFB	72
C–5 Leaves Lajes Field	77
C–5 at Lod Airport	79
USAF NCO Gives Food to Vietnamese Refugee Family	86
Operation BABYLIFT	87
Deplaning from a C–130 after Evacuation from Vietnam	89
Landing Zone "Hotel" in Phnom Penh	100
HH–53 Crews Prepare for EAGLE PULL	101
Marines Board a CH–53	107
Wreckage of U.S. Helicopters on Koh Tang	110
Moroccan Troops Prepare to Board a C–141	118
French Troops Observe a C–5	119
MC–130 Flying Low	128
MC–130 of the Type Used in the Rescue Attempt	131
C–130 Unloading at Point Salines	140
Army Rangers Board C–141	142
F–111F Bomber Based at Lakenheath	150
F–111F Takes on Fuel from a KC–135 Stratotanker	152
E–3 AWACS Provides Airborne Surveillance	163
KC-135 Refueling an F-16	164
U.S. Army Personnel Boarding C–5B	170
Peacekeepers Patrolling Perimeter of Howard AFB	173
Manuel Noriega in Custody of DEA Agents	176

CONTENTS

	Page
USAF Enlisted Men Prepare to Load a C–130	182
F–16 at Incirlik AB	187
F–16 Test Aircraft at Eglin AFB	192
437th Airlift Wing Globemaster	206
C–141 at Mogadishu	213
C–5 Unloads Vehicles in Somalia	215
NATO AWACS Aircraft over the Adriatic Sea	222
F–15 Refuels from a KC–135	223
C–130s Staging at MacDill AFB	233

Foreword

Since the fall of the Berlin Wall, a series of geographically localized crises caused by political, religious, or ethnic unrest; outright military aggression; and natural disasters has replaced the relative stability that characterized international relations for more than fifty years of the Cold War. For the United States Air Force (USAF), this has meant short-notice deployments, airlifts, and other operational missions conducted in reaction to local crises. Such missions—once of secondary importance to nuclear deterrence or preparations for theater war—have come to dominate Air Force operations. The result has been recognition that global aerospace power and mobility are central to effective American crisis intervention in the post-Cold War world. This recognition has led the U.S. Air Force to restructure itself as an Expeditionary Aerospace Force, exploiting diverse core competencies consisting of global air and space superiority, rapid global mobility, precision engagement, global attack, information superiority, and agile combat support. Via rapid-response air expeditionary forces, the U.S. Air Force can furnish global power and presence for humanitarian or combat purposes—"bombs or bread or both"—in hours to any spot on Earth. A traditional precept of USAF doctrine has been that the service must always be prepared to assess its roles and missions in light of new and ever-changing national policy and strategy. Recognizing that doctrine is largely a distillation of knowledge gained from historical experience, the Air Force Historical Research Agency has compiled this record of USAF contingency operations covering the last half-century.

This book is an effort to meet the needs of Air Force commanders and other decision makers for a useful reference work on contingencies. One of an ongoing series of reference works, it is organized in the style of the recently published *The United States Air Force and Humanitarian Airlift Operations, 1947–1994*. It adds to the history of the Air Force by providing statistics and narrative descriptions of the Air Force's most significant contingency operations over the last fifty years.

Decision makers, planners, logisticians, and educators may find in these pages examples of lessons learned or themes worthy of further analyses. Scholars, educators, journalists, and the general public may gain an understanding of how the Air Force meets its obligations in a rapidly changing world.

RICHARD P. HALLION
Air Force Historian

Preface

Air Force Basic Doctrine 1, September 1997, states, ". . . military operations other than war may deter war, resolve conflict, relieve suffering, promote peace, or support civil authorities."

Scope and Definition

Spanning the decades from the beginning of the Cold War to today's strategy of global engagement, the twenty-three operational summaries in this book illustrate each of the objectives for military operations other than war. The summaries deal with a particular type of military operation; that is, *contingency*, which is defined as an emergency caused by natural disasters, terrorists, subversives, or other unexpected events and involving military forces. A contingency requires plans, rapid response, and special procedures to ensure the safety and readiness of personnel, installations, and equipment. Such operations are as old as the U.S. Air Force, but professional interest in them has increased in direct proportion to their growing importance in the spectrum of post-Cold War operations. This book provides a reference resource that, hopefully, will also stimulate disciplined and analytical investigation of the subject.

The U.S. Air Force conducted each of these contingencies in a combat zone or area of serious civil disturbance. Armed raids, major evacuations, major rescue operations, movement of troops or equipment into foreign countries for peace operations or in support of war, or enforcement of no-fly zones are typical. In sum, the contingencies in this book represent the most significant Air Force flying campaigns undertaken in a hostile, potentially dangerous milieu short of war. The compilation is representative rather than comprehensive. Excluded are operations involving small numbers of aircraft and personnel, strictly humanitarian airlift operations, shows of force, peace operations not involving combat, and those contingencies in which the Air Force played a minor role. Most of the twenty-three entries deal with a single contingency, but several cover two, and occasionally even more, where the operations are closely related.

Arranged chronologically, each entry includes the dates—beginning with the first day of USAF involvement and ending with the last day of USAF operations. Also listed are the location or theater of operations and overseas air bases used. The list of USAF flying organizations involved includes from major command level, where relevant, down to the squadrons and flights, but the latter are recorded only if the parent wings did not physically participate. Also listed are the types of USAF aircraft used; in the narrative, the writer may also identify aircraft of other services and nations. A map of the area of operations shows geographical and political features affecting events. A brief narrative states the principal purposes of the campaigns, a summary of activities, and lessons learned.

Political/Military Environment

Until the collapse of the Soviet Union, most contingencies were either directly or indirectly associated with the Cold War. At least seven Cold War operations effectively countered Communist provocation. Breaking the Berlin Blockade by airlift marked the first Western victory over post-World War II Soviet expansionism. Thirteen years later, the Cuban Missile Crisis ended in a humiliating defeat for the Soviet Union with the forced withdrawal of its nuclear missiles from their bases in Cuba. Several contingencies in Africa, such as Operation NEW TAPE and Operations ZAIRE I and ZAIRE II served to prevent the expansion of Soviet and Cuban influence across the emerging nations of the continent. U.S. intervention in the Dominican Republic, Haiti, and Grenada not only countered Communist expansion but also introduced requisite political and economic stability, allowing democratic processes to take root. Eleven Cold War contingencies imposed political stability on chaotic nations or supported peace operations.

Principal Missions

USAF airlift capabilities have always been the cornerstone for U.S. global-projection missions. Twelve of the twenty-three entries in this book involved principally military airlift; such as transport of troops, their equipment, and other cargo to support combat operations. Virtually all twenty-three also included some humanitarian airlift; that is, transport of food, clothing, tents, medical supplies, or other cargo for the relief of a civilian population.

Although airlift played a significant supporting role, the basic missions in seven summaries entailed reconnaissance, air-to-air combat, air-to-ground attacks, or close air support of ground forces. The Air Force amply demonstrated its abilities to maintain air superiority with aerial victories over enemy aircraft during Operations SOUTHERN WATCH and PROVIDE COMFORT and by damaging or destroying enemy air defense systems during operations such as URGENT FURY and DENY FLIGHT. Operation DENY FLIGHT also saw the effective use of precision-guided munitions to force an end to violence and aggression. In addition, Air Force personnel usually provided critical combat-support elements such as reconnaissance, command and control of air traffic, logistics, and air refueling to other U.S. services and allied forces during most military actions.

Role of the Reserve Component

One of the clearest changes, illustrated through the study of contingencies, is the steadily increasing importance of the Air Reserve components—the Air National Guard (ANG) and Air Force Reserve (AFRES). For example, no ANG or AFRES unit participated in Operation VITTLES in 1948–49. During the Cuban Missile Crisis in 1962, personnel and aircraft from AFRES units supplemented active duty airlift capabilities within the United States. A short three years later, AFRES members voluntarily flew missions to the Dominican Republic, and an ANG unit provided aircraft to enhance long-distance communications. In the early 1970s, implementation of the Total Force Policy resulted in far greater Reserve participation, as was evident in Operations ZAIRE I and II in 1978. During those, at least three AFRES associate airlift wings participated. By Operation UPHOLD DEMOCRACY in 1994, the Air Reserve components were thoroughly integrated into the activities of the regular Air Force. Not only had they become a vital, integral part of the Air Force's airlift mission capability, but they also provided fighter, reconnaissance, air refueling, and other functions amounting to some 10 percent of deployed forces.

Joint and Combined Operations

In these twenty-three summaries, the U.S. Air Force operated alone in only three. The remainder were joint operations, involving one or more of the other U.S. armed services. Until enactment of the Goldwater-Nichols Department of Defense Reorganization Act of 1986, few joint contingencies had a true joint commander. Rather, the unified (i.e., joint) commander coordinated operations, with each armed services component commander retaining control of his forces. Prime examples included the Dominican Crisis and Operation URGENT FURY. But, every contingency since 1986 has benefited from a joint commander who exercised full command of all military forces in the area of operations, thus improving the integrated application of force, including air power, towards successful operations.

Fourteen summaries describe combined operations; that is, military forces from other nations cooperated or worked closely with U.S. armed services, and beginning with DESERT SHIELD/DESERT STORM in 1991, coalition force commanders have directed all contingencies. Ten entries involved multinational organizations, such as the United Nations, North Atlantic Treaty Organization, and the Organization of American States. Virtually all required cooperation from other nations to provide to the U.S. Air Force overflight rights, forward air bases, and other logistical support.

A. TIMOTHY WARNOCK
Chief, Organizational History Branch
Air Force Historical Research Agency

Acknowledgements

Robert T. Cossaboom, Chief, History Office, Air Mobility Command, and members of his staff; Daniel F. Harrington, Historian, History Office, United States Air Forces in Europe; Jacob Neufeld, Chief, Projects and Production Division, Air Force History Support Office (AFHSO); and Daniel R. Mortensen, Chief of Research, Airpower Research Division, College for Aerospace Doctrine, Research and Education, Air University, carefully read the manuscript, offering constructive, critical comments to improve it. Other readers at AFHSO were Richard Davis, Sheldon Goldberg, Perry Jamison, Priscilla Jones, Edward Mark, Roger Miller, Diane Putney, Wayne Thompson, George Watson, Herman Wolk, and Tom Y'Blood. Larry Benson, AFHSO, provided a copy of his background paper on "Historical Examples of USAF Operations Tempo," which proved very useful. Tammy Rodriguez, editorial assistant, Air Force Historical Research Agency (AFHRA) pulled the material into a single document and edited it for format and consistency. Frederick J. Shaw Jr., Chief, Research Division, AFHRA, arranged for editing and layout as well as provided expert advice to the editor. SrA Susan Beasley, AFHRA, scanned the photographs. Air University Press accomplished the copy editing and layout, including compilation of the illustrations. Specifically, Debbie Banker did an outstanding job of copy editing and layout, Susan Fair and Daniel Armstrong did the photographs, maps, and cover, and Linda Colson typeset the manuscript—all under the expert guidance of Steve Garst, Design Branch Division Chief, and Deputy Director, Tom Mackin. A word of appreciation is due Col. William E. Mathis, Commander, AFHRA, for his support and to Dr. Richard P. Hallion, Air Force Historian, as sponsor of the work. Errors of omission and commission ultimately rest with the editor.

Introduction
From Cold War to Global Engagement

On March 17, 1947, U.S. President Harry S Truman in a message to Congress requesting foreign aid to assist Greece and Turkey against Communist subversion established containment as the national strategy to counter Soviet expansionism. To halt Soviet expansion, the United States had to rely on a large professional military establishment and nuclear weapons, bolstered by international alliances to deter war. The explosion of the Soviet Union's first atomic device in August 1949 imparted greater urgency to U.S. efforts to develop and expand its nuclear capabilities. In the forty-year period of international tension that came to be known as the "Cold War," the containment of the Soviet Union and deterrence of nuclear war to a great extent depended on the ability of the United States to develop and maintain a credible nuclear deterrent force.

The potential for successful exploitation of nuclear weapons, the basis of deterrence, at first depended on bombers stationed overseas that were capable of hitting targets within the Soviet Union. Building a nuclear-capable fleet of strategic bombers was the responsibility of the United States Air Force (USAF), established as a separate armed service in September 1947. Considering strategic bombing its primary mission, the new service focused its resources on expanding the Strategic Air Command (SAC). While SAC slowly built its nuclear deterrent, the USAF's conventional forces remained comparatively weak, especially considering the massive conventional arsenals of the Soviet Union and its client states. Paradoxically, the nuclear stalemate engendered by successful deterrence increased the need for the conventional forces to resolve the Cold War's numerous crises.

The first Cold War contingency was the Soviet blockade of Berlin in June 1948, in a manner of speaking, the opening shot of the Cold War. The U.S. government determined to break the blockade by supplying the city by airlift. The effort began with C–47s, but the U.S. Air Force quickly moved to the larger

C–54s, stripping the Military Air Transport Service and other major air commands to build a fleet of 225 large transports for Operation VITTLES. The airlift broke the blockade, giving the West (embodied in the newly founded North Atlantic Treaty Organization [NATO]) its first victory of the Cold War. It also dramatically demonstrated the need for specialized military cargo aircraft capable of loading near ground level from the front or rear. In the early 1950s, the U.S. Air Force put into operation the four-engine C–124 aircraft to haul oversized military cargo long distances, as well as the twin-engine C–123 for intratheater airlift. In the latter part of the decade, the versatile C–130, initially a short-haul carrier of oversized cargo, entered service.

The invasion of South Korea by the North Koreans in June 1950 marked the beginning of another major Cold War crisis, requiring the exclusive use of conventional forces. Early in the war, the United States marshaled its diplomatic resources to obtain a United Nations (UN) condemnation of the Communist invasion and, under UN auspices, threw what forces it had in the Far East into the fray. Throughout the conflict, the United States and its Allies were unwilling to provoke a nuclear confrontation with the Soviet Union or risk adverse world reaction by employing nuclear weapons against conventional Communist forces. Under the UN Command, the Far East Air Forces (FEAF) employed its meager forces, although trained and equipped for the air defense of Japan, in interdiction and ground-support roles to help slow the enemy advance. Despite handicaps imposed by post-World War II neglect of tactical air support, the FEAF soon established and maintained air superiority over South Korea and most of North Korea. The USAF experience in Korea would have important consequences for addressing the requirements of the contingency mission.

In the aftermath of the Korean conflict, the Air Force, while continuing to emphasize the buildup of its nuclear forces, began improving its ability to deal with the crises and "brush fire" wars that it now recognized as Cold War "facts of life." In July 1955, it activated under Tactical Air Command (TAC) the Nineteenth Air Force as a planning headquarters for the newly established Composite Air Strike Force (CASF). Designed as a highly mobile tactical air force to be deployed to meet military emergencies anywhere in the world, the CASF drew its fighting forces from TAC's other numbered air forces. In July–October 1958, during Operation BLUE BAT, the CASF in its first crisis deployed to Lebanon. The C–124 and the newly operational C–130 aircraft proved their capabilities by transporting the CASF from bases in the United States to Incirlik, Turkey, within three days. Tactical fighter aircraft made the quick journey with the help of aerial refueling from KB–50 tankers. Among other lessons, the deployment revealed inadequate aircrew training for non-nuclear operations, significant joint command and control problems, and the inadequacy of forward air bases. The Air Force sought to alleviate the forward-air-base problem with the establishment of civil engineering teams, who could survey forward bases and install facilities to maintain and operate the deploying aircraft.

By the late 1950s, the dissolution of the European colonial empires was well advanced. Wars of national liberation, civil war, and political unrest clouded the twilight of imperialism. In July 1960, civil war in the newly independent Republic of the Congo, formerly a colony of Belgium, involved the U.S. Air Force in Operation NEW TAPE. During NEW TAPE's four year history, USAF transports airlifted refugees from the rebellion-wracked Congo, delivered UN troops to keep the peace, and flew humanitarian relief missions. Because of the inadequacies of the propeller-driven C–124s and C–119s, the Air Force instituted in October 1962 the use of the C–135, a civilian jet airliner converted to military use. The experience of Operation NEW TAPE added urgency to the procurement of a jet military transport and underscored the need to expand the airlift forces.

While USAF transports accomplished their mission in the Congo, a series of events unfolded that pushed the United States and Soviet Union to the brink of nuclear war, producing the most serious crisis of the Cold War. By the early 1960s, the dissolution of European colonial empires was exacerbating Cold War tensions. Guided by experience and Marxist-Leninist doctrine, Soviet Premier Nikita Khrushchev in January 1961 announced Soviet support for "wars of national liberation" to advance the triumph of world Communism in emerging nations. To counter the Soviet strategy, U.S. President John F. Kennedy, who took office the same month, directed that military response be made swiftly and in kind to the aggression encountered. Known as "flexible response," this defense posture acknowledged the importance of conventional forces and, among other improvements, led to a program to increase airlift capacity. The new policy also affected the employment of nuclear weapons. In June 1962, Secretary of Defense Robert S. McNamara refined massive retaliation to include a counterforce strategy based on a second-strike capability, emphasizing the destruction of military forces. In pursuit of this strategy, the administration planned to deploy Minuteman intercontinental ballistic missiles (ICBM) in hardened silos and Polaris nuclear-powered submarines equipped with sea-launched ballistic missiles.

Under tremendous internal pressure from Soviet hard-liners to balance U.S. initiatives, Premier Khrushchev saw opportunity when Cuba requested military aid to deter U.S.-sponsored invasions. In October 1962, U.S. intelligence received word that the Soviets were building sites for medium-range and intermediate-range ballistic missiles in Cuba. USAF reconnaissance flights confirmed the construction of missile sites and also discovered the presence of IL–28 medium-range bombers, capable of carrying nuclear bombs. In reaction, the United States brought its nuclear forces to full combat alert, and a CASF led the deployment of TAC units to bases in the Southeastern United States within range of Cuba. During tense diplomatic negotiations, the United States enforced a naval blockade of Cuba. Within a few days, facing a possible U.S. invasion of Cuba or general nuclear war, the Soviet leaders ordered the removal of nuclear weapons, withdrawal of ballistic missiles and bombers, and destruction of the missile sites. This crisis revealed the inadequate capabilities and shortages of USAF tactical aircraft and the need for development of modern tactical air reconnaissance systems capable of all-weather and darkness surveillance.

Shortly after the termination of the Cuban missile crisis, another emergency erupted; this one occurred on the border separating India from China. In November 1962, the People's Republic of China invaded the remote Himalaya region of India. The Indian government requested U.S. military support in the form of munitions, other war materiel, and tactical airlift.

During Operation LONG SKIP, the United States shipped the most urgently needed supplies by air from Europe and the United States. It also provided a squadron, with aircrews and maintainers, of C–130s that for over six months provided tactical airlift to the almost inaccessible disputed area. The C–130 proved its capability to operate successfully on short, primitive airfields at high altitudes. In less than a year, the Chinese forces had pulled back to China, vindicating U.S. containment policy.

The U.S. Air Force returned to the Congo in Operation DRAGON ROUGE from November through December 1964. C–130s transported Belgian soldiers from Belgium to the Congo, air-dropping some and landing others, to secure key towns and cities and rescue Europeans and Americans being held hostage by rebel forces. Numerous aircraft came under enemy fire that punctured fuel cells and tires but failed to impair operations significantly. The C–130 aircrews developed new landing and takeoff tactics that would be used later in Southeast Asia. Like NEW TAPE, Operation DRAGON ROUGE was a peace operations contingency.

As conventional U.S. responses to international crises became routine events, the Kennedy administration turned its attention to the growing conflict in Southeast Asia. At first, the U.S. government perceived it as a guerrilla war against South Vietnamese Communist rebels augmented by North Vietnamese troops. The Kennedy administration determined that it could be met through flexible response. However, it quickly evolved into a conventional war of attrition against North Vietnam. Kennedy's successor, President Lyndon B. Johnson, prosecuted a war of gradual escalation in Southeast Asia with little success. His successor, President Richard M. Nixon, began withdrawal of U.S. forces from Vietnam shortly after his inauguration in 1969. Conducting bombing campaigns against North Vietnam in 1972, the U.S. Air Force became the primary military instrument that forced the North Vietnamese to negotiate an end to the war in early 1973. Despite the formal cessation of hostilities, the Communists would attain most of their goals in Southeast Asia, capturing Laos, Cambodia, and South Vietnam within three years without opposition from the United States.

During the Vietnam War, U.S. forces deployed overseas to the Dominican Republic in 1965–66. In the Dominican Crisis, the U.S. government undertook military intervention to deter subversion of the Dominican government by Communist Cuba. This operation began with USAF C–130s airlifting the entire 82d Airborne Division from Pope Air Force Base, North Carolina, to Santo Domingo. The Air Force also deployed a tactical fighter squadron, a fighter-interceptor squadron, a reconnaissance squadron, and psychological-warfare elements to support the U.S. Army and deter Cuban reaction to the intervention. This could be considered the first nation-building contingency of the Cold War and one of several peace operations in the 1960s. It highlighted shortcomings in USAF contingency planning and in joint command and control.

As the Communists overran Southeast Asia in 1975, the U.S. Air Force became involved in three contingencies, marking the end of U.S. military intervention in that region. Two of these involved evacuations of refugees fleeing Communist forces. During the U.S. withdrawal from South Vietnam, April–September 1975, the U.S. military evacuated over 130,000 refugees, about 50,000 by air, over a period of several weeks. Carried out in mass confusion, panic, and fragmented command and control with no single military commander, the Vietnam evacuation resulted in the loss of a C–5 and a C–130. The Cambodian airlift and evacuation initially involved the airlift of supplies to besieged friendly forces in the Cambodian capital of Phnom Penh. The U.S. Air Force relied heavily on civilian-contract airlift for this operation. When the fall of Phnom Penh became imminent in April 1975, the U.S. ambassador implemented a plan with a USAF officer as commander of the joint evacuation force. In this highly successful operation, nearly 300 people took advantage of the chance to leave the country.

The third contingency in Southeast Asia during 1975 also involved Cambodia. In the Mayaguez Crisis, Khmer Rouge soldiers seized an American civilian merchant ship, the SS *Mayaguez*, traveling off the Cambodian mainland. U.S. President Gerald R. Ford decided to attempt a rescue of the crew. USAF reconnaissance aircraft found the ship but could not determine the location of its crew. Reconnaissance also failed to reveal the size of enemy forces on the island where the crew was mistakenly believed held. USAF helicopters inserted a U.S. Marine force on the island, where they came under intense fire from an entrenched, powerful enemy. After a significant delay, the Air Force provided effective close air support, enabling the helicopters to extract the marines. In this operation, the U.S. Air Force lost four helicopters, and U.S. forces lost forty-one lives. The limitations of reconnaissance, weaknesses of intelligence, and the tragic consequences that may result from both marked the last major U.S. military operation in Southeast Asia.

In the course of the Southeast Asian conflict, the U.S. Air Force brought its airlift capability to maturity, introducing the C–141 and C–5 transport aircraft into operational service. In the ensuing years, the role of aerial transport in projecting military power to contingency-conflict areas assumed critical importance. In 1977, the Department of Defense recognized the rising prominence of airlift by designating the U.S. Air Force the single manager for all transport aircraft. To meet this role, the USAF Military Airlift Command (MAC) became a specified command; that is, it came under the strategic guidance of the Joint Chiefs of Staff for air transport. Three contingencies of the 1970s illustrated the vital importance of strategic airlift to meet U.S. national policy objectives.

The first was Operation NICKEL GRASS, the aerial resupply of Israel's arsenal in October 1973. Armed with Soviet-supplied weaponry, Egypt and Syria attacked Israel, which, rapidly running short of munitions and equipment, appealed to the United States for supply. In addition to flying fighter aircraft to Israel, USAF C–141s and C–5s transported tons of cargo, including tanks, from the United States. Operation NICKEL GRASS convinced USAF leaders of the need to modify the C–141 for aerial refueling and to procure the KC–10, which was capable of transferring twice as much fuel as the venerable KC–135.

In the other two airlift contingencies of the decade, Operations ZAIRE I and II, May–June 1978, the U.S. Air Force returned to the Congo, now Zaire. In response to Zaire's request, the United States cooperated with France and Belgium to provide military aid against Marxist rebels. MAC set up an infrastructure to support the airlifters, and C–130s airlifted Belgian, French Foreign Legion, and later, African troops to Zaire, while C–141s transported needed supplies and equipment. This operation was noteworthy for the substantial numbers of USAF Reservists involved. It also exposed some recurrent problems, such as poor communication infrastructure and inadequate support facilities at forward air bases, but it did serve U.S. containment policy by helping thwart another Communist government in Africa.

A broad political consensus not to get involved in another third world "quagmire" like Vietnam dissuaded the United States from heavy involvement in contingencies during the last half of the 1970s. But in 1979, the excesses of a fundamentalist Moslem regime in Iran forced a U.S. reaction. When in November 1979 Iranians made U.S. diplomatic members in Tehran hostage, U.S. President James (Jimmy) E. Carter approved a rescue attempt. The Department of Defense devised a plan and assembled equipment and people to carry it out. In April 1980, the rescue force rendezvoused in the Iranian Desert, but the team leader called off the attempt because of helicopter failure. As the aircraft departed, an explosion destroyed a helicopter and an EC–130, killing eight people. This experience provided the impetus for the United States to create a Special Operations Command and to strengthen special operations forces in all armed services.

The next President, Ronald W. Reagan, announced a scant ten months after taking office in 1981 the rejuvenation of U.S. strategic forces. He sought the strengthening and modernization of land-based missiles, sea-based missiles, and bombers, the so-called strategic triad. For the U.S. Air Force, this meant the procurement of the B–1 strategic bomber, which President Carter had canceled several years previously. The missile force would see the introduction by the end of the decade of the Peacekeeper ICBM. President Reagan also instructed the services to equip and train for rapid response and flexible employment of conventional forces. The Department of Defense established a Rapid Deployment Joint Task Force (RDJTF), whose commander had operational control of certain U.S. Army and Air Force units, as well as planning responsibility for operations in Southwest Asia. In January 1983, the U.S.

Central Command, a unified command, replaced the RDJTF. Three months later, the U.S. Air Force merged its special operations forces with its Aerospace Rescue and Recovery Services under a new MAC organization, the Twenty-Third Air Force. This numbered air force had global responsibilities not only for rescue and recovery and special operations but also for weather reconnaissance, drone recovery, space-shuttle support, and support for SAC missile sites. The amalgamation of these missions proved fortuitous for the success of a major contingency later in 1983.

Following an anti-American coup of the government in Grenada, President Reagan acted quickly to protect U.S. citizens attending medical school on the island and to eliminate a growing Cuban military presence there. In Operation URGENT FURY, the U.S. Air Force on October 25 transported and air-dropped U.S. Army troops, while its special operations gunships, the AC–130s, provided close air support for the assault. The Air Force also provided close air support for U.S. Army and U.S. Marine operations over the next two days, while evacuating U.S. citizens to safety in the United States. Operation URGENT FURY met political and military objectives by expelling the Cuban military from the island, deposing an authoritarian regime, and laying the groundwork for the reestablishment of democratic rule. From the military perspective, it exposed recurrent problems with intelligence, flaws in joint command structure, and the reluctance of USAF major commands to yield operational control of aircraft. The Goldwater-Nichols Department of Defense Reorganization Act of 1986 addressed these discrepancies by reforming the Department of Defense and mandating a single commander in joint military operations.

Even as Congress debated this legislation, the United States successfully completed yet another major military campaign. In April, President Reagan ordered an air strike against Libya, which had sponsored several terrorist attacks worldwide against the United States and its allies. During Operation ELDORADO CANYON, U.S. authorities assigned targets to both the U.S. Navy and Air Force. The Air Force flew a force of F–111s, supported by KC–10 and KC–135 aerial tankers, from England to strike assigned targets in or near Tripoli, Libya, in close cooperation with the naval air strike as well as naval units supporting both strike forces. In spite of the loss of an aircraft and several aborted sorties, the USAF aircrews successfully destroyed their assigned targets with little collateral damage. President Reagan had proven the validity of a prepared and trained force for flexible response against terrorism.

Another crisis ripened in Panama during 1989 when dictator Manuel Noriega's policies jeopardized the U.S. commitment to transfer control of the Panama Canal to Panama. As U.S.-Panamanian relations worsened, the dictator terrorized internal opposition and increasingly harassed U.S. military members and citizens. U.S. President George H. W. Bush decided that U.S. interests required the ouster of Noriega, whom a U.S. grand jury had indicted on drug-related charges. The United States launched Operation JUST CAUSE in December. The Air Force airlifted U.S. Army troops from the United States, provided close air support, and transported supplies for the U.S. military, as well as humanitarian aid for displaced Panamanians. Another nation-building activity, JUST CAUSE resulted in the establishment of a pro-American democratic government in Panama.

The disintegration of the Soviet Union in 1989 spelled the end of the Cold War. Subsequently, the United States began to reduce its military forces, including its nuclear forces. The retreat from nuclear confrontation reached a historic milestone in July 1990 when the Strategic Air Command ended nearly thirty years of continuous airborne command-post operations known as Looking Glass. Then in September, President Bush ordered SAC to end its thirty-minute alert status; on September 28 the alert forces ceased operations. Henceforth, U.S. strategy would rely more heavily on tactical, conventional means of military operations. Ironically, the dissolution of the Soviet Union eliminated the stability imposed by nuclear stalemate and superpower understandings, unleashing dangerously pent-up tensions. To meet the resulting crises and those arising from other causes, the United States sent military forces on extended operations overseas even as it reduced its forces significantly.

The beginning of this new era was signaled as early as July 1987 with the commencement of Operation EARNEST WILL in the Persian Gulf. Increasingly, Iran and Iraq in their war with one another were attacking neutral shipping, particularly oil tankers, in the Persian Gulf. When the Kuwaiti government asked for protection for its ships, the United States agreed to register them as U.S. vessels and provide naval escort through the gulf. The U.S. Air Force provided airborne warning and control system surveillance support to other U.S. services, all of which operated under a single joint commander. U.S. forces successfully conducted sixty-six escort missions before Iran and Iraq declared a cease-fire in 1988.

Peace remained elusive in the Middle East. Within three years, the United States once again used its military forces on behalf of Kuwait against Iraqi aggression. In 1990, Iraq invaded Kuwait, declaring it an Iraqi province. The United States formed a coalition in Operation DESERT SHIELD/DESERT STORM to defeat quickly and decisively Iraqi aggression against Kuwait. Air power dealt precise blows against Iraqi infrastructure and armies to prepare the way for a short ground war that forced Iraq in February 1991 to withdraw from Kuwait and concede to terms for international weapons inspections.

Even in defeat, Iraq continued to threaten its neighbors and brutally repressed internal opposition, particularly its Kurdish minority. Operations PROVIDE COMFORT and SOUTHERN WATCH addressed the United Nations' concerns with Iraqi policies. PROVIDE COMFORT involved the enforcement of a no-fly zone over northern Iraq to protect the minority Kurds from Saddam Hussein's forces and discourage further Iraqi moves against Kuwait. The U.S. Air Force airlifted extensive humanitarian aid to the Kurds and transported some refugees to Guam. SOUTHERN WATCH was the enforcement of a no-fly zone over southern Iraq, which continued into 1998. These two exercises exacerbated USAF personnel problems with excessive deployment time overseas and a growing maintenance crisis due to much higher-than-planned use of equipment and aircraft.

Even as the United States sought to contain Iraq, in 1991–92, internal conflict in Somalia created a starving, diseased-ridden population. International agencies, including the United Nations, attempted to provide humanitarian relief, but thievery and violence among warlords often thwarted these efforts. The U.S. Air Force airlifted U.S. and later UN troops to keep the peace, as well as transporting humanitarian aid cargoes.

An event illustrating the importance of a capable air transport system to U.S. policy makers occurred in October 1993. The U.S. President, given a choice between a twenty-one-day sea lift and an eight-day airlift, chose the latter, proving the growing reliance of the modern world on air power for rapid delivery of humanitarian assistance and military forces.

In Southern Europe, the breakup of Yugoslavia generated old ethnic hatreds and conflicts that eventually led to UN and NATO intervention. The two contingencies involving USAF participation were Operations PROVIDE PROMISE and DENY FLIGHT. In the first, the U.S. Air Force airlifted humanitarian relief supplies to the besieged population of Bosnia. During the second operation, NATO and the United Nations enforced a no-fly zone over Bosnia to check Serbian aggression and protect PROVIDE PROMISE's humanitarian deliveries. Later, USAF and other NATO aircraft conducted air strikes, known as Operation DELIBERATE FORCE, to force the antagonists to negotiate an end to the war.

During Operation UPHOLD DEMOCRACY, a nation-building effort in Haiti, the United States used its military forces to stabilize the country following a collapse of government. The U.S. Air Force initially provided the airlift to transport Army troops to Haiti and to provide humanitarian relief to the population of the capital city. This contingency ended with the return of the exiled legitimate president to Haiti.

Given the contingency operation's respectable longevity, formal USAF doctrine has been slow to recognize its significance. In 1953, the USAF's first published doctrine focused on the delivery of weapons of mass destruction to an opponent's heartland to destroy the capacity to wage war. The resulting emphasis on building a nuclear deterrent diverted attention from preparation for more conventional operations. The realities of the Southeast Asian conflict forced attention on less traditional forms of air power. In 1964, USAF doctrine recognized counterinsurgency—with its potential for contingency operations—as a legitimate application of air power. Air Force doctrine further expanded in 1971 by defining for the first time support functions like psychological warfare, search and rescue, air refueling, and airborne command and control. Later iterations of doctrine carefully elaborated the importance of these and other functions, particularly as Cold War tensions declined and new technologies came to prominence. It remained for the September 1997 edition of *Air Force Basic Doctrine* to acknowledge the importance of the contingency operations to contemporary roles and missions. Devoting an entire section to "Air and Space Power in Military Operations Other Than War," it recognized that ". . . many strategic actions tend to be non-nuclear, conventional or special operations against more limited war or contingency operations objectives. . .." Recognizing the primacy of the contingency operation in current world affairs, it identifies the Air and Space Expeditionary Task Force as the most appropriate organization to meet this challenge. Recent deployments to Southwest Asia tested prototypes of the expeditionary task force.

Once eclipsed by nuclear deterrence and theater conventional warfare, the contingency operation has gained during the last decade of the Twentieth Century a conspicuous position in the overall mission of the Air Force. Spanning the universe of "operations short of war" from peacekeeping to humanitarian airlift, these operations are often conducted under joint service command or in cooperation with other nations. They are currently the USAF's primary means of protecting and projecting U.S. interests in the period of readjustment made necessary by the disintegration of the Soviet Union, localized conflicts, and continuing natural disasters. Finally assuming a prominence in formal USAF doctrine, the contingency operation is today driving the organization of the "Air Expeditionary Force." The contingencies described in the following pages encapsulate much of the USAF historical experience with this extremely challenging application of air power.

Berlin Airlift: Operation VITTLES

Daniel L. Haulman

DATES: June 26, 1948–September 30, 1949

LOCATION: Germany

OVERSEAS BASES USED: Burtonwood, England; Celle Royal Air Force (RAF) Station, Fassberg RAF Station, Kaufbeuren Air Force Base (AFB), Oberpfaffenhofen AFB, Rhein-Main AFB, Wiesbaden AFB, Germany; Tegel Airfield, Tempelhof AFB, Gatow Airfield, Berlin.

AIR FORCE ORGANIZATIONS:

TASK FORCES/DIVISIONS	GROUPS: (con't.)
Airlift Task Force (Provisional)	317th Troop Carrier
1st Airlift Task Force	1420th Air Transport Group (Provisional)
Combined Airlift Task Force	1422d Air Transport Group (Provisional)
7499th Air Division	
	SQUADRONS:
WINGS:	1st Air Transport (later, 1263d Air Transport)
Airlift Wing (Provisional)	3d Air Transport (later, 1273d Air Transport)
60th Troop Carrier	8th Air Transport (later, 1255th Air Transport)
61st Troop Carrier	9th Air Transport (later, 1256th Air Transport)
313th Troop Carrier	11th Air Transport (later, 1250th Air Transport)
317th Troop Carrier	12th Air Transport (later, 1251st Air Transport)
525th Air Transport (later, 1602d Air Transport)	17th Air Transport (later, 1258th Air Transport)
7150th Air Force Composite	19th Troop Carrier
7497th Airlift Wing (Provisional)	20th Troop Carrier
	21st Air Transport (later, 1266th Air Transport)
GROUPS:	22d Air Transport (later, 1267th Air Transport)
Airlift Group (Provisional)	23d Air Transport (later, 1268th Air Transport)
60th Troop Carrier	54th Troop Carrier
61st Troop Carrier	7169th Weather Reconnaissance
313th Troop Carrier	

AIR FORCE AIRCRAFT: C–47, C–54, C–74, C–82, YC–97

Operations

At the end of World War II, the victorious Allies divided Germany into four zones of occupation, one each for the United States, Great Britain, France, and the Soviet Union. They similarly divided Berlin. Unfortunately, the German capital lay in the center of the eastern Soviet zone. Highways, canals, railroads, and three air corridors connected the western sectors of Berlin with the American, British, and French zones that lay 110 miles to the west.

Following World War II, relations between the Soviet Union and its former allies deteriorated into the Cold War. In 1947, Soviet Premier Joseph Stalin denounced the American-sponsored Marshall Plan for the economic recovery of Europe. On June 18, 1948, the western powers announced currency reforms in their zones of Germany. Six days later, the Soviet Union severed all land routes between western Berlin and western Germany, isolating more than two million people. Berlin became an island in the Soviet zone.

The United States considered four options. Abandoning German currency reform would cripple European economic recovery. Abandoning Berlin to Soviet occupation would demonstrate appeasement and encourage further Communist expansion. Forcing an armored column through the Soviet zone of Germany would likely provoke a war in Europe against Soviet ground forces with overwhelming numerical superiority. President Harry S Truman approved a plan to airlift supplies from western Germany to Berlin to neutralize the blockade and buy time for a diplomatic solution.

The Berlin Airlift originated as an expedient. General Lucius D. Clay, USA, military governor of the American zone, asked Lt. Gen. Curtis E. LeMay, USAF, Commanding General, U.S. Air Forces in Europe (USAFE), to arrange an emergency airlift of coal and food to western Berlin. LeMay appointed Brig. Gen. Joseph Smith, USAF, at Wiesbaden as temporary commander of the operation. Americans called the airlift Operation VITTLES. The British conducted a parallel airlift, which they called Operation PLAINFARE.

The first USAF transports airlifting cargo to Berlin supplied only the U.S. garrison. Within days of the full blockade, the

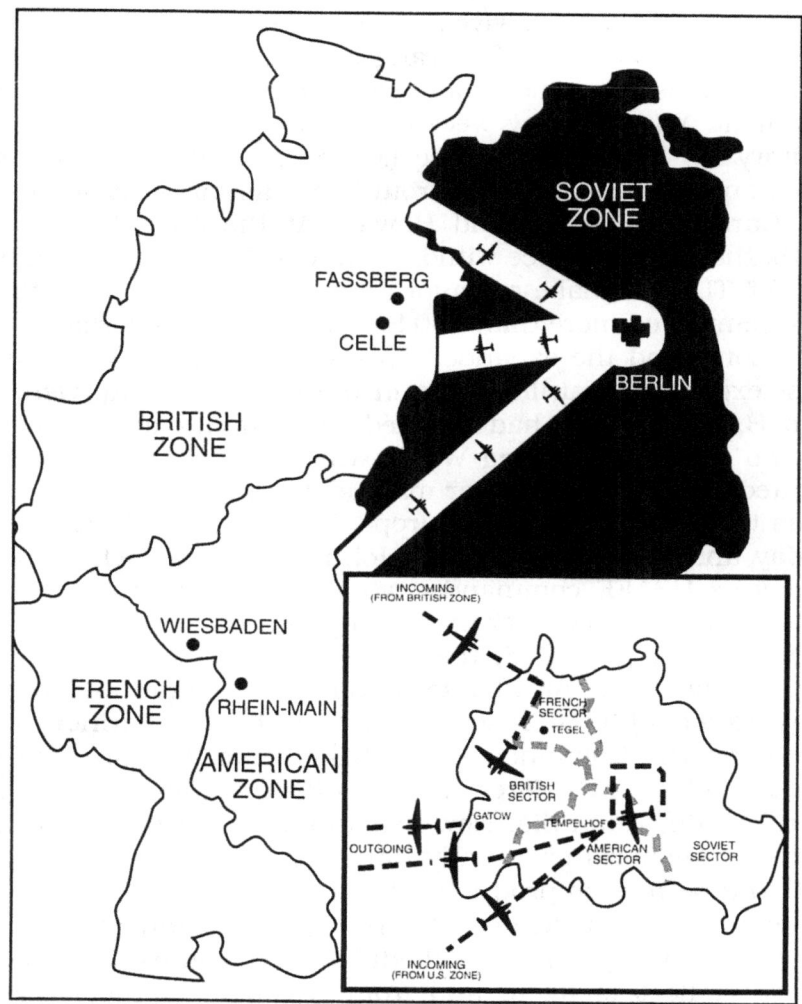

Germany during Berlin Airlift
Inset: Berlin during Operation VITTLES

60th and 61st Troop Carrier Groups began ferrying tons of VITTLES cargo to the people of Berlin. At first, USAFE performed the operation with C–47s, transporting coal and food from western Germany to Tempelhof Airport in Berlin. Smith increased deliveries to the besieged city, but the C–47s available were too small to transport the estimated forty-five tons of coal and food the city needed daily to survive. In June, General Hoyt S. Vandenberg, USAF Chief of Staff, arranged to augment the C–47s with C–54 Skymasters, which could carry three times as much cargo per flight. Within a few weeks, scores of Skymasters from the Military Air Transport Service (MATS) and at least four other commands joined the airlift from bases as far away as Alaska, the Caribbean, Texas, and Hawaii. At the end of September 1948, the U.S. Air Force withdrew all USAFE C–47s from Operation VITTLES to make room for more C–54s. Eventually, the Air Force employed more than 200 Skymasters on the airlift.

To command the expanded operation, Vandenberg chose the most experienced airlift expert in the Air Force, Maj. Gen. William H. Tunner. He had directed the complex and successful "Hump" operation during World War II, which in its last year airlifted 550,000 tons of war materiel from India over the Himalayas to isolated China. In Europe, Tunner worked closely with LeMay and later with Lt. Gen. John K. Cannon, who replaced LeMay as USAFE commander when the latter returned to the United States to take over the Strategic Air Command (SAC).

On October 15, 1948, the United States and Britain transformed the Berlin Airlift into a combined operation. The preponderance of U.S. resources assured that Tunner would command the Combined Airlift Task Force. British Air Commodore John W. F. Merer served as deputy commander. Pilots from Britain, Australia, New Zealand, and South Africa flying British transports eventually hauled most of the passengers, salt, and petroleum products on the airlift.

General Tunner turned the Berlin Airlift into an efficient machine. His system of schedules and routes allowed the transport fleet to fly to and from Berlin as if they were on conveyor belts. The general demanded a precise, rhythmic cadence. He replaced holding patterns and the stacking of aircraft preparing to land with straight-in approaches. He determined that Berlin flights would not be delayed if one airplane failed to land on its first attempt. Instead of circling around for another try, it would go back to its base of origin, allowing the next plane to land on schedule. Tunner insisted that the direction, altitude, and speed of each and every VITTLES airplane be strictly controlled, with pilots routinely following instrument flight rules. Radio beacons at several locations in western

Maj. Gen. William H. Tunner, Commander of the Berlin Airlift

Germany and Berlin controlled the routes of the airplanes. Precision was important because the corridors over the Soviet zone were only twenty miles wide. Eventually, an airplane landed in Berlin every three minutes. Ninety seconds after each transport landed, another took off. The transports flew at staggered altitudes to minimize the danger of collisions. At one point, pilots followed one of five different altitude tracks. Transports at the same altitude were spaced from six to fifteen minutes apart. As a result, there was only one mid-air collision during the entire operation. At the peak of the airlift, allied aircraft flew the northern and southern corridors from nine bases in the western zones of Germany to three airfields in western Berlin. The middle corridor carried airplanes from Berlin back to western Germany.

The U.S. Air Force used seven major air bases for Operation VITTLES: Rhein-Main, Wiesbaden, Fassberg, and Celle in western Germany, and Tempelhof, Gatow, and Tegel in western Berlin. Of these, only Rhein-Main, Wiesbaden, and Tempelhof were located in American zones. The British maintained and operated the airfields at Fassberg, Celle, and Gatow, and the

French administered Tegel, which was located in their sector of Berlin. The Allies constructed two new bases, Celle and Tegel, and built new runways at Tempelhof and Gatow. At Tempelhof, where high apartment complexes surrounded the airfield, airlift engineers constructed light towers in a nearby cemetery to guide the aircraft in bad weather.

Once an airplane landed in Berlin, a "follow me" jeep or a truck guided it to its unloading point. During unloading, aircrews remained near their aircraft so that they could take off again as soon as possible. Tunner arranged for vehicles with refreshments, briefing personnel, and maintenance men to meet the crews at their aircraft. Careful management reduced turnaround time in Berlin from an hour to only thirty minutes. A transport stayed on the ground only long enough for unloading and emergency maintenance. By the summer of 1949, unloading at Tempelhof took only fifteen minutes.

General Tunner devoted much of his attention to maintenance. Never designed for heavy cargo shuttling, the C–54s wore out quickly. After 200 flying hours, VITTLES aircraft flew to Oberpfaffenhofen, Germany, and later to Burtonwood, England, for inspection and repair. After 1,000 hours, the airlift transports flew to the United States for inspection and overhaul by civilian contractors. The largest USAF depot, Kelly AFB, Texas, overhauled 500 C–54 engines monthly for Operation VITTLES. Huge C–74 Globemasters ferried the engines to and from Germany. By increasing the utilization rate of his aircraft, Tunner was able to limit the number of aircraft needed.

General Tunner encouraged competition among units and the setting of new tonnage records. He insisted that the figures be published, despite objections from nervous security officers who wanted them classified. On the first anniversary of the Air Force, September 18, 1948, American aircraft alone transported 5,582 tons to Berlin. Ground teams also competed to see how quickly they could load the airplanes. On April 16, 1949, the Berlin Airlift delivered an incredible 12,941 tons of coal and food, the equivalent of 12 50-car trainloads, to Berlin in 24 hours. This "Easter Parade" involved almost 1,400 flights. Between May and August 1949, the airlift transported an average of 8,000 tons per day. Heavy loads departed Berlin with manufactured products, allowing factories there to stay in business. As the operation continued, the cost per ton-mile decreased consistently.

The Combined Airlift Task Force demanded thousands of trained airmen, who were in short supply. Each airplane required three three-man crews and seven maintenance men. By the end of 1948, MATS had furnished the operation with no less than 457 aircrews. Temporary duty assignments, originally set at forty-five days, eventually stretched to six months, challenging the family lives of pilots surprised by the emergency. Eventually, an aircrew replacement training unit at Great Falls AFB, Montana, provided substitutes. Maintenance, engineering, logistics, transportation, communication, weather, and other support personnel far exceeded in number the men in the aircrews. To reinforce the maintenance work force, Tunner employed German aircraft mechanics. In June 1949, almost 11,500 USAF personnel were assigned or attached to the operation.

Between August 1948 and August 1949, Operation VITTLES recorded hundreds of harassment incidents by Soviet forces, including buzzing by fighters, antiaircraft firing and air-to-air target shooting in the vicinity of the corridors, balloons in the corridors, and searchlights directed at aircraft taking off. Yet the Communists never seriously challenged the airlift. Remembering the failed German airlift to Stalingrad, Soviet officials might have assumed the operation would fail anyway. They were also aware that the United States had deployed some ninety SAC B–29 bombers to Europe during the crisis.

VITTLES was not only a combined but also a joint operation. Two U.S. Navy squadrons, flying R5D airplanes that were virtually identical to the USAF C–54s, participated in the airlift. The U.S. Army transported supplies by rail and truck to the airlift bases, constructed or repaired airfields, and supervised the loading and unloading of the VITTLES airplanes. The Airways and Air Communications System provided radio and telephone links among the bases and between the airfields and the aircraft.

Publicity focused the world's attention on the airlift. First Lt. Gail S. Halvorsen, USAF, inadvertently contributed to the propaganda value of the airlift with "Operation LITTLE VITTLES," in which he and his fellow pilots dropped candy attached to tiny handkerchief parachutes to the children of Berlin.

By late spring of 1949, Stalin had concluded that the blockade of Berlin was not working and was generating publicity contrary to Soviet interests. Operation VITTLES was uniting Germans in the western zones of Germany and Berlin against the Communists and in support of the West in this opening round of the Cold War. At the height of the airlift, in early April 1949, the North Atlantic Treaty Organization (NATO) was born, uniting the powers of North America and Western Europe. Frustrated, the Soviets reopened the land routes between western Germany and Berlin on May 12, 1949. Tunner continued the airlift through September 30 to stockpile fuel, food, and medicine in the city in case the Soviets changed their minds. The Combined Airlift Task Force airlifted over 2.3 million tons of cargo on more than 277,000 flights during the Berlin Airlift. The United States delivered more than 1.78 million tons.

Of all the lessons the Berlin Airlift taught, the most important was the need for larger cargo airplanes designed specifically for airlift. The C–54s were more efficient than the small C–47s that USAFE used when the airlift began, but even the Skymasters were too limited in capacity for such an operation to continue indefinitely at acceptable cost, and they were difficult to load and unload. Airlift demanded specialized aircraft, preferably with a giant door in the back or front and with landing gear that allowed it to sit close to the ground so that cargo could be rolled in and out. Larger transports would mean fewer trips, fewer crews, fewer bases, less maintenance and fuel, and fewer communications and traffic problems. Operation VITTLES, which tested the C–74 Globemaster, C–97 Stratofreighter, and C–82 Packet, stimulated the development and production of the C–124 Globemaster II cargo airplane, which revolutionized air mobility in the 1950s. During the Berlin Airlift, Tunner convinced Secretary of the Air Force Stuart Symington to support the acquisition of this twenty-five-ton-capacity airplane, which could carry two and a half times the cargo of a Skymaster.

Operation VITTLES demonstrated the value of cycled reconditioning of aircraft. The systematic and methodical maintenance methods used during the Berlin Airlift contributed to future military airlift operations and even to commercial aviation. The operation proved the value of an efficient depot and logistics network ready to respond to emergencies.

Moving coal from a truck to a C–54 destined for Berlin.

The demands of the Berlin Airlift produced shortages of aircraft and personnel in other theaters. MATS had to curtail airlift in the Pacific, the Caribbean, and Alaska. In all three areas, no more than 60 percent of airlift requests could be fulfilled in 1948. One lesson of Operation VITTLES was that the U.S. Air Force needed enough aircraft and crews to respond to contingencies without substantially degrading its normal operations elsewhere.

The Berlin Airlift experience taught its participants the need for reorganization. Sensing the prerequisite of centralized operational control of supporting elements, such as ground handling units, the U.S. European Command established an Airlift Support Command in April 1949. General Tunner struggled with shortages of manpower, materiel, supplies, and housing, partly because of friction with the USAFE leadership, which discouraged his direct communications with MATS or Air Materiel Command. He also recognized USAFE favoritism to occupation troops over rotating airlift personnel and noted inefficiency at depots beyond his control. After Secretary Symington visited Tunner in December 1948, the problems diminished but never completely disappeared. Air-mobility specialists noted the need for a single manager for airlift, but the designation of one command for both strategic and tactical airlift did not occur until 1974.

The transportation of coal to Berlin challenged the airlift more than the delivery of other commodities. Coal dust eroded equipment and demoralized crews. General Tunner oversaw the improvement of coal bags and the modification of aircraft to combat the problem, but it remained a persistent headache. At one point, Tunner discovered that coal sacks were being loaded beyond the one hundred pounds for which they were designed, resulting in overloading of the airplanes.

Operation VITTLES provided opportunities for the Air Force to improve air traffic control and ground-controlled approach techniques that benefited not only future military operations but also commercial airlines. It also demonstrated the need for improved materials-handling equipment, such as forklifts.

The Berlin Airlift cost in lives and property. Of the 126 U.S. accidents recorded, 70 were major. At least twenty-four USAF and British airplanes crashed, and more than thirty Americans, including twenty-two USAF pilots, lost their lives during the operation. Experts determined that Operation VITTLES cost the United States as much as $300 million.

It was worth the cost. Operation VITTLES achieved all of its purposes and more. It satisfied the needs of more than two million people, proving the ability of airlift to sustain a large isolated population. It was the first victory in a forty-year Cold War, demonstrating the resolve of the West in the face of the first major Communist challenge and encouraging the formation of NATO. It proved the continued ability of the United States and Great Britain to perform combined operations in the post-World War II era. It protected the economic recovery of Germany and planted the seeds for future unification as a noncommunist nation. The Berlin Airlift revolutionized the technology and methods of air power, proved the effectiveness of airlift as an instrument of national policy, and blazed the trail for hundreds of humanitarian airlifts around the world. It convinced many that the U.S. Air Force could move anything anywhere anytime. In terms of tonnage and sorties, Operation VITTLES remains the greatest airlift operation in history.

Lebanon Crisis: Operation BLUE BAT

David A. Byrd

DATES: July 14–October 24, 1958

LOCATION: Lebanon

OVERSEAS BASES: Adana (Incirlik) Air Base (AB), Turkey; Beirut International Airport, Lebanon; Furstenfeldbruck Field, Erding Field, Ramstein-Landstuhl AB, Rhein-Main AB, Germany; Evreaux-Fauville AB, France; Royal Air Force Sculthorpe, United Kingdom

AIR FORCE ORGANIZATIONS:

NUMBERED AIR FORCE:	WINGS: (con't.)
Nineteenth Air Force	363d Tactical Reconnaissance
	463d Troop Carrier
WINGS:	4505th Air Refueling
60th Troop Carrier	
63d Troop Carrier	**AIR DIVISION:**
86th Fighter-Interceptor	322d Air Division (Combat Cargo)
314th Troop Carrier	
317th Troop Carrier	**SQUADRONS:**
345th Tactical Bomb	498th Bomb
354th Tactical Fighter	7167th Air Transport

AIR FORCE AIRCRAFT: B–57, F–100, RF–101, RB–66, WB–66, F–86, T–33, C–130, C–124, C–119, C–54, C–131

Operations

In today's U.S. Air Force (USAF), the USAF Air Expeditionary Force (AEF), a tailored mix of airlift, reconnaissance, and attack aircraft with a myriad of responsibilities and capabilities, is central to the service's capacity to meet the combat aspect of its mission—the ability to attack anywhere, anytime. But, the concept of deploying significant U.S.-based air forces quickly is not new. Over forty years ago, the Air Force deployed its Composite Air Strike Force (CASF), a progenitor to the AEF, in response to the Lebanon Crisis. Featuring a wide range of

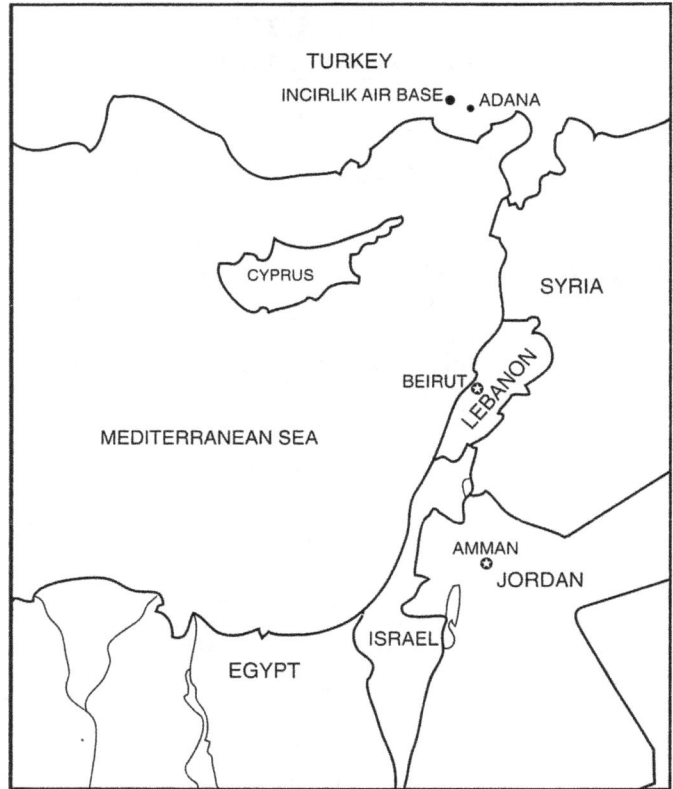

BLUE BAT Area of USAF Operations

aircraft from a number of different units, the CASF met the challenge of "anywhere, anytime."

Immediately following the Korean War, the United States adopted a military strategy acknowledging the ascendancy of the Cold War with the Soviet Union but also recognizing the threat posed by lesser conflicts. The U.S. Air Force developed the CASF as a flexible, mobile force, capable of meeting limited threats conventionally or with tactical nuclear arms. In the four years following the Korean War, the CASF command element, Headquarters Nineteenth Air Force, developed, implemented, and refined BLUE BLADE, the blueprint for CASF operations. The Air Force implemented the concept when trouble began brewing in the Middle East.

In May 1958, political instability in Lebanon led to armed rebellion. Well-equipped but politically divided Moslem rebels seized control of much of the country and demanded the removal of Camille Chamoun, the Christian president. Chamoun refused to resign, and the situation stalemated for several weeks. The overthrow of the Iraqi government on July 14 prompted President Chamoun, who feared the coup would spur renewed action by rebels in Lebanon, to immediately request military aid from the United States, France, and Britain.

Lebanese rebels stated that they had no hostile intentions against the United States, but the possibility of losing a pro-Western ally to an anti-Western regime was not palatable to U.S. policy makers. Several months before the unrest, the United States had announced its willingness to support any Middle Eastern government who requested aid against armed aggression. Besides, U.S. military preparations for assistance had begun as early as mid-May; consequently, response to Chamoun's request was swift. On July 14, U.S. President Dwight D. Eisenhower ordered the U.S. Navy's Sixth Fleet to land U.S. Marines at 3:00 P.M. local time the following day, thus implementing BLUE BAT, the operational plan for Middle East operations. The Air Force's involvement was divided into three distinct actions: Composite Air Strike Force "Bravo" deployed into Adana (present-day Incirlik) AB, Turkey. At the same time, the U.S. Air Forces in Europe (USAFE) airlifted U.S. Army troops and supplies to Lebanon. Finally, the Military Air Transport Service (MATS) deployed numerous aircraft from the United States to Europe to assist in the USAFE airlift.

The first of three U.S. Marine landing teams startled lounging, bikini-clad vacationers when it arrived on Lebanon beaches in the mid-afternoon hours of July 15. Within hours, they had assumed control of the Beirut International Airport and moved into the city itself early the next day. The marines encountered no resistance.

Before the marines waded ashore, the Air Force was ordering its units into action. C–124s from the MATS 63d Troop Carrier Wing (TCW) at Donaldson AFB, South Carolina, began flying out late on the evening of July 14. Twenty-six were in place at Rhein-Main AB, Germany, by July 16, and another ten from Donaldson arrived the following day. In addition to

USAF Troop Carrier C–54, typical of the C–54s used during Operation BLUE BAT.

the thirty-six aircraft en route, USAFE used eight MATS C–124s from the 63d TCW already on temporary duty to Europe. As the aircraft arrived in Germany, they were integrated into the 322d Air Division (AD), USAFE's combat cargo unit responsible for airlift.

On July 15, some C–124s, along with thirty-two C–130s from the 317th TCW, and nineteen C–119s from the 60th TCW—both wings assigned to the 322d AD—converged on Furstenfeldbruck and Erding Fields in Germany. The following day, the aircraft began moving the U.S. Army's "Task Force Alpha," consisting of 1,749 paratroopers and associated equipment, from there to Adana, Turkey. Although air sovereignty and landing rights issues with Austria and Greece complicated the seventy-two-sortie movement, Alpha was in Turkey ready for deployment by July 17. After a daylong delay caused by congestion at the airport in Beirut, Task Force Alpha arrived in Lebanon on July 19. While Task Force Bravo remained on twenty-four-hour alert in Germany, Task Force Charlie—made up primarily of support personnel—followed closely behind Alpha. Lack of ramp space at Adana delayed arrival of this unit in Turkey, although some aircraft made it through on July 19. These transports flew from Turkey to Lebanon the following day, and other 322d AD aircraft completed the movement of Charlie directly from Germany to Lebanon by July 26. All together in the 12-day period, aircraft under the control of the 322d AD flew 418 accident-free sorties and airlifted over 8 million pounds of troops and cargo.

The diverse mix of aircraft and units, the logistical difficulties associated with arranging and implementing airlift and aerial refueling, and the last-minute nature of the situation combined to make the deployment of the CASF the most challenging aspect of USAF operations in the Lebanon Crisis. Despite pending inactivation because of the ongoing phaseout of B–57Bs, the 345th Tactical Bombardment Wing at Langley AFB, Virginia, deployed one of its twelve-aircraft squadrons to Adana on July 15. It was the first U.S.-based tactical unit to depart. The first ten B–57s, assigned to the 498th Bomb Squadron, were in place by July 17; the final two arrived the next day.

Although originally not part of the CASF plan, nor the first aircraft to leave the United States, F–100s from the 354th Tactical Fighter Wing (TFW) were the first to arrive in Turkey. Of the initial twelve-ship package launched in the mid-afternoon of July 15, four arrived in Turkey around noon local time on July 16, twelve and one-half hours after takeoff from Myrtle Beach AFB, South Carolina. Air aborts and other logistical problems prevented all but three of the initial package from making it to Adana; aircraft from the second and third launches brought the total number of F–100s in Turkey to twenty-six. More would arrive in the weeks that followed.

The CASF also included RF–101s, RB–66s, and WB–66Ds from the 363d Tactical Reconnaissance Wing (TRW) at Shaw AFB, South Carolina. As with the 354th TFW, air aborts proved a problem for this package. Twelve RF–101s launched from Shaw, but five returned to base due to mechanical problems. The RB–66s had their problems as well, to include the loss of one aircraft 325 miles southeast of Lajes. Rescuers subsequently picked up the pilot and navigator but could not find the gunner. Despite the troubles, the whole reconnaissance force was in place by July 20.

The first RB-66 aircraft made. An aircraft like this was lost 325 miles southeast of Lajes where the pilot and navigator were rescued, but the gunner was never found.

The 463d and 314th Troop Carrier Wings provided most of the CASF airlift. Twenty-four C-130s from the 314th and nineteen from the 463d transported material and personnel ranging from the Nineteenth Air Force (command element for CASF) to support equipment and troops from Shaw, Langley, and Myrtle Beach AFBs. The short notice given the airlift wings caused some problems for the 314th. Some aircraft, positioned at Pope AFB, North Carolina, and Stewart AFB, New York, to perform other missions, deployed from those locations without all the required equipment. The C-130s returned to the United States after the initial airlift.

While airlift was generally satisfactory, problems during the deployment phase of CASF Bravo included inadequate planning, experience, and supplies. Most significant, however, was unsatisfactory air-to-air refueling availability and procedures. A lack of spares to replace aborted 4505th Air Refueling Wing KB-50s at the first refueling location left several of the 354th's F-100s short of fuel, and three were forced to abort to Greenwood

Field in Nova Scotia. One aircraft crashed there because of fuel starvation compounded by inclement weather; the pilot ejected safely. In addition to the aborts, the KB–50s carried reduced loads because runway repair at Langley prevented takeoff with full loads. Inclement weather, a refueling unit not qualified for night air refueling procedures, and aborts all contributed to a shortage of tankers at the second air-to-air refueling area near Lajes Field, Azores, and at the final refueling area over Europe.

Despite the difficulties, all CASF forces were in place at Adana on July 20. The fifty-five combat aircraft force included twenty-six F–100s, twelve B–57s, seven RF–101s, seven RB–66s, and three WB–66s. Nine F–86s from the 86th Fighter-Interceptor Wing (Ramstein AB, Germany)—technically not part of the CASF—provided air defense for the base. About 1,100 personnel also deployed. Four KB–50s of the 429th Air Reconnaissance Squadron deployed to Adana on July 21 as a last-minute addition in case air-to-air refueling was needed. They remained on one-hour alert throughout much of the deployment with aircrews initially sleeping under their airplanes.

Adm. James L. Holloway, USN, Commander in Chief, Specified Command, Middle East, oversaw U.S. military operations during the Lebanon Crisis. Elements of the Sixth Fleet, U.S. Army and Marine units, and the CASF and associated air units comprised American forces. Maj. Gen. Henry Viccellio, USAF, Commander of Nineteenth Air Force and of the CASF, also served as the Commander, U.S. Air Forces, and directed all USAF air operations.

Thanks to diminishing tensions in the area after the arrival of U.S. forces, the United States did not engage in combat during the Lebanon Crisis. Air employment operations consisted of mass fly-overs of Lebanon, reconnaissance, air defense, and a leaflet drop. In addition, the Air Force supported British troops in Jordan with an airlift.

The first CASF flights began on July 18 when six 354th TFW F–100s flew their initial combat sorties. From then until their departure on October 19, the F–100s flew a total of 874 sorties. Missions included combat air patrols, scrambles, and training. Operations were generally uneventful, although aircraft suffered

Composite Air Strike Force KB–50 tanker refueling F–100, F–101, and RB–66, all accompanied by two C–130s.

from a chronic lack of supplies and experienced a pair of landing accidents at Adana.

While the Super Sabres patrolled the skies during the day, USAFE F–86s provided air defense for the base after sunset. Their 506 sorties also provided training opportunities for the aircrews. Occasionally the F–86s augmented the F–100s during daytime operations or stood in for them during inclement weather.

The B–57s also began operations on July 18. Through the end of the deployment, they flew day and night visual reconnaissance, various training sorties, and other missions. Ten B–57s participated in show-of-force formations on July 23, 26, and 29. Maintenance crews of the often-balky aircraft maintained a surprisingly high in-commission rate of 87 percent during the deployment. One B–57 suffered small-arms fire damage, probably from a .30-caliber rifle.

The reconnaissance package of the 363d TRW bore the heaviest load during the CASF Bravo deployment, primarily in support of U.S. Army requests. Flights began July 21 and included weather, day photo, and visual reconnaissance missions. The package performed adequately, although the RB–66 aircraft, which had to be flown low and slow to perform its mission adequately, received small-arms ground fire on numerous occasions. No one was hurt, and damage was minimal.

Seven Air Force C–124s and 13 C–130s airlifted 247 tons of fuel to Jordan from Beirut during July 17–26. The airlift supported thirty-five British troops in that country performing much the same mission as U.S. forces in Lebanon. On July 24, more transports began carrying supplies to the British contingent, an airlift that lasted until August 10. Altogether, both airlift operations moved 2,277 tons of cargo into Jordan's capital.

In the last major deployment action of the crisis, 322d AD aircraft transported Task Force Delta (4,411 support personnel, including an Honest John missile battery) and Task Force Echo (668-man artillery unit) during the first two weeks of August, flying directly out of Germany to Beirut. When this phase of airlift was completed, the 322d AD had flown 13,997 hours without incident, airlifting over 8,200 tons.

Psychological warfare operations in Lebanon took the form of a leaflet drop July 21. Two escorted USAF C–130s dropped one million leaflets over the populated areas of Lebanon explaining the role of the United States in the country. In the end, the Lebanese people generally approved of American presence. One could argue that the pro-American leaflets helped; just as likely, however, was the stability the U.S. forces provided and the improved business climate that resulted.

The arrival of the Americans prompted intense political activity by the various Lebanese factions to solve the country's internal problems without bloodshed. Gen. Fouad Chehab, head of the Lebanese army, was elected to replace President Chamoun on July 31. Leading rebels as well as those in the government found him acceptable. By mid-August, the situation warranted the withdrawal of one Marine battalion. The WB–66s—generally not needed thanks to mostly clear weather during the deployment—departed in late August, followed by eight F–100s on September 4 and eight more on September 13. Chehab assumed governmental control on September 23, and remaining U.S. forces left Lebanon and Turkey in various stages over the next thirty days.

Dubbed Operation HATRACK, 322d AD transports began withdrawal of U.S. Army units on October 18. Heavy equipment went first, then personnel. C–130s and C–124s flew seventy-seven sorties in this phase of the redeployment. Altogether, the division airlifted 2,579 passengers and over 1,100 tons of freight without incident or accident. The operation ended October 28.

Operation SUNDANCE, the redeployment of the Composite Air Strike Force, began the day after USAFE started airlifting the U.S. Army out of Lebanon. The bulk of CASF aircraft, to include six F–100s and the remaining B–57s and RF–101s, departed Adana on October 19. USAFE F–86s followed them two days later. Twelve F–100s of the 353d Fighter Squadron stayed behind as part of a temporary rotational squadron. The air, land, and naval headquarters officially inactivated October 24, bringing BLUE BAT and USAF involvement in the Lebanon Crisis officially to an end.

The U.S. military establishment learned a number of lessons from its three-month action in Lebanon. In a February 1959 memo to the National Security Council, the Joint Chiefs of Staff (JCS) cited five lessons learned, two of which directly reflected problems the Air Force experienced during its operations. First, the JCS wrote that the early determination of overflight and staging rights hampered the USAF response. During the crisis, Greece, Israel, and Austria imposed restrictions that negatively affected initial airlift of ground forces and deployment of the CASF. During the airlift to Jordan, Saudi Arabia's restrictions forced the Air Force to airlift fuel from Beirut rather than Bahrain. Second, inadequate facilities seriously constrained operations, particularly during the early days of the operation. Although Adana was the best base available to meet the demands of the Lebanon Crisis, it was in fact inadequate in terms of size and prepositioned supplies. Additionally, the United States failed to notify Turkey of plans to use Adana; subsequently, the Turks began to apply strict controls on U.S. military activities in that country. Poor planning also negatively impacted USAF reaction to the crisis. For example, MATS was originally cast to provide CASF airlift, not Tactical Air Command's (TAC) own C–130 units. More significantly, the TAC F–100 unit that eventually deployed was not scheduled to go—the 354th TFW, which had just received a new designation and mission two weeks before, replaced the 832d AD with only a few hours notice. Although CASF crews were fully qualified for the delivery of nuclear weapons, the F–100 pilots had not shot rockets nor dropped conventional bombs. Only a few had strafing experience. Similarly, the B–57 crews lacked experience in conventional weapons delivery.

Despite the difficulties associated with Operation BLUE BAT, a number of positive results came from the deployment. Changes were made to later iterations of the CASF planning document to answer shortcomings. In addition, the Lebanon Crisis, as well as later emergency deployments of the late 1950s and early 1960s, led to the establishment of PRIME BEEF (Base Engineer Emergency Force) teams. PRIME BEEF's mission of providing force beddown and other essential civil engineer services marked an evolution in Air Force support doctrine that continues today.

In the end, the USAF response to the Lebanon Crisis proved to be a victory on a number of fronts, and its consequences continue today. Air power played a predominant role in furthering U.S. political aims, and the Lebanese government did not fall. Just as significantly, the Air Force proved it could deploy a large force quickly in response to a limited threat. Although the deployment revealed a number of flaws, the service implemented corrective actions that resulted in a force more capable of reacting to similar situations in the future. The lessons learned have been continually refined over the last forty years. The CASF and its descendants have evolved into today's Air Expeditionary Force. Like the CASF, the AEF draws its resources mostly from units based in the United States and deploys them overseas to meet current contingencies as quickly as possible.

Crisis in the Congo: Operation NEW TAPE

Daniel L. Haulman

DATES: July 8, 1960–June 30, 1964

LOCATION: Democratic Republic of the Congo

OVERSEAS BASES USED: Accra, Ghana; Addis Ababa (Harar Meda Airport), Ethiopia; Albertville, Coquilhatville, Elizabethville, Goma, Kamina, Kindu, Leopoldville (N'Djila Airport), Libenge, Luluabourg, Pointe Noire, Stanleyville, the Congo; Amman, Jordan; Asmara, Ethiopia; Bonn, Cologne, Rhein-Main AB, Stuttgart, Germany; Bordeaux, Evreux-Fauville AB, Chateauroux Air Station (AS), France; Brazzaville, Congo-Brazzaville; Brussels, Belgium; Cairo, Egypt (United Arab Republic); Clark Air Base (AB), Philippines; Conakry, Guinea; Copenhagen (Vaerlose Airfield), Denmark; Dakar, Senegal (Mali Federation); Dar es Salaam, Tanganyika; Dhahran, Saudi Arabia; Diredawa, Ethiopia; Djakarta, Indonesia; Dublin, Ireland; Entebbe, Uganda; Freetown, Sierra Leone; Garoua, Cameroon; Harmon, Malmo, Stockholm (Arlana Airport), Sweden; Kano, Lagos, Nigeria; Karachi, Pakistan; Khartoum, Sudan; Kuala Lumpur, Malaya; Lome, Togo; Luanda, Angola; Mildenhall, Prestwick, United Kingdom; Monrovia (Roberts Field), Liberia; Nairobi, Kenya; Bombay, New Delhi, Jamnager AB, India; Oslo, Norway; Pisa, Italy; Salisbury, Rhodesia; Sidi Slimane AB, Morocco; Tehran, Iran; Trenton, Ontario, Canada; Tunis (El Aouina Airfield), Tunisia; Vienna, Austria; Wheelus AB, Libya

AIR FORCE ORGANIZATIONS:

DIVISION:	WINGS: (cont.)
322d Air (USAFE) (later, MATS)	1602d Air Transport
	1607th Air Transport
AIR FORCES:	1608th Air Transport
Eastern Transport Air Force (MATS)	1611th Air Transport
Western Transport Air Force (MATS)	MATS Air Transport Wing, Provisional (Europe)
WINGS:	**SQUADRONS:**
62d Troop Carrier	MATS Air Transport Squadron, Provisional (Europe-1)
63d Troop Carrier	MATS Air Transport Squadron, Provisional (Europe-2)
317th Troop Carrier	MATS Air Transport Squadron, Provisional (Europe-3)
464th Troop Carrier	MATS Air Transport Squadron, Provisional (Europe-4)
1501st Air Transport	

AIR FORCE AIRCRAFT: C–130, C–124, C–118, C–119, C–135, C–133, C–121, C–54

Operations

Independence brought chaos to the Congo. Within days after Belgium granted the country independence on June 30, 1960, various factions within the new nation began fighting among themselves. As early as July 5, elements of the Congolese army mutinied, demanding promotions, pay raises, and the removal of Belgian officers. Various tribes across the country demanded independence for their provinces. The breakdown of law and order led to riots and looting in the cities. Mobs threatened Europeans, who began a mass exodus from the country. To protect those who remained, Belgium reinforced a 2,500-man garrison it had left, by treaty, in the Congo.

On July 11, Moise Tshombe declared Katanga Province independent and asked for Belgian military support. The Congolese government, headed by President Joseph Kasavubu and Premier Patrice Lumumba, appealed to the United Nations (UN) to send troops to replace those of Belgium. They threatened to turn to the Soviet Union if the UN failed to do so. On July 14, two days after the request, the UN Security Council resolved to airlift peacekeeping troops to the Congo. None of these troops would come from any of the five permanent members of the Security Council, which included the United States and Soviet Union.

Since July 8, the U.S. Air Force (USAF) was already evacuating Americans and airlifting desperately needed food to the Congo in an operation called SAFARI. U.S. President Dwight D. Eisenhower agreed to airlift most of the UN troops as well, and the operation was renamed NEW TAPE. The operation would last four years, rotating troops between their countries and the Congo, delivering food to where it was most needed, and evacuating refugees.

The 322d Air Division of the U.S. Air Forces in Europe (USAFE), then under command of Col. Tarleton H. Watkins, USAF, operationally controlled military transports in Europe and Africa. Three C–130 Hercules squadrons at Evreux-Fauville AB in France and Military Air Transport Service (MATS) C–124 Globemaster IIs at Chateauroux AS, France, were available for the initial phases of Operation NEW TAPE. The division set up

Combat Airlift Support Units around Africa to direct and track the movements of C–130s south of the Sahara Desert. Lt. Col. Francis E. Merritt, USAF, commanded the support unit at Leopoldville, capital of the Congo. At the same time, MATS set up Movement Control Teams at various bases around Africa to coordinate the movements and maintain intratheater C–124s. Col. Paul C. Steinle, USAF, commanded the most important team, at Brazzaville, just across the Congo River from Leopoldville.

On July 18, MATS set up a provisional wing alongside the 1602d Air Transport Wing at Chateauroux to support Operation NEW TAPE. The provisional wing, which initially embraced four C–124 air transport and two maintenance squadrons, served under Col. Marshall H. Strickler, USAF, until July 25. Then Col. William H. Schwartz Jr., USAF, Commander, 1602d Air Transport Wing, assumed command of the provisional organization as well.

Some of the Operation NEW TAPE flights were especially memorable. In one four-day operation in 1960, C–124s from Chateauroux picked up Moroccan troops at Sidi Slimane in North Africa, refueled at Dakar on the west African coast, and stopped at Accra, Ghana. After twenty-seven hours of duty, the crew rested for twelve hours. The Globemasters continued on to Leopoldville, where they unloaded, refueled, and underwent routine maintenance checks. The crews stopped at Dakar for rest on the way back. By the time the airplanes returned to Chateauroux, they had covered 11,200 miles. Another mission from Chateauroux landed in Egypt to load Swedish troops, who had been patrolling the Gaza strip on the border with Israel, and carried them via Wheelus AB, Libya, and Kano, Nigeria, to Leopoldville. That round-trip covered 11,720 miles. It compared in distance to forty-four Berlin Airlift flights, or twenty-two World War II "Hump" missions.

Crews faced many dangers on these missions, not the least of which was flying for hundreds of miles over the world's largest desert. They were not necessarily safe when they landed in the Congo. At Stanleyville on August 27, 1960, Congolese soldiers pulled a C–124 crew off their airplane and severely beat them, apparently mistaking them for Belgians.

Despite these challenges, USAF aircraft airlifted 20,000 passengers, including refugees and more than 16,000 troops,

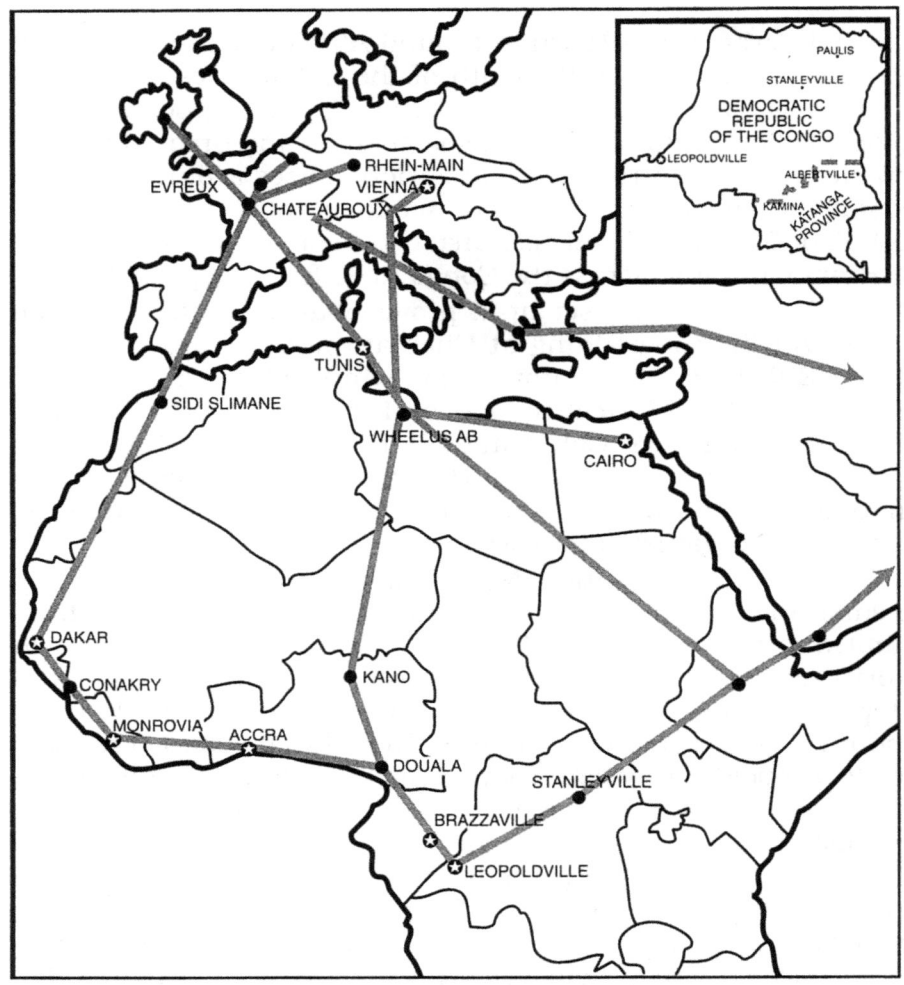

Operation NEW TAPE Routes
Inset: Democratic Republic of the Congo

during the first 3 months of Operation NEW TAPE. They also transported more than 3,300 tons of cargo, including UN military equipment and over 1,100 tons of food. After September 1960, the number of C–130 and C–124 airplanes needed in Africa declined. The MATS provisional wing based at Chateauroux disappeared, and only one provisional air transport and one provisional maintenance squadron remained alongside the 1602d Air Transport Wing.

American transports airlifted more than food and UN military equipment to the Congo. In December, 5 C–130s and 6 C–124s carried 112 Austrian medical personnel and 122 tons of medical equipment and supplies from Vienna via Libya, Nigeria, and Uganda to Goma in the Congo. The flights took sixteen hours.

Operation NEW TAPE fluctuated with events in the Congo. In September 1960, President Kasavubu and Premier Lumumba fired each other, and Col. Joseph Mobutu, Congolese army chief of staff, took over the government. Tshombe continued to fight for the independence of Katanga Province, and Albert Kalonji led a new secession movement in Kasai Province. After the assassination of Lumumba in February 1961, the UN Security Council voted to use force to end the Congolese civil war and prevent the secession of two valuable provinces. The United States airlifted more troops from around the world to the Congo. In June, the United Nations convened a new Congolese Parliament, and Kasavubu was renamed president, with Cyrille Adoula as new premier.

In September 1961, MATS gained operational control of the C–124s that had served USAFE's 322d Air Division while in Africa. After September 21, NEW TAPE missions became MATS special assignment airlift missions. UN Secretary General Dag Hammarskjold was killed in an aircraft crash, and his successor, U Thant of Burma, pursued a UN war in the Congo, attempting to establish stable political institutions while at the same time suppressing secession in Katanga and Kasai. Assisted by a predominantly American airlift of UN forces from countries around the world, he achieved some degree of success. Most of the troops came from Ethiopia, Ireland, Tunisia, Sweden, Nigeria, Morocco, India, Liberia, and Ghana. In December, MATS discontinued its provisional air transport and maintenance squadrons at Chateauroux, but the 1602d Air Transport Wing remained there with C–124 squadrons.

On January 8, 1962, France withdrew its support of the UN Congo operation; consequently, the Air Force could no longer fly from Chateauroux and Evreux-Fauville to Africa. Portugal followed France's example and also denied overflight clearances for aircraft on UN Congo missions. Thus, USAF flights from Britain, Germany, or Scandinavia followed new routes over the Brenner Pass in the Alps, using Wheelus AB as a staging base on the way to the Congo.

In October 1962, the USAF used jet-powered C–135s for the first time in the Congo operation. The faster Stratolifters were more comfortable and required fewer stops than their propeller-driven predecessors. They carried Swedish troops from Stockholm to the Congo, stopping only for fuel at Wheelus AB and flying over Kano, Nigeria, on the way.

During the second half of 1962, rotations of UN troops from other nations to central Africa continued, but more and more airlift missions were needed within the Congo, as UN forces drove into secessionist Katanga Province. By 1963, MATS C–124 airplanes shuttled troops within the Congo, while C–135 Stratolifters moved them among the scores of nations from which they came. Eventually, the C–135s carried more UN troops from the Congo to their native lands than the other way around. By 1964, NEW TAPE was tapering off. The 322d Air Division transferred from USAFE to MATS and moved to Chateauroux, and MATS officials discontinued the 1602d Air Transport Wing. A crisis in Cyprus between Turks and Greeks demanded the diversion of UN troops from central Africa to the Mediterranean, and by June 30, 1964, UN forces were out of the Congo. MATS continued to serve Leopoldville with a channel route from Charleston AFB, South Carolina.

C–130s at Wheelus AB, Libya, during Operation NEW TAPE.

Both USAFE and MATS learned many significant lessons from the NEW TAPE airlift experience. The Congo emergency was a surprise, and the Air Force was not fully prepared for the operation. In October 1960, MATS published a revised mobility manual recommending Quick Reaction Forces with equipment for rapid deployments. The forces would precede the main airlift force to a crisis area and arrange base support, schedule aircraft movements, and note suitability of airfields. NEW TAPE taught the Air Force to expect contingencies in all parts of the world and to prepare for operations in regions lacking modern facilities or equipment.

Operation NEW TAPE was the beginning of the end for the C-124 Globemaster IIs, and the end of the beginning for new jet cargo airplanes, such as the C-135 Stratolifter. Globemaster IIs were not suitable for many of the African airfields because they needed long and strong runways that were not always available. The piston engines of the C-124s operated poorly at airfields at high elevation, such as those in Ethiopia, or with high temperatures, such as those in the Sahara Desert. Slower and more costly to operate than the turboprop C-130s, the C-124s were also more particular about the fuel they drank.

In many ways, NEW TAPE was a much more demanding operation than the Berlin Airlift. For one thing, the distances

USAF crew members dine on a Congo airstrip.

were enormous! The voids of the Mediterranean Sea and Sahara Desert and the scarcity of adequate airfields in sub-Saharan Africa made extremely long flights necessary. From Evreux to Cairo, Egypt, was 1,765 miles. Tunis, Tunisia, to Kano, Nigeria, was 1,498 miles. The trip from Wheelus AB, Libya, to Kano required seven flying hours. An aircrew took 6 hours to fly the 1,200 miles between Kano and Brazzaville.

This operation was more demanding than the Berlin Airlift in other ways, as well. Many of the African airfields lacked the communication and navigational facilities that were common in Europe. Runways were often short or weak, and there was a shortage of ramp space, maintenance facilities, and materials-handling equipment such as forklifts. At some of the airfields, refueling equipment was nonexistent, and personnel had to manually pump fuel from fifty-five-gallon drums. To solve such problems, USAFE and MATS set up field maintenance teams at many locations in central Africa. Three C–124s shuttled among airfields with spare engines, propellers, and other parts, and after about a month of operations, there were thirteen repair kits in the theater. Quality maintenance contributed to a very low accident rate.

Shortages of personnel plagued Operation NEW TAPE. At Leopoldville, there were only twenty-five aerial port men, where almost four times as many were needed. During the first phases of the operation, twelve-hour workdays and seven-day workweeks were common. Resultant fatigue threatened morale and safety.

Hostile fire challenged some of the airlift flights over the Congo. In December 1961, some transports were hit by small-arms fire. MATS responded by temporarily suspending flights to the zone where the incidents occurred and by acquiring fighter escorts for a time. Future airlifts into hostile zones would face similar challenges.

Navigation and communication were problem areas. Air Force personnel originally lacked the maps and charts they needed to carry out flights to various sub-Saharan airfields. Absence of radio signals and landmarks over much of the African landscape forced crews to rely on celestial navigation, and even that was difficult in areas of dust storms. Weather information had to come from a Strategic Air Command base in Spain. Belgian and French airlines sometimes provided the necessary information. At first, the 322d Air Division and MATS lost track of some aircraft after they crossed the Sahara Desert because of the absence of radio communication facilities. The Air Force had to establish new radio and Teletype stations in Africa to alleviate the problem.

Command and control for Operation NEW TAPE was initially confused. At Brazzaville, Colonel Steinle was at first unaware that the airlift had expanded from food deliveries and refugee evacuations to airlift of UN troops, that MATS was augmenting the number of C-124s in Europe and Africa, and that the 322d Air Division of USAFE had operational control of his airplanes. Airplanes landing at Leopoldville or Brazzaville were often diverted from their flight schedules to carry out emergency refugee evacuations at the request of Clare H. Timberlake, U.S. ambassador to the Congo.

There was also a language problem, because air traffic controllers in the Congo initially could not communicate in both French and English. Troops from more than thirty countries eventually rode aboard USAF transports in Operation NEW TAPE, and many of them could not talk with each other or with the aircrews that were transporting them. Some of the cargo was mislabeled or was labeled in metric quantities with which all participants were not familiar.

Sanitation became a persistent problem with passengers who had never flown before or who had never seen an aircraft latrine. Ground personnel had to disinfect the planes routinely. Because of insects, aircraft had to be fumigated on a regular basis. Many nations required aircrews to show proof of immunization against seven dangerous diseases common in equatorial Africa and quarantined those who could not show such proof. This led to some flight delays. Despite precautions, MATS crews suffered eleven cases of malaria.

Unlike the machine-like Berlin Airlift, Operation NEW TAPE suffered irregularity because there were no steady cargo flows to Chateauroux or Evreux-Fauville. Some staging bases ran out of aircraft fuel, and rerouting was necessary. Field units in Africa, such as the Combat Airlift Support Units and Movement Control Teams, enjoyed the financial support of the U.S. Department of State but often lacked adequate billeting or messing facilities. Heat, disease, insects, and poor sanitation challenged people on the ground.

French and Portuguese denial of overflight clearances for Congo airlift missions early in 1962 encouraged the United States to develop longer-range and faster cargo airplanes and to consider aerial refueling for large transports to accommodate longer flights. Congress pressed for development of the C-141 Starlifter as a replacement for the C-124.

Operation NEW TAPE, the largest USAF airlift since the Berlin Airlift of 1948–49, covered much greater distances and carried more tons per aircraft. The monumental operation proceeded under three American presidents: Eisenhower, John F. Kennedy, and Lyndon B. Johnson. It supported the largest deployment of UN troops since the Korean War. In duration and in ton-miles, Operation NEW TAPE surpassed even the vaunted Berlin Airlift. MATS alone moved 63,899 passengers and 18,806 tons of cargo among at least 24 nations in the 4 years between July 1960 and June 1964. By the end of 1962, USAFE's 322d Air Division and MATS together had already moved more than 94,000 passengers and over 21,000 tons of cargo on NEW TAPE missions. By 1964, eight kinds of airplanes had taken part, including giant C-133s and jet C-135s. No previous airlift had transported troops from so many nations over such long distances. American transports shuttled troops, refugees, and food among more than sixty different airfields.

Operation NEW TAPE allowed the United Nations to achieve many goals in the Congo, including preserving the country's unity, preventing a return to Belgian colonial rule, avoiding a Cold War confrontation in central Africa by preventing a unilateral Soviet intervention, and bringing some law and order in place of anarchy and chaos. The operation also prevented mass starvation by delivering thousands of tons of food, prevented genocide by evacuating thousands of refugees, and preserved international access to key raw materials, such as uranium, cobalt, and copper. The United States and other western nations depended on some of these for national defense. For both strategic and humanitarian reasons, Operation NEW TAPE succeeded, paving the way for other such operations in the future.

Cuban Missile Crisis

Edward T. Russell

DATES: October 13–November 15, 1962

LOCATION: Cuba

OVERSEAS BASE USED: Guantanamo Naval Air Station, Cuba

AIR FORCE ORGANIZATIONS:

MAJOR COMMANDS:	WINGS:
Strategic Air Command	55th Strategic Reconnaissance
Tactical Air Command	62d Troop Carrier
Military Air Transport Service	363d Tactical Reconnaissance
Continental Air Defense Command	1501st Air Transport Wing (Heavy)
Air Force Reserve	4080th Strategic

AIR FORCE AIRCRAFT: C–124, C–133, C–135, RB–47, RF–101, U–2

Operations

Early in 1962, the Premier of the Soviet Union, Nikita S. Khrushchev, could not match the United States in nuclear weapons or strategic delivery systems nor push the western nations out of Berlin. In the east, the Chinese constantly harassed him concerning Soviet weakness. In his frustration and frantic search for an opportunity to alter the strategic imbalance, he turned to Cuba. In 1959, Fidel Castro had overthrown the dictator, Fulgencio Batista, and assumed power. Initially promising free elections, he soon instituted a socialist dictatorship. Hundreds of thousands of Cubans fled their island, many coming to the United States. From his rhetoric and actions, Castro proved he was a Communist. Consequently, in late 1960, the President of the United States, Dwight D. Eisenhower, authorized the Central Intelligence Agency to plan an invasion of Cuba using Cuban exiles as troops. Ultimately, Eisenhower hoped that in conjunction with the invasion, the Cuban people would overthrow Castro and install a moderate, pro-U.S. government. Eisenhower's second term ended before the plan could be implemented. The new president, John F. Kennedy, eager to prove that he was more aggressive than his predecessor, ordered the invasion to proceed. In mid-April 1961, the Cuban exiles landed at the Bay of Pigs and suffered a crushing defeat. Not only did the Cuban people not rise to help them, but Castro's forces killed some 200 and captured close to 1,200 invaders.

Following the Bay of Pigs fiasco, Khrushchev increased Soviet aid, including military supplies to Cuba. In August 1962, the Soviet Union, with Cuban cooperation, began to build intermediate-range (IRBM) and medium-range ballistic missile (MRBM) sites on the island. The American intelligence community, suspicious of the construction on the island, needed tangible proof and called for photographic reconnaissance. On October 11, 1962, Headquarters Strategic Air Command (SAC) notified the 4080th Strategic Wing at Laughlin Air Force Base (AFB), Texas, to "freeze" two officers, Maj. Richard S. Heyser and Maj. Rudolf Anderson Jr., for a special project. They reported to Edwards AFB, California, where they received orders to conduct strategic reconnaissance flights over Cuba. On October 13, Major Anderson deployed to McCoy AFB, Florida, to join a U–2 aircraft ferried in for the special mission. Meantime, Major Heyser launched from Edwards AFB in a U–2 equipped to photograph suspect sites on the island. He arrived over the island during daylight on October 14. The next day, Major Anderson made his flight from McCoy. Photographs obtained on these flights confirmed that Soviet/Cuban crews had launch pads under construction that, when completed, could fire nuclear-armed IRBMs with a range of approximately 5,000 miles and MRBMs with a range of approximately 3,000 miles.

While the U–2s flew high-altitude reconnaissance missions, the staff of the 363d Tactical Reconnaissance Wing at Shaw AFB, South Carolina, made aware of the potential need for low-level flights over Cuba, began planning such flights and preparing target folders. On October 21, Tactical Air Command (TAC) ordered the 363d to deploy to MacDill AFB, Florida. The wing began immediately to move RF–101 and RB–66 aircraft, personnel, and photographic equipment to Florida. By the next morning, the aircraft were at MacDill, cameras cocked, ready to carry out any reconnaissance missions. While aircrews went on alert, support personnel expanded the

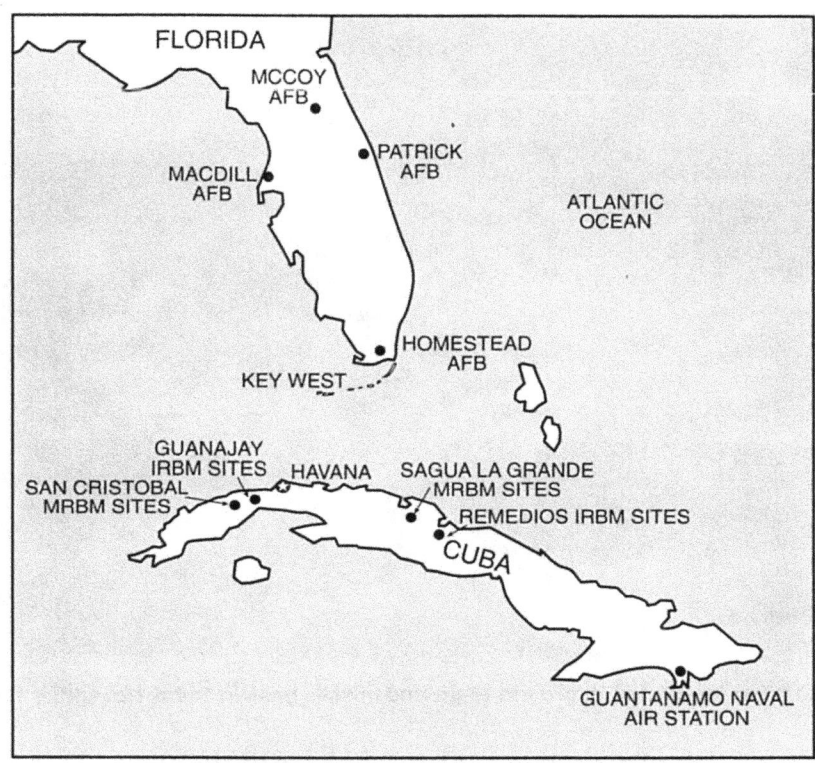

Area of USAF Operations in Cuban Missile Crisis

base photo-laboratory facilities and installed photo vans and darkrooms. Because of a shortage of adequate facilities, aircrews and other airmen occupied temporary, inadequate, wooden barracks that hampered crew rest. After trying off-base housing, the aircrews moved to permanent airmen's quarters on the base for the remainder of the deployment.

On October 26, the wing launched the first flight of two low-level reconnaissance aircraft. For the next three weeks, wing aircraft, by photographic and visual reconnaissance, gathered vital data, including prestrike intelligence, air-surveillance verification of Cuban buildup, and subsequent dismantling of the IRBM and MRBM sites and Soviet IL–28 aircraft. Because of the possibility of alternate sites and concealed storage facilities, the wing initiated intensive low-level aerial search efforts. Other flights returned with highly significant

Photo taken by RF–101 of ground-to-ground missile base in Cuba, November 1962.

photographs of missiles and related equipment on docks at Cuban ports, the loading of Soviet freighters, and the deck cargo of Soviet ships entering and leaving Cuban ports. Consequently, the President of the United States was constantly aware of Soviet actions regarding the withdrawal of the missiles from Cuba.

Analysis of the 363d photographs provided a wide range of essential intelligence concerning Cuba. Frequent sorties over major Cuban airfields provided daily information on the number, type, and specific location of Cuban aircraft. Photos also revealed the number and location of assembled, partially assembled, or unassembled IL–28 Soviet twin-engine tactical bombers with a range of 1,500 miles. This information was vital to establish immediate air superiority if strike forces went into action. On one of these missions, the 363d discovered the first evidence of the existence of infrared homing air-to-air missiles (Soviet AA–2s). Surface-to-air missile (SAM) sites proved to be prime targets for low-level reconnaissance missions. The wing also garnered extensive intelligence concerning Cuban ground equipment, military encampments, cruise-missile sites, and possible landing beaches.

SAC ordered continual U-2 reconnaissance flights over Cuba, and at the same time, in order to make room for fighter aircraft, ordered the deployment of medium and heavy bombers and tanker aircraft from MacDill, McCoy, and Homestead AFBs in Florida. Meanwhile, TAC began deploying F-84, F-100, F-105, RB-66, and KB-50 aircraft to bases in Florida, while Continental Air Defense Command (CONAD) began flying missions to protect bases in the southeastern United States. SAC, alerted to the possibility of war with the Soviet Union, dispersed nuclear-armed B-47 aircraft to approximately forty airfields in the United States and kept numerous B-52 heavy bombers in the air and ready to strike. In addition, all available intercontinental ballistic missiles (ICBM) stood ready for a launch countdown. These included the first ten solid-fueled Minuteman I ICBMs, which became operational on October 27.

While TAC continued to deploy fighter aircraft to MacDill, McCoy, and Homestead AFBs, the Military Air Transport Service (MATS) not only flew bombs and ammunition into bases in the southeast but also responded to airlift requests from the U.S. Army and Marine Corps. On October 20, 1962, for instance, the Joint Chiefs directed the Air Force to move nearly 2,000 marines and 1,400 tons of equipment to the U. S. Naval Air Station at Guantanamo, Cuba. Air Force C-124s, C-133s, and C-135s completed this task in two days.

In the midst of these preparations, President Kennedy and his advisors debated the sanest course of action. The President outlined the general goals: remove all Soviet missiles from Cuba, avoid a nuclear war, prepare for Soviet countermoves in Berlin, and preserve national honor. He formed an executive committee, which included the Attorney General Robert F. Kennedy, to give him advice. The committee examined several options such as launching a nuclear attack against the missile sites, launching a conventional strike against the sites followed by an invasion of Cuba, or instituting a naval blockade to prevent Soviet supplies from reaching the island. Fear of Soviet reaction soon eliminated talk of a nuclear strike, but support for a conventional air strike followed by invasion continued to grow. While the invasion forces gathered in Florida, Kennedy ordered the state department to develop a plan for civil government in Cuba. Former Secretary of State Dean Acheson and the Joint Chiefs favored an invasion, but Robert Kennedy vehemently opposed that plan and instead advocated a blockade. The President listened to his brother, and on October 22, 1962, appeared on television to explain to America and the world that the United States was imposing a strict quarantine on offensive military equipment being shipped to Cuba. Kennedy also warned Khrushchev that the United States would regard any missile attack from Cuba as an attack from the Soviet Union and would retaliate against the Soviet Union. SAC increased its alert posture by placing more B–52s on airborne alert.

Khrushchev responded belligerently. In a letter received in Washington on October 23, 1962, he accused the United States of degenerate imperialism and declared that the Soviet Union would not observe the illegal blockade. Nevertheless, the quarantine began on October 24. Tension mounted as the Soviets continued to work on the missile sites and their ships continued moving toward Cuba. Then on October 26, Khrushchev sent another message in which he offered to withdraw or destroy the weapons in Cuba, provided the United States would lift the blockade and promise not to invade the island. Before the presidential advisors could decide on an answer, another message arrived raising the price. Now the Soviets wanted the United States to withdraw all missiles from Turkey. On October 27, an RB–47 from the 55th Strategic Reconnaissance Wing located the Soviet freighter *Grozny* and reported its location. Meantime, Major Anderson failed to return from a U–2 reconnaissance mission. The Joint Chiefs recommended an immediate air strike against Cuba, but the President decided to wait.

The increasing tempo in the military, however, continued unabated. SAC ordered over sixty B–52 bombers to continue on airborne alert. TAC forces in Florida assumed a one-hour alert and prepared to go to a fifteen-minute alert, which involved pilots waiting in aircraft for launch orders. The Army placed six divisions on alert and called on MATS and the Air Force Reserve for airlift support. The U.S. Navy, in addition to tracking every known Soviet submarine in the Western Hemisphere, patrolled the high seas waiting for the Soviet ships to arrive.

In Washington, the President's advisors examined the Khrushchev letters and debated the appropriate action. The launch pads in Cuba were almost finished, and there were already missiles on the island. Furthermore, the Soviet ships carrying additional missiles were fast approaching the island and the quarantine cordon of the U.S. Fleet. Something had to be done. Robert Kennedy proposed that the President ignore Khrushchev's last message and instead answer the message offering to exchange the removal of the missiles with an American promise not to invade Cuba. After a heated debate, the advisors recommended that the President follow this proposal while Robert Kennedy met with the Soviet Ambassador, Anatoly Dobrynin, and in effect, promised to remove the American missiles from Turkey. This promise was sufficient. The next day the Soviet Union informed the United States that the missiles in Cuba would be withdrawn. The Soviets began turning their ships around, packing up the missiles in Cuba, and dismantling the launch pads. As the work progressed, the Air Force started to deploy aircraft back to home bases and lower the alert status.

The Air Force response to the crisis must be rated as outstanding. On October 19, 1962, the Air Force followed its normal peacetime posture. Within the following week, American airmen evacuated SAC bombers and tankers from Florida to make room for tactical fighters and defense forces. They placed B–52 forces on airborne alert, dispersed the B–47 fleet to predetermined military bases and civil airports, and brought the SAC airborne force (approximately 1,400 bombers and 900 tankers) to full combat alert. In addition, SAC initiated shipping surveillance assistance fifteen hours after receiving the request from Commander in Chief Atlantic. Throughout the crisis the Air Force flew daily high- and low-level reconnaissance flights to keep the U.S. leadership apprised of activities on the island of Cuba and on the high seas. Concurrently, TAC, which had 140 tactical fighters in Florida, increased this number to 511 fighters, 72 reconnaissance aircraft, and 40 tankers. At the same time, Air Force leaders

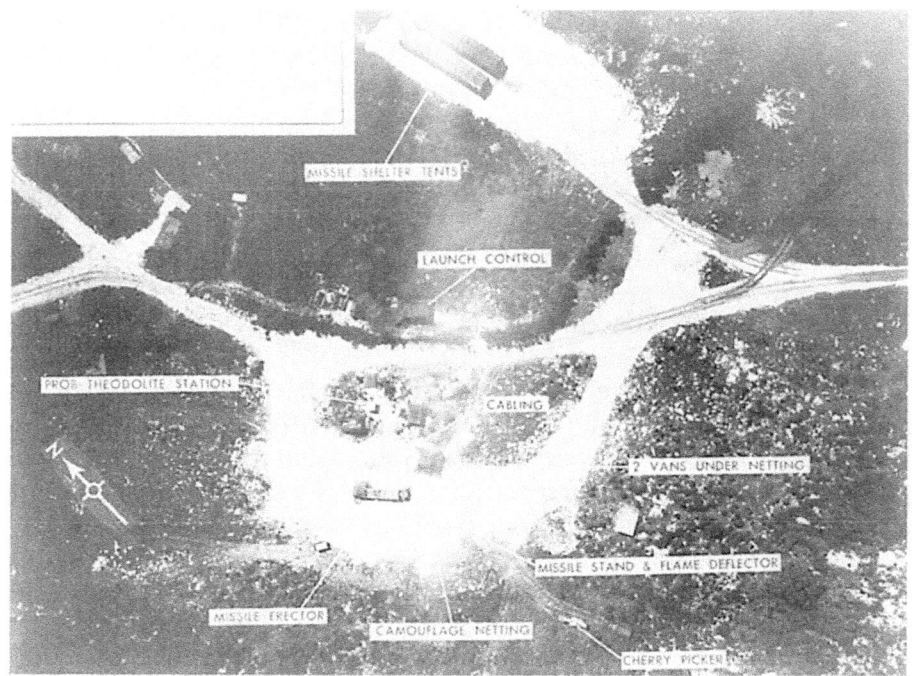

Missile site in Cuba, November 1962.

formulated a plan to augment the European force with ten additional fighter squadrons. At the beginning of the crisis, CONAD had 240 aircraft on normal air defense alert. Within 48 hours, it increased the force in Florida to 82 aircraft (F–101s, F–102s, and F–106s) and the total number on alert to 520 aircraft.

The airlifters of Military Air Transport Service, Tactical Air Command, and the Air Force Reserve played a vital role during the crisis. They airlifted several Marine battalions from points in the United States to Guantanamo Bay, Cuba, TAC support units from bases all over the United States to bases in Florida, and Army units from various locations to the southeastern United States. In addition to moving personnel, the airlifters carried bombs, rockets, ammunition, tanks, and other materiel. Some of this materiel came from as far as Turkey and the Philippines. MATS estimated that it airlifted 6,738 tons of cargo and 5,018 passengers in direct support of the Cuban requirements.

In examining the crisis, Secretary of Defense Robert S. McNamara noted deficiencies in the conventional forces. For example, there were not enough aircraft available to locate every Soviet ship moving toward the Western Hemisphere. In addition, because of a shortage of transport aircraft, the government called up approximately 14,000 Reservists and utilized approximately 400 obsolete aircraft to accomplish the airlift mission. Finally, McNamara noted the shortage of fighter aircraft, pointing out that air defenses in other parts of the United States had been stripped because of the need in the southeastern part of the country.

The Cuban Missile Crisis brought the world dangerously close to nuclear war, and the world breathed a sigh of relief when it ended. The strategic and tactical power of the U.S. Air Force, coupled with the will and ability to use it, provided the synergy to deter nuclear war with the Union of Soviet Socialist Republics and convince the Soviet leaders to remove the nuclear weapons from Cuba.

Indo-Chinese Conflict: Operation LONG SKIP

William J. Allen

DATES: November 2, 1962–August 31, 1963

LOCATION: India

OVERSEAS BASES USED: Dum Dum Air Base (AB), Calcutta; Palam Airport, New Delhi; and Leh Airfield, Ladakh, India; Rhein-Main AB, Germany

AIR FORCE ORGANIZATIONS:

AIR FORCES:	WINGS:	DETACHMENTS:
Eastern Transport	317th Troop Carrier	U.S. Air Attaché - Iran
Western Transport	1501st Air Transport	U.S. Air Attaché - Turkey
	1602d Air Transport	U.S. Air Attaché - Saudi Arabia
DIVISIONS:	1611th Air Transport	
322d Airlift		

AIR FORCE AIRCRAFT: VC–47, C–124, C–130, C–135

Operations

In 1962, the subcontinent of Asia was a huge, but undeveloped, giant. Its population exceeded the combined populations of Africa and South and Central America, and when compared to the United States, it contained nearly three times as many people! Its size alone made it an area of importance in the Cold War's balance of power. Moreover, the region's strategic importance increased with the economic expansion taking place. The world's policy makers could not ignore the potential that existed there.

Deeply entrenched in the Cold War, the United States constantly adjusted its foreign policy in the region in an attempt to keep two neighbors, India and Pakistan, from warring against each other and disrupting the balance of power. However, on October 20, 1962, India's and Pakistan's larger, more dangerous neighbor, the People's Republic of China, threw the subcontinent into turmoil. Communist Chinese troops attacked India across long-disputed Himalaya borders each shared.

Only a small portion of the 2,400-mile India-China border was officially or precisely defined, although the traditional boundary stood uncontested with no serious problems until 1955. At that time, the Chinese built a road across the Aksai Chin Plateau in northeastern Ladakh effectively seizing control of about 10,000 square miles of territory in Kashmir claimed by India. The Chinese exerted pressure with occasional light clashes along the disputed border between 1959 and 1962. Chinese activities on the Indian border increased after mid-1962, and heavy skirmishing broke out on August 20, when Chinese troops moved into India's Northeast Frontier Agency and the area around Ladakh. Here are some of the highest and most inaccessible territories in the world. In these areas, only airlift provided adequate supply lines into isolated valley landing fields.

On October 26, after a series of military reverses suffered by India during the first days of fighting, Prime Minister Jawaharlal Nehru wrote a letter to U.S. President John F. Kennedy outlining India's position on the border dispute and asking support in combating open Chinese aggression. President Kennedy's reply on October 28 promised solidarity with India and suggested talks between U.S. Ambassador J. Kenneth Galbraith and Indian officials about practical assistance. In conversations with Galbraith the following day, Nehru formally asked the United States for military assistance. By November 2, India had already received military assistance from the United Kingdom and Canada. After Nehru's request, the U.S. Department of Defense (DOD) established a small advisory team to refine and speed Indian military assistance requirements. The team reported directly to the Ambassador and the Secretary of Defense and operated within the U.S. Embassy since its chief was a member of the Country Team. The U.S. Air Force (USAF) and Army Secretaries and the Director of Military Assistance nominated one officer each to the team.

Arriving in New Delhi on November 1, the team reached agreement with Indian defense officials that same day concerning a list of the highest priority items for initial air shipment to India. Based on their availability and Indian ability to use them with the least delay, they included: 20,000 antipersonnel mines, machine guns, ammunition, mortars, and spare parts for the weapons. The United States expedited delivery by rounding out mine and ammunition quantities for aircraft loading capacity and waiving combat serviceable, packing, and preservation standards where necessary. The arms shipments included essential manuals and nomenclature lists.

Beginning its first all-jet cargo airlift on November 2, USAF Military Air Transport Service (MATS) delivered over 1,000 tons of required military items during the initial phase of LONG SKIP. From Rhein-Main AB, Germany, the first 2 C–135s from the 1611th Air Transport Wing took off for Calcutta's Dum Dum Airport, some 6,200 miles away. From Travis AFB, California, 3 C–135s from the 1501st Air Transport Wing flew to Calcutta with a 22-man maintenance team, small arms, and equipment; flying time was 22 hours, covering 10,600 miles. Deployed personnel from the 1602d Air Transport Wing at Chateaurox AS, France, constituted the LONG SKIP operations staff, including the airlift task force commander. Additionally, from Rhein-Main AB, Germany, the 322d Air Division (Combat Cargo), a U.S. Air Forces in Europe (USAFE) organization, launched two C–130s from the 317th Troop Carrier Wing and two rotational C–124s from the 15th Air Transport Squadron to Calcutta. These aircraft flew in support equipment needed for communications and maintenance.

Although the C–135s delivered to India its initial requirements (plus an additional fifty tons) by November 5, separate Indian government agencies submitted additional requests to U.S. representatives. Each increased the tonnage of arms, ammunition, and supplies to be flown in by the C–135 crews. On November 7, the Indian government provided the U.S. Ambassador a formal list of additional requirements that totaled approximately $65 million. By November 14, C–135 crews had airlifted major military-assistance items to India valued at approximately $3.7 million. During the 14-day airlift, 48 C–135 missions arrived in Calcutta carrying a total of 1,035 tons of arms, ammunition, and equipment. C–124s, C–130s, and a C–135 also flew eight additional support missions into Calcutta. The DOD team at New Delhi recommended further shipments estimated at fifty-one million dollars to Bombay by sea lift.

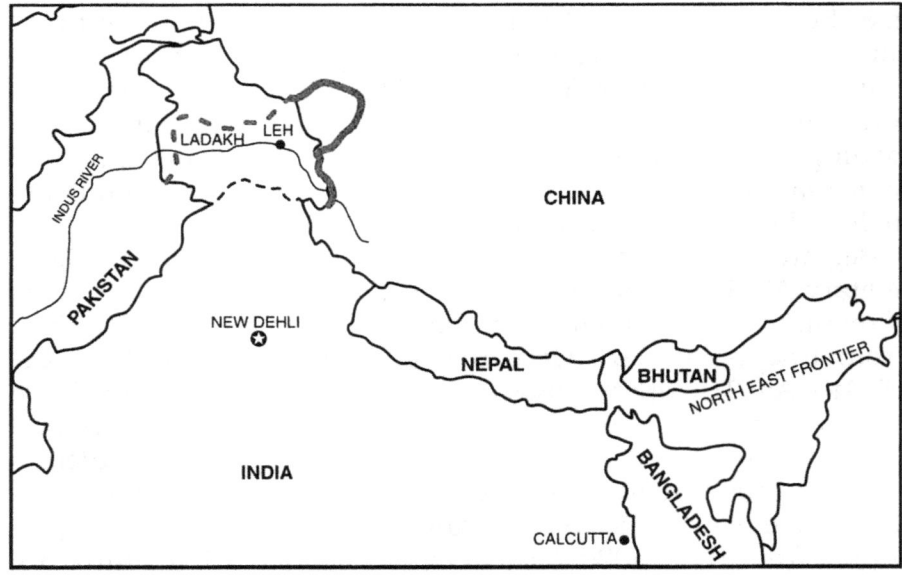

Area of USAF Operations for LONG SKIP

After the initial airlift, Indian army and air force officers briefing the DOD team on November 18 reported that use of Indian military aircraft plus requisitioned civilian planes could provide only 20 percent of the airlift urgently required to supply Indian troops in the combat areas. On November 20, Ambassador Galbraith requested U.S. air-transport assistance within India. The following day, the U.S. Department of State advised that twelve C–130s would be provided for this purpose.

On November 21, crews and support personnel for twelve C–130s from the 317th Troop Carrier Wing received alert orders for deployment to India. Within six hours, the first aircraft was airborne from Evreux-Fauville AB, France. The Hercules transports flew via Athens, Greece, and Tehran, Iran, reaching New Delhi's Palam Airport forty-eight hours after takeoff from France.

The first mission aircraft carried a Combat Airlift Support Unit (CALSU) package tailored to support the intra-India airlift operations. Consolidation of 20 USAFE radio technicians at Calcutta with 39 additional 2d Mobile Communications

Squadron technicians deployed to New Delhi brought the total CALSU strength to 166. Installed with the CALSU in a hangar at Palam Airport, the communications team established a double Teletype line via Wheelus AB in Libya to Evreux, a single Teletype circuit to Headquarters USAFE at Wiesbaden, and a radio link with the USAFE communications network.

Given very little advance notice of the departure for India, the first crews had not known what support, if any, they could expect. Accordingly, the 322d Airlift Division made use of its mobility cells, designed to make aircraft independent of the support normally furnished by USAF bases. Made up of supplies, equipment, and personnel, the cells provided all essentials: medical care, kitchen facilities, office supplies, and aircraft maintenance. Although the Indian government was generous in its efforts to support the operation, the decision to bring the mobility cells on the first aircraft proved to be a wise one. The CALSU personnel rotated every thirty days, the aircraft every sixty days.

Palam's 10,000-foot runways and 400-mile Instrument Landing System were suitable for commercial Boeing 707 operations. Ramp space was adequate for the twelve C–130s, but no hangar was large enough for the C–130's wingspread. When the aircraft was jacked up for maintenance, it had to be done between buildings with an eye to the wind. The Indian Air Force (IAF) was well trained and very cooperative. However, apparently the Indian government had not expected the quick arrival of the C–130s. No loads were available in the first three days; therefore, the Task Force Commander surveyed the forward airfields in India.

Developed mostly during World War II, India's air facility system comprised 176 airfields, most with permanently surfaced runways. Some forty-one of the fields north of 22° N were primary fields, which might be used in the India-China border dispute. Five of these, Agra, Ambala, Palam, Barrakpore, and Dum Dum, had permanently surfaced runways over 8,000 feet in length. The remaining 36 fields in this area had 3,000- to 8,000-foot runways.

In the first 14 days of operations in India, the USAFE C–130s flew 211 sorties and logged 50 hours. These initial C–130 intra-India airlift missions transported two 2,200-man

Loading a C–124
C–124s transported communications and maintenance equipment for Operation LONG SKIP.

C–124 in flight

Indian army brigades and their equipment to forward airfields in the disputed northeast and Ladakh areas. By the end of December, the C–130s had flown 1,927 hours, transporting 7,206 passengers and 3,407 tons of cargo. Among the passengers were Prime Minister Nehru, Defense Minister Y. B. Chavan, Ambassador and Mrs. Galbraith, and U.S. Secretary of Commerce Luther B. Hodges.

USAFE also provided VC–47s and crews to transport within India a high-level U.S. group after their arrival on November 22. This group, headed by W. Averill Harriman, Assistant Secretary of State for Far Eastern Affairs, included Paul Nitze, Assistant Secretary of Defense; William Sullivan, UN Advisor, Bureau of Far Eastern Affairs; and General Paul D. Adams, USA, Commander in Chief, Strike Command. The group quickly learned that the original Indian army stocks in the forward areas had been inadequate and were still marginal. Supply efforts up to that time had provided only the minimum essentials to troops in contact with Chinese forces. Indian military authorities, principally army, directed the transporting of supplies during the urgent beefing up of defenses in the North East Frontier area. Later, the Indian military devoted its entire use of the C–130 airlift to strengthening the northwestern area of Ladakh, which was more difficult to reach. Almost all supplies for Indian troops in contact with the Chinese forces in the area had to be airlifted or air-dropped to them. The Indian army estimated that supplies for the Ladakh area could only be airlifted to the airfield at Leh (at 11,500-foot elevation) and that it would take until June 1963 to accumulate what was needed.

The operation stabilized during the first few months of 1963. A liaison officer from the 322d Airlift Division worked with the Indian army to prepare loads and plan sorties for the following day. Indian army trucks brought the supplies and troops to Palam, where the CALSU had been established. Heavy tire use resulting from frequent landings at high-altitude fields became a major C–130 operational problem. The estimated cost was an average of one and a half tires per landing. The Task Force Commander suggested to the IAF that the C–130s make five airdrops and five landings per day to reduce tire damage. Thus, by the end of February, the C–130s were regularly making five landings a day at Leh and flying eight airdrops to two drop zones in the Indus River Valley.

Other problems encountered during this early period included keeping a sufficient number of crews trained at any given time for the difficult landing techniques required at Leh. Further, the daily airdrops quickly depleted the supply of standard USAF cargo-extraction parachutes. With improvisation the order of the day, the use of Indian parachutes began after a release system and bomb shackles were manufactured for the C–130s. Operations and maintenance personnel wrote plans to standardize rigging and dropping techniques, thus ensuring that replacement crews learned quickly. Other plans and information developed and made available to crews included routing and navigational procedures, emergency procedures for the Himalaya regions, operation schedules, and data concerning drop and landing zones.

Another operational improvement was the reservation of certain hours of the day for the IAF aircraft—C–47s, C–119s, and Soviet-built AN–12s—to fly into Leh. The total IAF airlift capability was about 100,000 pounds per day, far less than the 322d Air Division's 12 C–130s. Comparatively, the 4-engine turboprop AN–12 carried only 12,000 pounds into airfields at 11,000-feet while the 4-engine reversible turboprop C–130 airlifted 30,000 pounds. The deployed C–130s delivered about 260,000 pounds more per day than the entire IAF's transport fleet. Additionally, top echelons of the IAF had no clear picture of Indian tactical air support and air defense capabilities. The IAF made no realistic plans for airlift operations, apparently in the belief that the United States would provide additional air transport assistance, as well as combat and training aircraft.

Consequently, after several months of routine operations, the main problem became one of finding a diplomatic way to end the airlift. The task force had originally been sent for ninety days, but at the request of the Indian government, the United States extended this period several times. There were indications that the Indian government wanted the airlift to continue indefinitely.

The road from Srinagar into the Ladakh area was open only from July to October. The United States argued that it could be put into proper shape, and the airstrip at Leh rebuilt to take an increased number of Indian aircraft every day. Since work had progressed satisfactorily on the Srinagar-Ladakh road, the U.S. government decided that before sending the C-130s back to France the airlift would continue just long enough to transport heavy equipment and supplies to Leh. These would be used to build an airstrip big enough to handle the highest-tonnage cargo planes that the IAF could field.

Cement and other supplies had been flown into Leh since the first of 1963, along with the supplies for the Indian army. By May, the planeloads consisted mostly of construction items based on a list of available U.S., British, Japanese, and Indian equipment and supplies. In June, the number of C-130s deployed in India progressively dropped to six. By the end of August, after all items on the list had been transported, the remaining aircraft, crews, and ground personnel returned to France.

The 322d Air Division's nine-month-long portion of Operation LONG SKIP ended the last week in August 1963, when the division commander flew the last C-130 out of Leh back to New Delhi and from there to France. From November 1962 through August 1963, the 322d C-130 crews had flown over 1,800 sorties and 10,000 hours, transported over 20,000 passengers and troops, and delivered over 25,000 tons of supplies and equipment.

In both phases of Operation LONG SKIP, emergency and intratheater airlift, USAF forces deployed quickly with minimal notice, successfully endured frequent changes in airlift requirements, and in the end, found a diplomatic way to cease operations. In the face of foreign assistance to India, the Chinese had pulled back to their original positions on November 20, 1962, except in the Ladakh area where they continued to occupy some small villages. The U.S. contribution ensured no further Chinese aggression against India and was a major factor in maintaining peace and order in the region.

Rebellion in the Congo: Operation DRAGON ROUGE

Daniel L. Haulman

DATES: November 17–December 2, 1964

LOCATION: The Democratic Republic of the Congo

OVERSEAS BASES USED: Evreux-Fauville Air Base (AB), France; Kleine Brogel AB, Belgium; Moron AB, Spain; Ascension Island (United Kingdom); Kamina AB, Stanleyville, Paulis, Leopoldville, Congo

AIR FORCE ORGANIZATIONS:

DIVISION:	SQUADRON:
322d Air	52d Troop Carrier
WING:	
464th Troop Carrier	

AIR FORCE AIRCRAFT: C–130

Operations

After four years of attempting to prevent civil war from tearing the Congo apart, the last United Nations (UN) troops left the country on June 30, 1964. They left an unstable central government, headquartered at Leopoldville in the western Congo, under President Joseph Kasavubu and Prime Minister Cyrille Adoula. Neither Kasavubu nor Adoula was very popular. Late in 1963, Kasavubu had dissolved the Congolese Parliament and granted Adoula full legislative powers. Adoula attempted to redistrict the country into a host of new provinces. Opposition members crossed the Congo River to Brazzaville and revived the party of the late socialist Patrice Lumumba. During the summer of 1964 under Gaston Soumialot and Nicholas Olenga, rebel warriors who called themselves "Simbas" (lions) took over some towns in the eastern Congo, including Albertville. Christophe Gbenye,

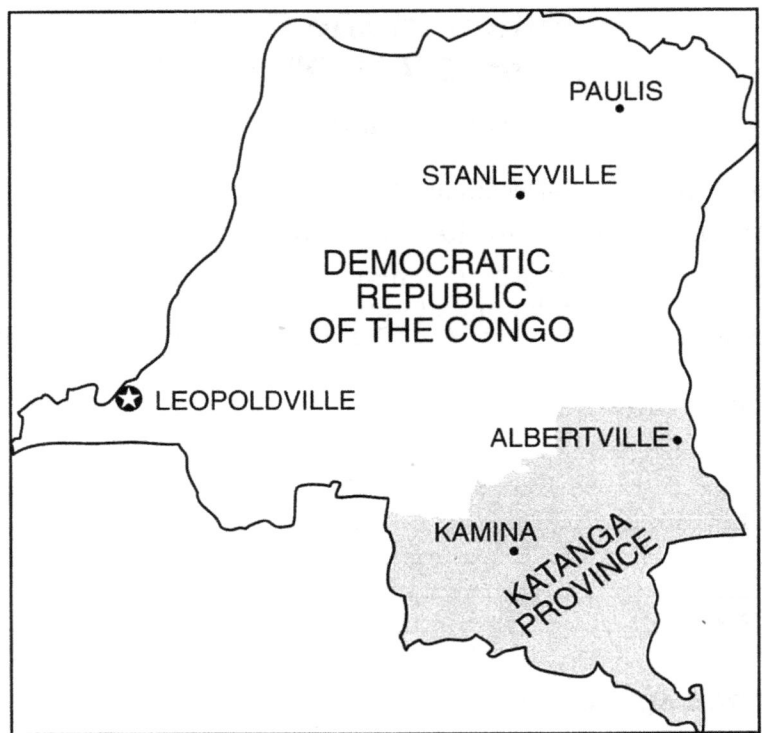

Democratic Republic of the Congo

leader of the Lumumbists at Brazzaville, named Soumialot head of a provisional government in the eastern Congo.

The rebel soldiers wore primitive clothing, had little education, and regarded with disdain those who did. They looked upon Europeans and Americans in the Congo, including Christian missionaries, as enemies. Although the Simbas carried shields and spears, they were not averse to using bullets and guns that they captured from the demoralized government forces they defeated. The Soviet Union and Communist China also sent weapons and ammunition to the rebels through Burundi and Uganda, located on the eastern border of the Congo.

To quell the rebellion, President Kasavubu in early July replaced Prime Minister Adoula with Moise Tshombe, who had just returned from exile in Europe. Tshombe had led a secession movement in mineral-rich Katanga Province in the south, and as premier he could attract the support of that part of the country for the central government at Leopoldville. Under Kasavubu and Tshombe, Gen. Joseph Mobutu served as military leader of the Congolese army. On July 20, Tshombe flew to Stanleyville, located in the northeast Congo, to negotiate with the rebels, but they refused.

In early August, Olenga's Simbas captured Stanleyville. They burned government records and began to execute Congolese loyalists in the province. Some of the executions were particularly brutal. Intellectuals and the wealthy were favorite rebel targets. On August 19, the rebels captured Paulis, another important town 225 miles northeast of Stanleyville. By the end of the month, with much of the eastern Congo under his control, Soumialot proclaimed a People's Republic of the Congo, with Stanleyville as capital and Christophe Gbenye as president. Soumialot was named defense minister and Olenga commander of the army. Within three months, the rebels had executed thousands of black Congolese in Stanleyville and Paulis.

After years of civil and intertribal war and recent defeats at the hands of the Simbas, the Congolese army was weak and demoralized. Tshombe and Mobutu contracted with white mercenaries from South Africa, Rhodesia, and Europe to help reconquer lost territory. They hired Maj. Mike Hoare, a South African, to lead the mercenaries. In response, Soumialot announced he could no longer guarantee the safety of whites in his area of the Congo. The rebels took as hostages over 1,500 white foreigners from several different nations. Among the hostages were about 60 Americans, 300 Britons, and over 1,000 Belgians. Many of these were Christian medical missionaries following in the footsteps of Dr. Albert Schweitzer.

Olenga met with Michael Hoyt, American consul at Stanleyville, about U.S. support of Tshombe, which could affect the safety of Americans in rebel hands. Hoyt assured Olenga that U.S. combat troops were not in the Congo. The United States also encouraged Tshombe to replace white mercenaries in his army with black African troops from neighboring countries. Tshombe tried that, but neighboring countries refused to participate in the defense of his regime. He and Mobutu continued to rely on the mercenaries to regain territory lost to the rebels in the east.

In September, UN Secretary General U Thant unsuccessfully urged the rebels to allow the hostages to leave the country, and Kenya's Prime Minister Jomo Kenyatta, head of the Organization of African Unity, attempted peace negotiations between representatives of Tshombe and Gbenye. He did not have much success, either. During the same month, a diplomatic crisis strengthened Tshombe's support in Leopoldville, the Congolese capital. When Tshombe attempted to attend a conference of nonaligned nations in Cairo in the United Arab Republic, Egyptian President Gamal Abdel Nasser put him under house arrest. Tshombe's government immediately put the United Arab Republic representatives in Leopoldville under house arrest until Tshombe was released. Despite this diplomatic slap in the face from Egypt, Tshombe refused to sever relations, because he knew Nasser was eager for an excuse to recognize the rebel government instead.

During October, Congolese government troops and mercenaries won control of Bukavu, Beni, and Bumba, liberating Belgian Roman Catholic priests and nuns and clearing the way for an offensive against the rebel capital. At the end of October, as more and more Congolese died at Stanleyville and Paulis and as rebel threats against whites there intensified, Hoare began to move against the rebel heartland.

Hoare's mercenaries reached Kindu on November 5, just in time to save 220 European hostages whom Olenga had ordered exterminated. At the news of the rebel defeat at Kindu, Gbenye announced that Belgian and American civilians would be treated as "prisoners of war." The Belgian and American consuls at Stanleyville, including Hoyt, were imprisoned and beaten. The rebels refused to allow International Red Cross representatives to examine the condition of the hostages. On November 16, the rebels announced that Dr. Paul Carlson, an American Protestant missionary who had been in the country three years and whose wife and children had recently fled the country, would be executed as a spy. When government troops took the town of Kibombo, they found three dead European civilians.

At this point, the United States and Belgium began to fear that the overland advance of the Congolese army and its mercenaries would not be rapid enough to save the hostages. With the approval of Premier Tshombe, they began preparing a contingency rescue mission called DRAGON ROUGE. U.S. President Lyndon B. Johnson and Secretary of Defense Robert S. McNamara refused to commit combat troops, but they were willing to airlift Belgian forces.

The United States provided aircraft and crews under the command of Col. Burgess Gradwell, USAF, Commander, 322d Air Division, Detachment 1 at Evreux-Fauville, France. At his disposal were C–130 Hercules aircraft of the 776th and 777th Troop Carrier Squadrons of the 464th Troop Carrier Wing, which were serving on rotation to Europe. The C–130s were excellent tools for the special mission. Each airplane could carry more than 22 tons of payload more than 1,750 miles at a cruising speed of 291 knots.

On November 17, 1964, fourteen 464th Troop Carrier Wing aircrews flew their C–130Es from Evreux-Fauville AB in France to Kleine Brogel AB in Belgium. After loading 550 Belgian soldiers of the First Paratroop Battalion under the command of Col. Charles Laurent, the airplanes flew to Britain's Ascension Island in the Atlantic Ocean, refueling at Moron AB, Spain, which was en route. Ascension was 7 hours, and slightly more than 2,500 miles, by air to Stanleyville. The move, designed to put more pressure on the rebels to release the hostages, was no secret to the world press. Gbenye postponed the execution of Dr. Carlson.

When negotiations between the United States and rebel representatives in Nairobi, Kenya, proved fruitless, Operation DRAGON ROUGE proceeded. The Belgian paratroops flew from Ascension Island to Kamina, a strong loyalist base in the southern Congo. On November 24, twelve of the C–130s, loaded with hundreds of combat-ready Belgian troops, took off from Kamina for the assault on Stanleyville. Five of the U.S. airplanes air-dropped Belgian paratroops, who secured the airport and cleared the runway, littered with gasoline barrels standing on end and vehicles without wheels. Less than an hour later, the other seven C–130s delivered the remaining Belgian troops.

The airlifted troops quickly secured two roads leading from the airport to the center of Stanleyville. When the rebels learned of the landings, they herded some of the white hostages from a hotel into the street in front of the Lumumba monument. Gbenye and Soumialot fled, leaving the fate of the prisoners in the hands of Soumialot's bodyguard, who killed twenty-two men, women, and children and wounded forty others. Among the dead was Dr. Paul Carlson. As the Belgians approached, the rebels retreated. In another section of the rebel capital, the paratroopers discovered bodies of thirty more white civilians who had been beaten or hacked to death.

With or without the rescue operation, hostages would have died. Survivors agreed that the quick arrival of the Belgian paratroopers in the center of Stanleyville saved many lives. The Belgians took the liberated hostages to the airport for aerial evacuation to Leopoldville, located about 750 miles to the southwest. The rebels had wounded many of the hostages, requiring twenty-eight of them to be carried. During the rescue, hostile gunfire hit several of the Hercules airplanes, but none of the crew members was injured, and all of the airplanes were able to take off. In addition to the twelve C–130s that landed troops, two others arrived to help evacuate survivors to Leopoldville. The USAF crews transported more than 1,200 of the Stanleyville hostages to the Congolese capital. Among the hostages were Consul Hoyt and his aides, along with about thirty other Americans.

Later in the day, units of the Congolese army, including Hoare's mercenaries, linked up with the Belgians. They fought off rebel counterattacks and secured the city for the Tshombe regime. The rebels retreated in the direction of Paulis, and the Belgian paratroopers returned to Kamina to prepare for the liberation of another town.

Two days later on November 26, about 250 Belgian commandos and paratroops struck again. This time they flew on 7 USAF C–130s to Paulis, where 270 whites, including 44 Roman Catholic missionaries and 7 Americans, were being held hostage. Despite bad weather on the route and fog at the objective, the paratroops air-dropped successfully and secured the 4,100-foot airfield. They established a combat control team to direct the C–130 landings, but heavy enemy gunfire at the

C–130 lands to evacuate rescued hostages and Belgian paratroops from Paulis.

approach end of the runway delayed landings about fifteen minutes while the commandos cleared the area. As at Stanleyville, the C–130s sometimes landed and took off under hostile fire, which damaged several airplanes, piercing fuel cells and tires. But all returned safely to Kamina AB. Rebels massacred eighteen hostages before the rescue mission was complete. At Paulis, the Belgian paratroopers rescued about 250 people of many nationalities.

On November 27, the American C–130s withdrew the Belgian troops from both Stanleyville and Paulis to Kamina AB, and, under the protection of government troops, continued to evacuate refugees to Leopoldville. The next day, an advance party of Americans and Belgians redeployed to Ascension Island to coordinate support for the requirements of the main force, which began redeploying from the Congo on November 29. By the end of December 2, redeployment was complete. The 464th Troop Carrier Wing C–130s returned to Evreux-Fauville AB in France, after taking the Special Forces back to Belgium.

Reaction to the missions of November 24 and 26 was mixed. Americans, Belgians, the former hostages, and countrymen of the hostages interpreted Operation DRAGON ROUGE as a heroic rescue. Britain, having allowed the use of Ascension Island,

Belgian paratroopers prepare to board a C-130 on Ascension Island.

praised the operation as a humanitarian necessity. On the other hand, Communist nations such as the Soviet Union and China condemned the operation as "imperialist aggression." They had hoped that the rebels would establish a new Communist state in central Africa, and they wanted to attract the loyalty of nonaligned nations such as Egypt and Algeria, which opposed the Tshombe regime. Remembering that Belgium had recently ruled the Congo as a colony, many African states also condemned the rescue operation as a revival of Western imperialism. Even some black political activists in the United States, such as Malcolm X, condemned the operation and blamed President Johnson for the deaths of some of the hostages.

Operation DRAGON ROUGE was significant politically. First of all, it freed more than 1,400 hostages, including dozens of Americans. Only three Americans died. The rescue attracted the admiration of many people around the world. The operation strengthened the central government of the Congo by helping it crush a rival regime, forestalling secession and revolution. At the same time, it demonstrated the solidarity of Belgium and the United States and their ability to conduct successful combined missions. It also revealed the crucial importance of friendly support and staging areas; for example, British-controlled Ascension Island.

DRAGON ROUGE was significant in other ways. It was the first example of American C-130 airlift operations in a tactical combat situation under enemy fire. All of the Hercules aircraft, even those with damaged fuel cells or tires, survived. With less than twenty-four hours of maintenance, they were ready to fly again. For the first time, C-130 crews successfully tested new formation procedures for landing and taking off in combat. Such tactics would be used again in Southeast Asia, when C-130s were committed there in 1965.

During Operation DRAGON ROUGE, the 322d Air Division did not augment aircrews, and there was minimal crew rest. Had the operation lasted longer, personnel fatigue might have become a problem. Operation FULL STRIKE, launched during DRAGON ROUGE, deployed twenty more 464th Troop Carrier Wing C-130 crews and sixteen C-130s from Pope Air Force Base, North Carolina, to Moron AB, Spain. They supplemented U.S. Air Forces in Europe resources while some C-130s were in Africa and could have reinforced aircraft and aircrews of Operation DRAGON ROUGE.

Dominican Crisis: Operation POWER PACK

A. Timothy Warnock

DATES: April 29, 1965–September 21, 1966

LOCATION: Dominican Republic

OVERSEAS BASES USED: San Isidro Air Base (AB), Dominican Republic; Ramey Air Force Base (AFB), Roosevelt Roads Naval Air Station, Puerto Rico

AIR FORCE ORGANIZATIONS:

MAJCOM:	WINGS: (con't.)	GROUPS:
USAF Southern Command	363d Tactical Reconnaissance	908th Troop Carrier Group, Medium
	433d Troop Carrier Wing, Medium	910th Troop Carrier Group, Medium
CENTER:	442d Troop Carrier Wing, Heavy	
USAF Special Air Warfare	452d Troop Carrier Wing, Medium	**SQUADRONS:**
	463d Troop Carrier Wing, Medium	28th Air Transport Squadron, Heavy
WINGS:	464th Troop Carrier Wing, Medium	331st Fighter-Interceptor
1st Air Commando	512th Troop Carrier Wing, Heavy	353d Tactical Fighter
62d Air Transport Wing, Heavy	514th Troop Carrier Wing, Medium	
63d Troop Carrier Wing, Heavy	516th Troop Carrier Wing, Medium	
137th Air Transport	1607th Air Transport Wing, Heavy	
313th Troop Carrier Wing, Medium	1608th Air Transport Wing, Heavy	
314th Troop Carrier Wing, Medium	1611th Air Transport Wing, Heavy	
317th Troop Carrier Wing, Medium		

AIR FORCE AIRCRAFT: C–130, C–124, C–97, C–47, C–123, U–10, F–100, F–104, RF–101, RB–66, KC–135, EC–135

Operations

The Dominican Republic shares with Haiti the island of Hispaniola, located about 700 miles southeast of Miami, Florida, between Cuba and Puerto Rico. Not only is the island near the United States, it occupies a strategic position as a gateway to the Caribbean Sea and an approach to the Panama Canal. Consequently, the United States has historically been involved militarily and politically in the Dominican Republic. Thus, U.S. President Lyndon B. Johnson decided on intervention when in late April 1965 the country fell into anarchy following a military overthrow of the existing government. He feared that Cuban Communism would subvert the government, thereby enhancing Soviet influence in the Western Hemisphere.

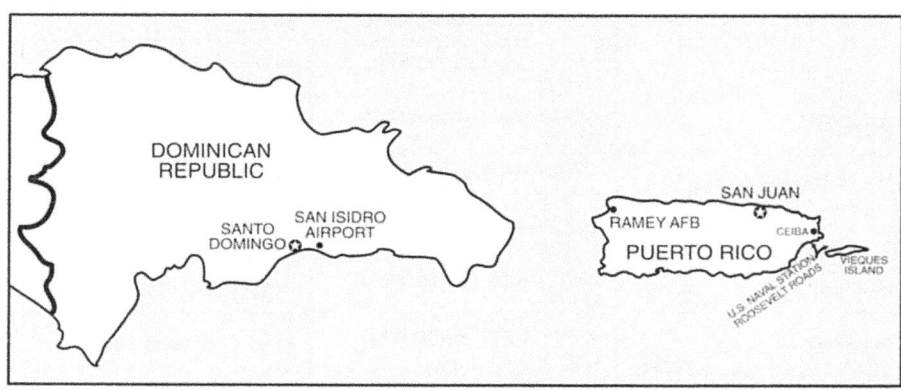

Area of USAF Operations during Dominican Crisis

On April 26, 1965, the U.S. Joint Chiefs of Staff, with presidential approval, moved a U.S. Navy task force off the Dominican coast and alerted the U.S. Army 82d Airborne Division for possible deployment to the Dominican Republic under the code name of POWER PACK. The next day, U.S. Marines from the naval task force began evacuation of U.S. and other foreign nationals from the capital, Santo Domingo. On the 28th, the current military junta requested U.S. military assistance to maintain order. President Johnson immediately authorized U.S. armed forces to protect American lives. Five hundred Marines landed to protect the U.S. Embassy and continue the evacuation. The President then decided to send the entire 82d

Airborne Division to the Dominican Republic to establish order and a friendly, non-Communist government.

The Nineteenth Air Force formed an Airlift Task Force (ALTF) at Pope AFB, North Carolina, to manage the airlift of the division, a force four times larger than conceived in contingency plans. After receiving approval from Maj. Gen. Robert H. York, USA, Commander, 82d Airborne Division, the ALTF staff coordinated activities with Brig. Gen. Robert L. Delashaw, USAF, Vice Commander, Nineteenth Air Force, at Seymour Johnson AFB, North Carolina. The ALTF staff had to locate more aircraft and crews, schedule arrivals at Pope, devise a parking plan for the overcrowded base, compute new loading plans, find sufficient personnel to load the aircraft, billet the hundreds of aircrews and other personnel arriving, and work out flight plans. To meet these demands, the ALTF commander, Col. William L. Welch, USAF, Commander, 464th Troop Carrier Wing (TCW), established a command post at the Consolidated Airlift Support Unit, which ordinarily staged, scheduled, and controlled airlift transport.

On April 28 and 29, Tactical Air Command (TAC) and Military Air Transport Service (MATS) deployed eighty-five C–130s within twelve hours from their home bases to Pope AFB to join the seventy aircraft already there. MATS also deployed C–124s to Seymour Johnson AFB, where the 82d loaded its heaviest equipment aboard six aircraft. The concentrated and sustained airlift operation at Pope overwhelmed support capabilities normally geared to supporting a single troop carrier wing. Billeting facilities proved totally inadequate, forcing officials to house transient personnel in unheated, open-bay barracks on nearby Fort Bragg. In addition, an airdrop exercise at Pope was not canceled until the day before, thus delaying the loading and reconfiguration for POWER PACK of several aircraft that had been participating in the exercise. To accommodate 148 aircraft at the same time, Pope authorities resorted to nose-to-tail parking, using all available ramp space and even taxiways. The resulting congestion impeded the refueling, loading, and launching of aircraft; for example, crews had to tow aborting aircraft clear before remaining aircraft could taxi. Movement of Army equipment to be loaded on the aircraft added to ramp congestion, and a lack of loading tables delayed preparation of cargo and equipment for airlift and airdrop. Cargo delivered out of sequence complicated the expeditious loading of aircraft. Nevertheless, within 18 hours, Air Force loaders put 1,754 paratroopers and their equipment and supplies aboard 144 C–130s.

General Delashaw, as commander of the Air Force Tactical Force formed to control USAF participation in POWER PACK, arranged for fighter escort, reconnaissance, and communications support. He then flew from Seymour Johnson to Ramey AFB, Puerto Rico, aboard the TAC Airborne Command Post (EC–135) to set up a Tactical Air Control Center and Command Post.

Colonel Welch commanded POWER PACK's assault airlift phase, code-named RED FOX. The first aircraft departed Pope AFB on April 29 at 7:54 P.M. Launched in a two and a half-hour period, the RED FOX force flew in four high-altitude in-trail formations with a continuous stream of red running lights visible for miles in the night sky. Within the formation, pilots flew sometimes at 250 knots and other times at 100 knots in efforts to maintain aircraft separation. While RED FOX was in mid-flight, the U.S. Embassy reported that friendly forces controlled San Isidro Airport, fourteen miles east of downtown Santo Domingo. Consequently, Colonel Welch diverted from the planned landing at Ramey to San Isidro. As the RED FOX force changed its heading, General Delashaw took the EC–135 from Ramey to a designated orbit near the Dominican Republic to control the landing of the assault force. Meanwhile, Vice Adm. Kleber S. Masterson, USN, the Joint Task Force Commander aboard the USS *Boxer* off the Dominican coast, learned from a Dominican leader friendly to the United States that the San Isidro control tower was unmanned and the runway unlighted. Admiral Masterson sent his aide and two U.S. Marine officers to man the tower, turn on the lights, and prepare for the arrival of the first C–130 landings. Because of the changed destination, the ALTF traveled the 1,200 miles to the Dominican Republic in about 7 hours, a good 2 hours more than would have been normally required.

Colonel Welch touched down aboard the lead C–130 at 2:00 A.M. on April 30, hitched a ride with a jeep-load of armed Dominicans to the control tower, assumed command of the airfield, and directed landing operations of thirty-three C–130s carrying troops and forty-six others with equipment. Within an hour, the airlifters had unloaded the 82d Airborne's soldiers, but unloading the equipment took longer. Since aerial-port equipment and manpower were unavailable, U.S. Army and Air Force personnel cut nylon webbing and honeycomb packing with axes before rolling stock could be driven off the aircraft and ramps. For lack of equipment, cargo clogged taxiways, impeding aircraft movement. Consequently, sixty-five C–130s, unable to land on the crowded base, diverted to Ramey AFB for refueling and rerigging. At Ramey, a Strategic Air Command (SAC) base, 300 SAC personnel physically manhandled the cargo off the aircraft, derigged (removing parachutes, nylon webbing, and honeycomb packing) it, and reloaded it for shipment to San Isidro. Finally, some five and one-half hours after the initial assault force had landed, San Isidro began accepting cells of nine aircraft, each arriving at fifteen-minute intervals from Ramey. Eighteen hours after the arrival of the initial assault force at San Isidro, an Aerial Port Detachment and a Consolidated Airlift Support Unit arrived with equipment and people to handle cargo and passenger loading and unloading.

Taking off from San Isidro, most aircraft returned to Pope AFB. In the first few days of the operation, Pope transit alert operations had difficulties handling so many returning aircraft in spite of the assistance of Enroute Support Teams from participating airlift units. As aircraft landed at intervals of one or two minutes, ground crews had to park, refuel, and prepare them for new flights. Confusion ensued, with some C–130s being loaded before receiving maintenance. As a result, crews had to transfer those loads to other aircraft that were ready for flight, thus raising the 464th Wing's turnaround time to excessive levels. Consequently, on the fourth, MATS began sending its POWER PACK aircraft to Charleston AFB, South Carolina, for maintenance prior to flying to Pope for loading.

In spite of these difficulties, the Air Force flew over 1,361 accident-free sorties and moved 12,000 passengers and 17,250 tons of cargo within 5 days from Pope to San Isidro. From April 30 through May 3, USAF members at San Isidro handled 651 C–130 sorties. Between May 4 and 6, they received 502 C–130 and 47 C–124 flights. The airlifters flew

Tents housed facilities at San Isidro AB, Dominican Republic. These included a field-ration mess and medical unit to support actions in that area. Parked on the ramp near the tents is a C–130E of the 464th Troop Carrier Wing.

forty-nine sorties on May 7, and then the 464th TCW flew resupply missions at the rate of about nine each day until the last week in May. They also transported to San Isidro a one-hundred-bed field hospital, as well as tons of beans, condensed milk, and flour for relief of the embattled Santo Domingo population. After May 7, ships provided most of the support for the military operation. In June, MATS established a scheduled flight from Charleston AFB to San Isidro Airport.

On May 1, Maj. Gen. Marvin L. McNickel, USAF, Commander, Ninth Air Force, assumed command of the Air Force Task Force at Ramey AFB. On May 5, he established at San Isidro Airport the Joint Air Control Coordination Center controlling all task force activities under the direction of U.S. Forces, Dominican Republic, the joint command headed by Lt. Gen. Bruce Palmer Jr., USA. Responsibility for providing forces, controlling movement to and from the Dominican Republic, and supporting them remained with the component commands, coordinated by the Commander in Chief, Atlantic Command.

Tactical air units, deployed to Ramey AFB for mission combat support, included a tactical fighter squadron, a fighter-interceptor squadron, and a composite reconnaissance squadron.

On May 2, the 354th Tactical Fighter Wing deployed aircraft, pilots, and support personnel totaling 400 people to Ramey and San Isidro. As part of this deployment, the wing's 353d Tactical Fighter Squadron sent its eighteen F–100s from Myrtle Beach AFB, South Carolina, to Ramey AFB. SAC tankers refueled the fighters en route. At Ramey, ground crews configured the aircraft for combat air patrol missions, intended primarily to deter possible air support from Cuba for the leftist rebels. On May 6, Air Defense Command sent twelve F–104s of the 331st Fighter-Interceptor Squadron from Webb AFB, Texas, to Ramey to augment the F–100s. Two fighter aircraft flew over the Dominican Republic at all times through the month of May. Between May 28 and June 3, the 354th Tactical Fighter Wing and the 331st Fighter-Interceptor Squadron redeployed their aircraft and personnel to the home stations.

The 363d Tactical Reconnaissance Wing deployed a composite squadron with six RF–101s, three RB–66s, an augmented photo-processing cell, and maintenance elements to provide reconnaissance support for POWER PACK. The aircraft deployed from James Connally AFB, Texas, to Ramey AFB and began operations on May 2. The wing had already sent 132 supporting personnel and 6 tons of equipment aboard C–124 transports. The first sorties targeted airfields throughout the Dominican Republic. Reconnaissance missions over Santo Domingo suffered because aircraft had to fly above 1,500 feet to avoid small-caliber ground fire. To counter this problem, the squadron obtained oblique photographs, a process that negated the necessity to fly over the city. It also photographed and updated reconnaissance of the entire country, including main lines of supply, rivers, and approach valleys, completing the project on June 3. The RB–66s flew thirty-one and the RF–101s ninety-six missions during the deployment.

At Ramey, excessive demand for aerial photography, primarily from the U.S. Army, overwhelmed the photo-processing cell. It met requirements after May 7 only because General McNickel ordered an arbitrary reduction by 50 percent of print production and distribution. Time to deliver developed photography averaged better than five hours, an unacceptable delay during a crisis. The photo-processing cell developed the photography at Ramey and delivered it by air to San Isidro, where jeeps distributed it to military users. The reconnaissance wing redeployed to Texas between May 21 and June 4.

Besides the fighter and reconnaissance units, the U.S. Air Force also deployed air control and communications elements. TAC's airborne command post directed the initial assault airlanding at San Isidro in a seven-hour mission and then for the next three days, coordinated air operations and relayed communications in twelve-hour missions. When the EC–135 was not on station, a C–130E configured as an Airborne Battlefield Command and Control Center or a similarly configured C–97 belonging to the Air National Guard (ANG) took over those functions. The 507th Tactical Control Group, stationed at Shaw AFB, South Carolina, deployed 264 airmen and 17 officers to San Isidro. By May 1, the group's long-range mobile radars and communications equipment tracked and controlled arriving and departing aircraft. Initially, flight patterns went over Santo Domingo, but the controllers quickly changed these to avoid the city after several aircraft received ground fire.

In the early phase of the Dominican Crisis, airborne communications proved absolutely essential, since ground-based communications did not have the range to reach offshore, much less provide links with U.S. national leaders. The 137th Air Transport Wing, an Oklahoma ANG organization, deployed C–97 "Talking Birds" to provide long-range communications until an adequate ground-based communications station could be installed. Also, the Air Force landed a specially equipped C–130 at San Isidro to provide long-range communication. These aircraft proved their usefulness to General Palmer and the U.S. Embassy staff during the first week because no other direct communications link to Washington existed.

The Special Air Warfare Center at Eglin AFB, Florida, played a key role in psychological operations by furnishing speaker-equipped C–47s, four C–123s, two U–10s, and a small photographic laboratory to support the U.S. Information Agency. Personnel from the 1st Air Commando Wing operated the C–47s from San Isidro, dropping leaflets and broadcasting messages. They began on May 3 with 2-hour missions, 3 times a day, at no more than 1,500 feet, at times receiving small-arms fire that wounded 1 crewman.

On April 30, a casualty-staging facility deployed to San Isidro to arrange aeromedical evacuation of patients from military medical facilities, principally the U.S. Army's 15th Field Hospital at Santo Domingo. Meantime the 1st Aeromedical Evacuation Group at Pope organized in-flight medical teams to send to San Isidro and Ramey. From April 30 until August 25, the group evacuated by C–130 some 500 patients, including 152 battle casualties, from Santo Domingo.

The 354th Tactical Fighter Wing at Myrtle Beach deployed a combat support group who established operations at San Isidro on May 1. During the first few days, personnel slept in tents, ate C rations, suffered from a lack of potable water, and worked twelve- to eighteen-hour days. Later, living conditions improved as civil engineers constructed shower and eating facilities. The combat support group included police, supply, transportation, and civil engineering members.

At the urging of the United States, the Organization of American States on May 6 formed an Inter-American Peace Force (IAPF) composed of U.S. and Latin American troops to restore order in the Dominican Republic. This gave an aura of legitimacy to U.S. military forces there and vindicated President Johnson's strong anti-Communist position. The U.S. Air Force in Operation PRESS AHEAD airlifted IAPF troops from Central and South America to Santo Domingo. On May 14–15, USAF Southern Command and TAC transports airlifted Honduran, Nicaraguan, and Costa Rican troops along with almost thirty tons of cargo to the Dominican Republic. Then on May 24–29, USAF and Brazilian airlifters carried 1,130 soldiers and their equipment from Santa Cruz, Brazil, to San Isidro. During this operation, USAF aircraft flew 65 missions, carrying 1,382 passengers and 734 tons of cargo. For over a year, USAF airlifters subsequently resupplied the IAPF and transported people rotating into and out of the Dominican Republic. At its peak, the IAPF numbered over 25,000 soldiers, the majority being U.S. troops.

With the arrival of Latin American troops, the United States gradually reduced its military presence. Military and diplomatic efforts soon resulted in establishment of an interim government under auspices of the Organization of American States. On September 9, 1965, the U.S. Air Force provided a

C–130 to transport General Elias Wessin y Wessin, commander of conservative Dominican forces and a major obstacle to the interim government, from San Isidro to Howard AFB, Panama Canal Zone. The next day, the general flew to exile in Miami, Florida.

By October, only 8,500 U.S. military personnel remained in the Dominican Republic. In June 1966, Dominican citizens elected Joaquin Balaguer as their new president. The last U.S. troops flew home on September 19, and the IAPF formally ended its operation the next day. The 464th TCW flew its last mission from San Isidro to Pope on September 21, 1966, thus ending Operation POWER PACK.

In assessing POWER PACK, General Palmer cited the Air Force for a successful airlift. Among lessons the Air Force learned was the importance of Reserve forces in supplementing active-force operations. Continental Air Command assigned about a fourth of Air Force Reserves' airlift forces to TAC and MATS. These aircraft and crews flew 1,844 missions, including as

Members of the 82d Airborne Division return to Pope AFB following service during the crisis in the Domincan Republic. C–130E aircraft assigned to the 464th Troop Carrier Wing at Pope flew troops to and from the island.

many as 300 to San Isidro, in support of POWER PACK between May 1 and July 5, 1965. Also, Continental Air Command and ANG airlift resources alleviated shortages within the United States by assuming regular TAC and MATS routes and flying them long after POWER PACK ended.

One of the most important lessons was that contingency plans should be current and flexible enough to deal with fluctuating force levels and unexpected, changing situations. In this crisis, existing contingency plans envisioned a mission one-fourth the size of POWER PACK. Consequently, the Air Force had to improvise, resulting in confusion and much heavier workloads than expected. Plans must also be flexible enough to incorporate restrictions on military actions, since national leaders are likely to supervise closely any political-military operation such as the Dominican Crisis. For example, political considerations prevented the use of the Santo Domingo International Airport, only ten miles from the city, even though crowded and rather primitive conditions at San Isidro imposed considerable difficulties on air operations. The operation also taught the need for a diversity of airpower assets. The U.S. Air Force provided airlift, fighter, and reconnaissance aircraft and support. It also aided in disaster relief, conducted psychological operations, took part in civil affairs, and provided aeromedical and civilian evacuation.

U.S. activities during the Dominican Crisis illustrated the Quick Reaction Concept. U.S. forces quickly deployed to a critical area to stabilize a government and prevent unfriendly elements from taking it over. The United States successfully used joint military forces to achieve limited political objectives. In a study of the Air Force's role a year later, the Air University's Aerospace Studies Institute outlined the basic lesson of POWER PACK: that in the future, a principal operational demand on military forces would be stability or peace operations in disturbed areas of the world. Today's USAF Air Expeditionary Forces reflect the prophetic character of that statement.

Military Airlift to Israel: Operation NICKEL GRASS

Edward T. Russell

DATES: October 14–November 14, 1973

OPERATION: Israel

OVERSEAS BASES USED: Lajes Field, Azores; Lod Airport, Israel

AIR FORCE ORGANIZATIONS:

NUMBERED AIR FORCES:	WINGS:
Twenty-First	60th Military Airlift
Twenty-Second	62d Military Airlift
	63d Military Airlift
	436th Military Airlift
	437th Military Airlift
	438th Military Airlift
	443d Military Airlift

AIR FORCE AIRCRAFT: C–5, C–141

Operations

Since 1967, when Israel seized the Sinai Peninsula and the Golan Heights in a six-day war, Egypt and Syria had been eagerly waiting to strike back at Israel to wipe out the humiliation of the earlier defeat and regain their lost territories. In January 1970, Egyptian President Gamal Abdel Nasser made a secret journey to the Soviet Union, returning with a Soviet promise of equipment and advisors. Shortly thereafter the equipment began to arrive: MiG–21 interceptors, battalions of surface-to-air missiles (SAM), banks of electronic equipment designed to counter enemy intruders, and high-altitude reconnaissance aircraft and the crews to man them. Nasser died in 1971; President Anwar el-Sadat succeeded him. While Soviet armaments continued to flow into Egypt, Sadat grew increasingly unhappy with the Soviet presence and soon expelled most Soviet advisors. Meantime, he enlisted the Syrians, to whom the Soviets had also provided equipment, in a planned attack on Israel. Sadat also persuaded other countries, including Iraq, Morocco, Kuwait, Saudi Arabia, and Tunisia, to move token forces to the Suez Canal area. At the time of the attack, Arab strength was approximately 350,000 soldiers and 2,800 tanks, of which 250,000 men and 2,000 tanks belonged to Egypt.

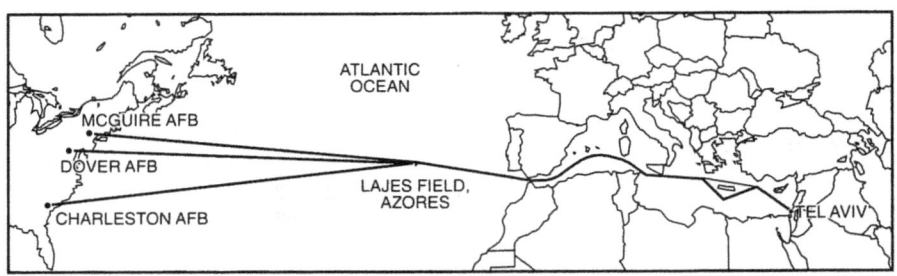

USAF Flight Route during Operation NICKEL GRASS

On October 6, 1973, Egyptian and Syrian forces made simultaneous attacks on Israel. Egyptian forces crossed the Suez Canal and quickly overran the Israeli fortresses, which were protecting the eastern bank. The Soviet-built antiaircraft and wire-guided antitank missiles and rocket-propelled grenades effectively blunted initial Israeli air and armor counterattacks. To the northeast, Syrian forces overran the major Israeli stations on Mount Hermon and then conducted a frontal assault against Israeli positions on the Golan Heights. Following a devastating artillery attack, the Syrians, manning hundreds of Soviet-built T–55 and T–62 tanks, virtually annihilated the outnumbered Israeli defenders.

As the Israelis recovered, they were able to stop the Arab attacks, but the attrition rate was enormous. Both sides began to run out of ammunition within a week. The Israelis required vast numbers of high-explosive antitank shells, sabot-discarding antitank rounds, and above all, antitank missiles. In the air, they needed replacement aircraft, parts, armament, and electronic equipment to detect and defeat the new Soviet antiaircraft batteries. Since many of their tanks, planes, and heavy guns were American-made, the Israelis naturally turned to the United States for resupply. At the same time, the Arab belligerents appealed for military resupply to the Soviet Union, which organized an airlift to Egypt and Syria.

After the Israeli government made the initial request, the United States hesitated, primarily out of concern that Arab nations would retaliate by interrupting the region's oil exports, but finally President Richard M. Nixon ordered the resupply to begin. However, the intensity of the war meant that there would not be enough time to manufacture and ship new weapons to Israel. Supplies would have to come from American inventories.

In preparation for Operation NICKEL GRASS, as the airlift was known, General Paul K. Carlton, USAF, Commander in Chief, Military Airlift Command (MAC), immediately notified his Twenty-First and Twenty-Second Air Force commanders to plan airlifting over 4,000 tons of materiel to Israel. He also sent Brig. Gen. Kelton M. Farris, USAF, to Lajes Field, Azores, in the mid-Atlantic Ocean, to direct airlift operations there. Lajes, the major en route station, would also prove to be a choke point. General Carlton ordered a buildup of petroleum supplies at Lajes to enable the airlift to continue. MAC also increased security

A C–5 leaves Lajes Field in the Azores; the major en route station and the key to the Israeli resupply operation.

forces at Lajes and other points to protect aircraft and essential fuel supplies. In rapid succession, Headquarters MAC activated its Contingency Support Staff, canceled all but essential training, designated the Twenty-First Air Force as the controlling organization, and placed all C-141 and C-5 aircrews on alert. Together, the C-141 and C-5 aircraft could carry almost any piece of equipment that the Israeli armed forces needed. The C-141 could accommodate ammunition, supplies, aircraft parts, and many vehicles, while the C-5 could carry tanks, aircraft fuselages, helicopters, and large guns.

As the airlift began, politics and geography became major factors. Most of the European nations, fearing a reduction in their oil supplies, chose to be neutral in the Arab-Israeli conflict. Thus West Germany, Spain, Italy, Turkey, Greece, Malta, and Cyprus denied overflight approval and use of their airfields. In addition, MAC aircraft could not land and refuel in Iceland, Greenland, Scotland, or England. Only Portugal agreed to help by allowing the U.S. Air Force to use Lajes Field, Azores. After entering Mediterranean airspace, U.S. pilots faced the hostility of Moslem states on the northern coast of Africa, particularly Libya and Egypt, and had to avoid flying over any country on either side of the sea. The final and perhaps most dangerous leg, approaching Israel, required particular caution because of its proximity to Egypt and Syria.

Because of the distance from the United States to Israel, the frequency of flights, the nature of the cargo, the necessity for picking up material at over twenty pick-up points, and the risks of the Mediterranean route, MAC had to use stage crews, augmented crews, and navigator pools. The stage crew would relieve the tired initial crew and fly on to the next destination. MAC used stage crews primarily in the C-141 aircraft. The C-5 aircraft flew, for the most part, with augmented crews. They had a third pilot, a second engineer, a second navigator, and an additional loadmaster. These crews flew as much as twenty-eight hours without rest, going from the U.S. east coast, or one of several other bases, to Lajes and then to Lod and back through Lajes. Then, the crew would change.

The USAF airlift began on October 14. The giant aircraft loaded their cargoes as close as possible to the source of supply within the continental United States then proceeded to

The first MAC aircraft to land at Lod Airport was a C–5, tail no. 0461, assigned to the 60th MAW at Travis AFB, California.

one of several major bases on the east coast, where they refueled and departed for the Azores. At Lajes Field, they refueled again, and rested aircrews took over the controls. The aircraft entered the Mediterranean over the Strait of Gibraltar and flew south of Sicily and Malta, then north of Crete, and then along the boundary that separated Greek and Libyan airspace to dodge the majority of civilian traffic and reduce any Arab threat. Avoiding Egypt by the greatest distance possible, the American aircraft then proceeded to Lod Airport, Tel Aviv, Israel. For the last 190 miles of the journey, Israel provided fighter aircraft as armed escort. According to the MAC study *Flight to Israel* by historian Kenneth L. Patchin,

> The whole airlift from start to finish was fraught with potential danger—danger at home due to the explosives carried and sometimes lack of sufficient parking—danger from possible terrorist attacks when security was questionable at Lajes—danger from hostile North African Arabian aircraft—danger of being attacked by missiles supposedly poised in Egypt for Israel's heartland—danger of conflict with Russian [sic] aircraft which did not always follow Greek controller instructions—and the ever present danger of aircraft problems occurring over so much open water.

On October 14, the ammunition-starved Israelis eagerly welcomed the first C–5 Galaxy. Since another C–5, carrying the special ground-handling equipment, had aborted to Lajes, the Israelis manually unloaded the 194,000 pounds of cargo themselves. Reflecting the urgency of the situation, they completed the job in three and one-half hours. Within three days, Military Airlift Command was delivering, on a daily basis, nearly 1,000 tons of critically needed ammunition, medical supplies, missiles, aircraft parts, helicopters, F–4 fuselages, 175-millimeter cannons, 155-millimeter howitzers, and even M–60 and M–48 tanks. As the Israelis stabilized the Syrian front and turned their attention to the Sinai, the airlift requirement increased from four C–5s and twelve C–141s daily to six C–5s and seventeen C–141s. From that point until the end of the war, the airlift flow remained fairly stable.

During the crisis, two factors became apparent: first, the "magic" weather, and second, the outstanding performance of the C–5. The only bad weather included excessive winds at Lajes in the beginning and severe fog at Lod Airport midway through the operation. The C–5 presented a few mechanical problems, but its logistics reliability turned out to be 95 percent. The C–141 had an even higher 98 percent reliability rate, but having flown since the mid-1960s, this was a time-proven aircraft.

The airlift to Israel lasted thirty-two days. In that period, 567 MAC flights carried approximately 22,300 tons of cargo, including numerous tanks. These shipments helped to reverse the imbalance of military power created by the vast shipments of Soviet war materiel to the Arab nations and led to a cease-fire. USAF airlift capability had made a strong contribution to an American national objective—peace in the Middle East. Perhaps the most meaningful assessment of the airlift came from the Israeli Prime Minister, Golda Meir, who expressed the thought that for generations to come Israel would remember the giant airplanes from America that brought the materiel that meant life to the Israeli people.

On October 24, the belligerents agreed to a cease-fire and silenced the guns. On January 18, 1974, they signed a disengagement agreement that called for Israeli forces to withdraw from the west bank of the Suez Canal, while a limited number of Egyptian forces occupied a strip along the eastern bank. Eventually, in April 1982, Israel returned control of the Sinai to Egypt.

In examining the airlift, American airmen quickly realized the crucial need for complete air refueling capability. The refusal of NATO allies to allow U.S. aircraft use of their airfields and airspace to deliver supplies to Israel could have been disastrous. In fact, if Portugal had denied the use of Lajes Field, NICKEL GRASS would have been virtually impossible. Without forward bases, the only alternative was in-flight refueling. The C-5 aircraft were equipped for it; however, in late 1973, MAC had only nineteen crews trained and proficient in this dangerous task. MAC planners had considered sending the C-5s directly to Tel Aviv from bases in the United States. The aircraft had enough range to go the distance with only 20 tons of cargo, but this would have increased the necessary number of sorties from 145 to over 500. To make matters worse, the C-5 could not return to the United States nonstop because of headwinds on the westbound journey. Considering the number of sorties needed to airlift the supplies that Israel required and the number of C-5s in the U.S. Air Force at the time, the airlift would not have succeeded if flown directly from the United States.

The C-141 aircraft was not equipped, at the time, for in-flight refueling and could not participate in the airlift without a forward base. Shortly after Operation NICKEL GRASS, Air Force leaders moved to modify the C-141 for in-flight refueling and train the aircrews for the task. They also pushed ahead with development of a new tanker aircraft, the KC-10. Known as the Extender, the KC-10 could unload twice as much fuel as the KC-135, fly longer distances, and receive fuel in flight. By teaming the KC-10 and KC-135, the distance to which fuel can be delivered is limited only by the number of supporting tankers available and the endurance of the crews.

Vietnam Evacuation: Operation FREQUENT WIND

Daniel L. Haulman

DATES: April 4–September 16, 1975

LOCATION: Republic of Vietnam (South Vietnam)

OVERSEAS BASES USED: Tan Son Nhut Air Base (AB), Saigon, Vung Tau, South Vietnam; U-Tapao Royal Thailand Air Base (RTAB), Thailand; Clark AB, Philippines; Andersen Air Force Base (AFB), Guam; Wake Island

AIR FORCE ORGANIZATIONS:

DIVISION:	WINGS: (con't.)
3d Air	436th Military Airlift
	437th Military Airlift
WINGS:	438th Military Airlift
3d Tactical Fighter	443d Military Airlift
18th Tactical Fighter	446th Military Airlift
22d Bombardment	514th Military Airlift
43d Strategic	
56th Special Operations	**GROUPS:**
60th Military Airlift	3d Aerospace Rescue and Recovery
62d Military Airlift	9th Aeromedical Evacuation
63d Military Airlift	
307th Strategic	**SQUADRONS:**
314th Tactical Airlift	16th Special Operations
374th Tactical Airlift	40th Aerospace Rescue and Recovery
388th Tactical Fighter	56th Aerospace Rescue and Recovery
432d Tactical Fighter	

AIR FORCE AIRCRAFT: A–7, AC–130, EC–130, HC–130, C–130, C–5, C–9, C–141, CH–53, HH–53, F–4

Operations

U.S. combat troops left the Republic of Vietnam in 1973 according to the terms of a peace agreement that temporarily ended more than a decade of war. The fighting had ended for American forces, but the North Vietnam Communist government re-equipped its army and escalated the ground war in Vietnam. Meantime, the U.S. government continued aid to South Vietnam at a greatly reduced level. Consequently, several thousand U.S. citizens remained, many employees at the Defense Attaché Office (DAO) complex at Tan Son Nhut Airport, at the U.S. Embassy compound in downtown Saigon, or at four consulates at Da Nang, Nha Trang, Bien Hoa, and Can

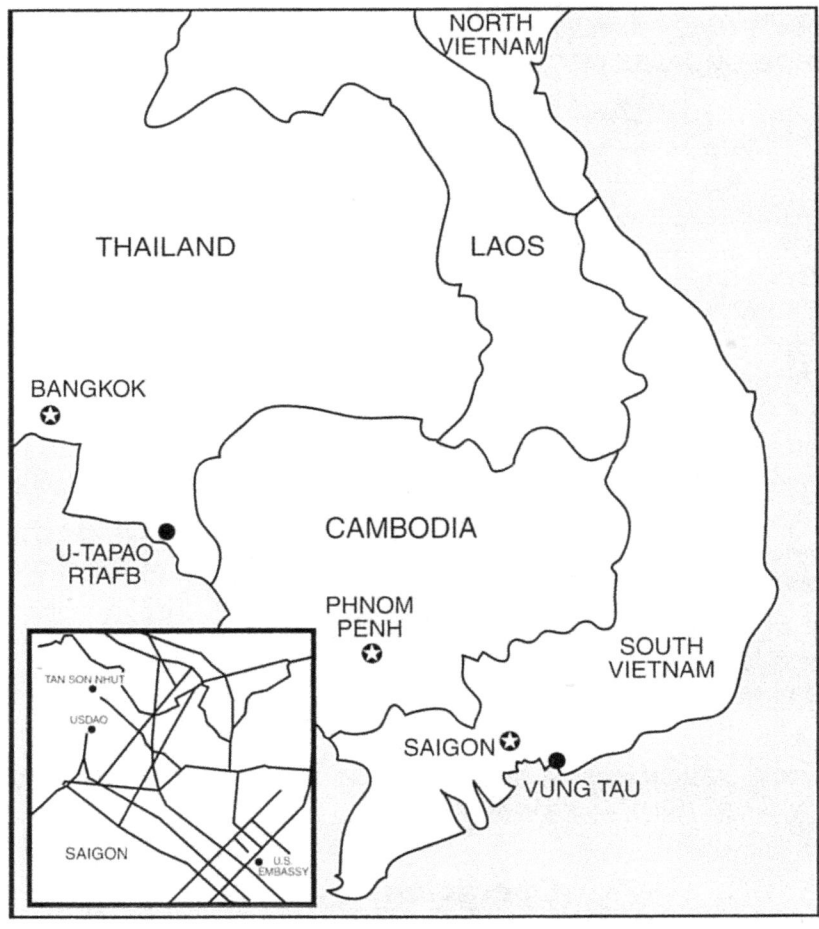

Southeast Asia during the Vietnam Evacuation
Inset: Saigon during Operation FREQUENT WIND

Tho. Each of these sites retained a handful of U.S. Marine guards. In August 1974, Maj. Gen. Homer D. Smith, USA, assumed command of the DAO. He reported to Graham A. Martin, U.S. Ambassador to South Vietnam, and to Adm. Noel A. M. Gaylor, USN, Commander in Chief, Pacific Command.

Early in 1975, Communist military forces in Vietnam prepared for a major offensive. Such an offensive was not likely to provoke a powerful American military response, such as the one launched in 1972, because President Richard M. Nixon had resigned in 1974 in the wake of the Watergate scandal. The U.S. Congress showed little willingness to approve more aid for South Vietnam, much less a reintroduction of American forces into the conflict. During the first week in March, the North Vietnamese Army attacked key bases in the central highlands of South Vietnam. Ban Me Thuot, on the highway between Saigon and the north central highlands, fell on March 14, persuading South Vietnamese President Nguyen Van Thieu to withdraw his forces from Pleiku and Kontum. A chaotic retreat followed. By the end of the month, enemy forces had captured the strategic bases of Quang Tri, Hue, Tam Ky, and Da Nang, the last three on the northern coast.

The evacuation of Da Nang was chaotic. Communist forces had cut off land escape routes, leaving refugees and military forces alike dependent on sea lift or airlift. Ships evacuated thousands southward to other coastal bases. Commercial airlines under contract to evacuate American citizens were forced to carry panic-stricken Vietnamese soldiers and their families. The last airplane to depart, a World Airways 727, carried out 290 passengers, at least 7 in its wheel wells. The aircrew could not even retract the airliner's landing gear.

During the first week in April, other key South Vietnamese coastal bases, including Cam Ranh Bay and Nha Trang, fell to the North Vietnamese. Sea lift carried thousands more refugees to Vung Tau, on the coast just southeast of Saigon, and Phu Quoc Island. Although some South Vietnamese fully expected U.S. air strikes against the Communists, President Ford refused to order them. He did announce on April 3 that American military transports delivering military cargo to Saigon would on return flights to the United States evacuate Vietnamese orphans.

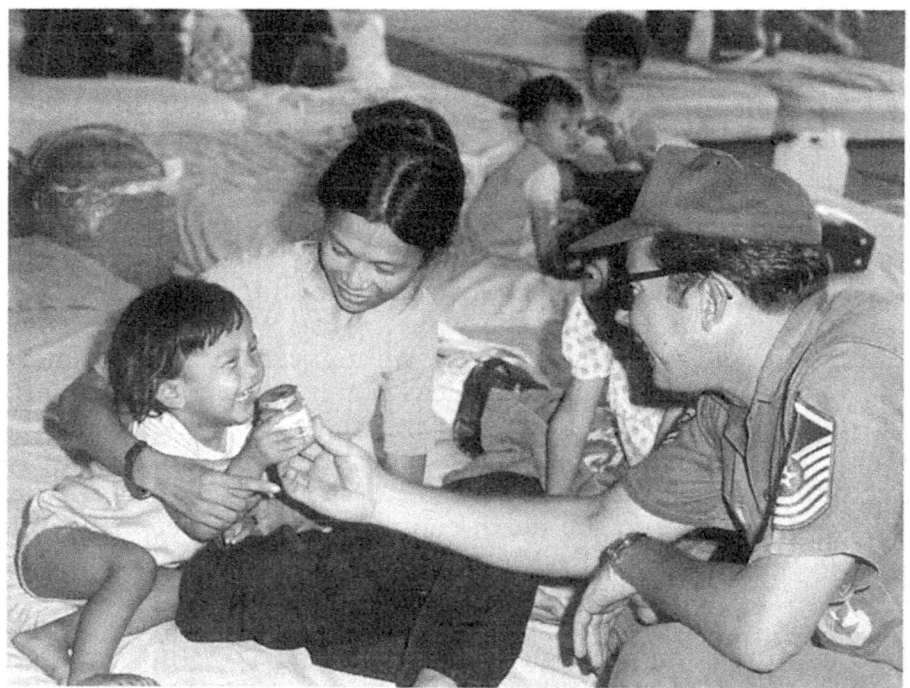

A USAF NCO gives food to a Vietnamese refugee family in Guam.

This operation, called BABYLIFT, began tragically. On April 4, a giant C–5 Galaxy, then the largest airplane type in the world, landed in Saigon with artillery for the South Vietnamese army. It took off with more than 200 orphans, escorted by 37 female DAO employees. Not long after taking off from Tan Son Nhut Airport, about the time it crossed the coast near Vung Tau, the C–5 suffered an explosive decompression in its rear cargo door area. Deprived of controls to the massive airplane's tail, Capt. Dennis Traynor, USAF, attempted to fly back to Saigon using the ailerons alone. Despite his best efforts, the huge airplane crash-landed in rice paddies short of Tan Son Nhut. Miraculously, 175 of the 330 aboard the C–5 survived the explosion and crash. Thus began the airlift evacuation of American citizens and Vietnamese refugees from Saigon.

Although sabotage was never proven, fear of it slowed the airlift from Saigon. The U.S. Air Force used no more C–5s and tightened luggage inspections. BABYLIFT was not a total failure.

MAC crew members cradle South Vietnamese infants during Operation BABYLIFT.

Other airplanes, including military transports and commercial airliners under contract, eventually evacuated more than 2,600 Vietnamese orphans to Hawaii and on to the continental United States.

A number of factors contributed to declining South Vietnamese morale during April. North Vietnamese forces continued to advance all across the country. On April 9, they attacked Xuan Loc, only thirty-eight miles from Saigon. That same week, Communist Khmer Rouge forces captured Phnom Penh, capital of neighboring Cambodia, and U.S. Marine Corps helicopters had to evacuate Americans there. If the trend continued, Saigon would also fall.

Ambassador Martin wanted to preserve an atmosphere of normality and calm in the South Vietnamese capital. He feared that a sudden massive American evacuation would lead to the kind of panic that had erupted in Da Nang, and he wanted to prevent the collapse of the South Vietnamese government. During the first part of April, USAF C–141 Starlifters landed in Saigon with increased frequency to deliver military cargo to the South Vietnamese. Available to evacuate U.S. citizens, third country nationals, and selected Vietnamese, at first they carried only a small fraction of their passenger capacity. U.S. citizens with Vietnamese dependents refused to leave without them, and Vietnamese dependents faced time-consuming paperwork. They also wanted to take their extended families with them. Lines grew to a mile or more, and some people waited for more than twenty-four hours. C–141s often landed at Tan Son Nhut more frequently than they could take off because of time-consuming passenger processing and baggage checks. Consequently, at one time, four vulnerable Starlifters sat on the ground at Tan Son Nhut. By April 19, only about 6,000 evacuees had flown out of South Vietnam.

The fixed-wing evacuation went into high gear between April 20 and 28. Admiral Gaylor and Ambassador Martin simplified the paperwork that had delayed so many evacuees. President Ford authorized the evacuation of tens of thousands of "at risk" Vietnamese, even if they were not American dependents. In addition to the C–141s, USAF C–130s from the 374th Tactical Airlift Wing at Clark AB in the Philippines began flying to and from Saigon on April 21. The air evacuation became an around-the-clock operation, with about twenty C–141s taking off every day and about twenty C–130s every night. Neither airplane type was authorized to carry more than 100 passengers, but each one, in the later stages of the airlift, carried 180 or more.

There were other reasons for the accelerated aerial evacuation. By April 21, two-thirds of the country's land area and twenty-one of forty-four South Vietnamese provincial capitals were in enemy hands. The defenders of Xuan Loc began withdrawing to Saigon. The North Vietnamese Army cut the main highway between Saigon and Vung Tau and took crucial points along the Saigon River, precluding a massive sea lift. On April 21, President Thieu resigned, hoping new South Vietnamese leadership would persuade the Communists to negotiate. But North Vietnam was not in a mood for compromise. The Communists sensed total victory and hoped to occupy

Saigon completely by the time of Ho Chi Minh's birthday in May. The North Vietnamese publicly announced that they would not oppose an American aerial evacuation of Saigon but only if it took place immediately.

On April 22, more than 3,000 evacuees flew out of Saigon. There were more each day. On April 26 and 27, about 12,000 departed Tan Son Nhut on 46 C–130 and 28 C–141 flights. Two 374th Tactical Airlift Wing C–130s evacuated 250 dependents of South Vietnamese marines from Vung Tau on the 27th. Shortly afterwards, more C–130s entered the operation, having deployed from the 314th Tactical Airlift Wing in Arkansas to the Philippines. Maj. Robert S. Delligatti, USAF, and later Col. Earl E. Michler, USAF, of the Seventh Air Force supervised the airlift at Tan Son Nhut, working in the Evacuation Control Center at Tan Son Nhut. They collaborated with Col. Garvin McCurdy, USAF, DAO Air Attaché, and Brig. Gen. Richard T. Drury, USAF, Pacific Theater Airlift Manager. By the end of April, the DAO had processed over 40,000 people for aerial evacuation.

Initially, most evacuees flew to Clark AB in the Philippines, but on April 23, Philippine President Ferdinand Marcos an-

Americans and Vietnamese deplane from a C–130 after evacuation from Vietnam.

nounced that he would permit no more than 200 Vietnamese refugees in his country at a time. There were already more than 5,000 there. His new policy forced the U.S. Air Force to airlift refugees to Andersen AFB, Guam, and to Wake Island in the central Pacific, where the U.S. military services hastily constructed huge camps.

On April 27, enemy rockets hit Saigon for the first time in years. They set off a huge fire that left 5,000 people homeless. The attack ended the C–141 airlift because the Starlifters were more expensive and vulnerable than the C–130s and because they were needed for shuttling passengers from the Philippines to Guam and Wake. The C–130 airlift continued, but not for long. The next day, Communist pilots in captured A–37s bombed Tan Son Nhut, temporarily halting the Hercules evacuation after only 18 flights had carried out 3,500 people. Ambassador Martin hoped to use sixty C–130 flights to complete the aerial evacuation of Saigon on April 29, but Communist rockets frustrated his plans. A predawn artillery attack destroyed one C–130 and forced the last two to take off immediately, one with refugees and one with the burning C–130's crew. The runways also became full of evacuating South Vietnamese military aircraft and mobs of people demanding to be taken away. By dawn on April 29, the fixed-wing evacuation of Saigon was over.

Between April 1 and 29, the U.S. Air Force flew 201 C–141 and 174 C–130 sorties in the evacuation. Between April 5 and 29, these aircraft had airlifted more than 45,000 people from Saigon, including more than 5,600 U.S. citizens. Thousands of refugees and many U.S. citizens, including the ambassador, his staff, and many DAO members, remained in Saigon when the last C–130s departed. Fourteen North Vietnamese Army divisions armed with antiaircraft weapons surrounded the city. At this point, President Ford ordered the final aerial evacuation of Saigon by helicopter, Operation FREQUENT WIND.

At dawn on April 29, a fleet of Air America UH–1 helicopters began shuttling evacuees from preselected Saigon rooftops to the DAO at Tan Son Nhut or to the American embassy. At the same time, a fleet of buses moved selected evacuees from predetermined Saigon assembly points to the DAO or to the embassy. Large Marine Corps CH–53 and CH–46 helicopters gathered on ships of the Seventh Fleet off the Vietnamese coast to transport Marine Corps security forces to protect the DAO and embassy and to extract evacuees. Each CH–53 could carry as many as sixty-five passengers.

The U.S. Air Force played a key role in Operation FREQUENT WIND. Ten USAF CH–53 and HH–53 helicopters from the 56th Special Operations Wing and the 40th Aerospace Rescue and Recovery Squadron in Thailand had deployed earlier in the month to the USS *Midway* in the South China Sea. Operation FREQUENT WIND was the first major operation involving the use of USAF helicopters from an aircraft carrier. Nine flew with the Marine Corps helicopters to Saigon for the final aerial evacuation. Col. Loyd J. Anders Jr. commanded the USAF contingent. The U.S. Navy provided fighters from aircraft carriers as air cover for the helicopters, and the U.S. Air Force flew fighters and gunships, including F–4s, A–7s, and AC–130s, from bases in Thailand. Some of the F–4s attacked enemy antiaircraft artillery sites near the encircled capital. The Air Force also provided KC–135 tankers to refuel the fighters and C–130 airborne command and control aircraft to handle the air traffic.

Despite careful planning, Operation FREQUENT WIND did not proceed on schedule. Crowds of panic-stricken Vietnamese blocked bus routes in downtown Saigon and surrounded the embassy and DAO complex. South Vietnamese military forces at Tan Son Nhut demanded evacuation for themselves and their families. Enemy raids on the airport had knocked out the Air America helicopter refueling facility, forcing the UH–1s to fly all the way to the fleet to refuel. Many more refugees gathered at the U.S. Embassy than expected, and evacuation from that site did not begin until almost dark. There was confusion over scheduling with cover flights arriving in Saigon some three hours before the large helicopters from the fleet. Bad weather complicated an already confused operation.

During FREQUENT WIND, 71 American military helicopters flew 662 sorties between Saigon and elements of the Seventh Fleet. The operation succeeded in extracting more than 7,800 evacuees from the DAO and U.S. Embassy on April 29 and 30, not counting the U.S. Marines that had landed that day. On 4 round trips between the *Midway* and Saigon, USAF helicopters evacuated more than 1,400 people. Counting fighter, tanker, and command and control flights, the U.S. forces flew a total of 1,422 sorties over Saigon the final day. The operation ended before 9:00 A.M. on April 30. Shortly after noon, Communist flags were flying from Saigon's Presidential Palace.

Although FREQUENT WIND, the final air evacuation of Vietnam, was over, the airlift of Vietnamese refugees to islands in the Pacific continued. Refugees congregated at Clark AB and the naval base at Subic Bay in the Philippines, Andersen AFB in Guam, and Wake Island. More than 400 Military Airlift Command (MAC) flights transported 8,556 tons of cargo to the refugee camps during the spring of 1975. Starlifters carried most of the supplies, including bedding, tents, and food. Of the camps, Guam was by far the most significant. MAC C-141s and C-130s made 135 flights to move at least 31,000 refugees from the Philippines to Guam. By mid-May, the island sheltered more than 50,000 Indochinese refugees.

In an operation called NEW ARRIVALS, MAC transports and commercial airliners transported tens of thousands of refugees from the Pacific island camps to refugee reception centers in the continental United States. The movement, which lasted through the end of summer, took about 600 flights. Refugees landed at one of several military bases that had been prepared for them, including Fort Chaffee, Arkansas; Camp Pendleton, California; and Eglin AFB, Florida. To reduce the refugee population on Guam, which became increasingly vulnerable as typhoon season approached, the Department of Defense opened a fourth reception center at Fort Indiantown Gap, Pennsylvania. In Operations NEW LIFE and NEW ARRIVALS, about 130,000 Indochinese refugees eventually settled in the United States.

Members of the armed services drew several lessons from the evacuation experience. Fragmented command and control hindered the operation, especially during FREQUENT WIND. A single military commander, and not the ambassador, should have controlled all military forces involved in the final phases of the evacuation. Not all participants in FREQUENT WIND agreed on scheduling, leading to confusion over the launch time of the large helicopters. A single agency should have defined the reference hour for execution. The definition of who qualified for airlift evacuation kept changing, which routinely expanded the number of refugees to be evacuated. The Vietnamese evacuation demonstrated the value of a single theater airlift manager, the effectiveness of integrating strategic and tactical airlift resources, and the critical importance of adequate ground-support personnel to mission success.

The aerial evacuation of South Vietnam was the largest in history. More than 50,000 people fled by air, the majority on USAF aircraft. Almost all U.S. citizens left by air. Operation FREQUENT WIND ended more than twenty years of U.S. involvement in Vietnam.

Cambodian Airlift and Evacuation: Operation EAGLE PULL

Daniel L. Haulman

DATES: April 11, 1973–April 17, 1975

LOCATION: Cambodia (Khmer Republic)

OVERSEAS BASES USED: Korat, Nakhon Phanom, Ubon, Udorn, and U-Tapao Royal Thai Air Force Bases (RTAFB), Thailand; Tan Son Nhut Air Base (AB), South Vietnam; Clark AB, Philippines

AIR FORCE ORGANIZATIONS:

WINGS:	GROUP:
56th Special Operations	3d Aerospace Rescue and Recovery
60th Military Airlift	
307th Strategic	**SQUADRONS:**
374th Tactical Airlift	7th Airborne Command and Control
388th Tactical Fighter	21st Special Operations
432d Tactical Fighter	40th Aerospace Rescue and Recovery

AIR FORCE AIRCRAFT: C–130, AC–130, EC–130, F–4, RF–4, HH–53, CH–53, A–7, OV–10, KC–135, C–141

Operations

During the late 1960s, as the war in Vietnam intensified, Viet Cong and North Vietnamese troops infiltrated neighboring Cambodia to build Communist supply bases for attacks in South Vietnam. Cambodian ruler Prince Norodom Sihanouk seemed unwilling or unable to stop the infiltration. In March 1970, while Sihanouk visited the People's Republic of China, Lt. Gen. Lon Nol seized power in Phnom Penh, the Cambodian capital. Nol depended on the United States for aid and announced his opposition to the Communists. In May, he allowed U.S. and South Vietnamese troops to enter Cambodia to wipe out the Viet Cong and North Vietnamese supply bases. When those troops left Cambodia later that year, Lon Nol still faced a combination of antagonists, including Communist

"Khmer Rouge" forces and supporters of Sihanouk, who remained in China.

During the early 1970s, the Cambodian Communists attempted to take Phnom Penh in a series of frontal attacks. Failing in this, the Khmer Rouge embarked on a new strategy of cutting all supply lines to the Cambodian capital. They gained increasing amounts of Cambodian territory and threatened to cut all major highways between Phnom Penh and the countryside. The Cambodian capital survived only with supplies shipped up the Mekong River from South Vietnam and by a USAF airlift.

In April 1973, the 374th Tactical Airlift Wing began flying C–130s carrying rice, ammunition, and fuel from U-Tapao Royal Thai Naval Airfield, Thailand, into Phnom Penh's Pochentong Airport. The wing also air-dropped weapons and food to twenty-five major enclaves across Cambodia, including Kampong Seila and Neak Luong. By October 1974, the U.S. Air Force had airlifted about 100,000 tons of cargo from Thailand to Cambodia on over 6,000 flights.

In 1974, U.S. President Gerald R. Ford and his advisors grew increasingly cautious about the possibility that American aircrews would be shot down over Communist-held territory. The Cambodian (Khmer) air force could not take over the airlift because its C–123 aircraft were not large or numerous enough to carry the needed cargo. To continue the airlift and yet reduce the presence of American military forces in Cambodia, the Military Airlift Command (MAC) contracted in September with a private company called Birdair to furnish aircrews. In early October, Birdair civilians began to fly all the USAF C–130s on the Cambodian airlift, continuing to deliver rice, ammunition, and fuel from U-Tapao to Pochentong and dropping the same kinds of cargo to the enclaves. The Birdair crews, some with USAF experience, learned to air-drop with precision, despite high-altitude and high-velocity flights. The 374th Tactical Airlift Wing continued to furnish and maintain the airplanes.

This arrangement worked well until early 1975, when Communist offensives in both South Vietnam and Cambodia closed the Mekong River supply line. The last Mekong River convoy turned back to Saigon on February 5, when it encountered a

CAMBODIAN AIRLIFT AND EVACUATION

Area of USAF Operations during Cambodian Airlift and Evacuation

barrage of enemy gunfire and mines. Airlift alone could sustain Phnom Penh, as it had Berlin, but only if it was vastly expanded. Birdair had been flying about ten missions a day, using five aircrews. Experts estimated that Cambodia would need a daily minimum of 30 missions, because Phnom Penh alone required more than 1,000 tons of supplies per day.

The United States reacted to the emergency by increasing the number of C–130s available for the Cambodian airlift and expanding the Birdair contract. Birdair doubled the number of aircrews and tripled the number of sorties by the end of February, moving impressive amounts of food, munitions, and fuel from U-Tapao in Thailand to Phnom Penh and the enclaves. Still it was not enough. Phnom Penh had a population of more than two million people, equivalent to that of Berlin in the late 1940s, and only an airlift on the scale of the one for Berlin in 1948–49 would allow it to survive. Moreover, Phnom Penh needed additional supplies to fight off military attack.

More was needed, but President Ford, aware of growing opposition in Congress, refused to reintroduce USAF aircrews into the Cambodian airlift. He had asked for about $220 million in additional aid for Cambodia, but Congress refused to approve it. Some congressmen, who expected Cambodia to fall in any case, even demanded a June 30 cutoff for all aid to the country.

To augment the Birdair C–130 airlift, MAC contracted with two airlines, Airlift International and World Airways, for DC–8 flights. On February 15, they began transporting war materiel from Thailand to Phnom Penh. By the end of February, the DC–8s were flying about 550 tons of rice daily on a new route from Saigon to Pochentong Airport in the Cambodian capital. In March, MAC contracted with three additional DC–8 airlines, Trans International, Flying Tiger Line, and Seaboard World, to carry more food from Saigon to Phnom Penh. At the same time, Birdair C–130s continued to transport war materiel from U-Tapao to Pochentong. MAC personnel supervised the double airlift from South Vietnam and Thailand.

The expanded Cambodian airlift allowed the Lon Nol regime to survive through March, but the Khmer Rouge continued to tighten the ring around Phnom Penh, and more enclaves fell. By April, the end was near. Lon Nol departed Cambodia for Indonesia on April 1, turning the government over to acting President Saukham Khoy. On April 4, the United States began the aerial evacuation of Phnom Penh. The same C–130s and DC–8s that delivered ammunition and rice from Thailand and South Vietnam began to transport selected evacuees from Pochentong Airport. A few C–130s flown by USAF crews on routine administrative flights to Phnom Penh also participated in the fixed-wing evacuation of the Cambodian capital. Between April 4 and 11, about 875 Cambodians flew to Thailand on USAF C–130s. Most of them found shelter at a large refugee camp at U-Tapao. Among the Cambodian evacuees were fifty-two orphans, whom the U.S. Air Force flew from Thailand to the Philippines on a 60th Military Airlift Wing C–141. They flew on to the United States on a MAC contract flight.

Between January 1 and the middle of April 1975, an estimated 2,500 enemy artillery and rocket rounds hit in the vicinity of Phnom Penh's airport. DC–8 pilots demanded changes in ramp space to avoid areas most often hit. Increased Khmer Rouge shelling of Pochentong ended all C–130 and DC–8 air-land flights on April 11. Since mid-February, DC–8s had flown 770 missions from Saigon to Phnom Penh, delivering over 36,000 tons of rice, ammunition, medical supplies, and other cargo. During the same period, Birdair flew more than 1,000 missions to deliver over 20,000 tons of cargo, mostly war materiel, from Thailand. Deprived of these lifelines, the Lon Nol government had no hope of survival.

At the time U.S. airplanes stopped flying to Phnom Penh, the Khmer Rouge appeared ready for the final assault on the Cambodian capital. John Gunther Dean, U.S. Ambassador to Cambodia, decided to implement Operation EAGLE PULL, the final evacuation of U.S. citizens, Cambodian employees of the U.S. government, and third-country nationals from Phnom Penh. Eager to avoid a repetition of the chaotic aerial evacuation a couple of weeks earlier from Da Nang, South Vietnam, Dean and military planners prepared to use helicopters to lift the evacuees from a defensible soccer field just a few blocks from the U.S. Embassy. Lt. Gen. John J. Burns, USAF, Commander, Seventh Air Force, served as commander of the joint operation. He reported to Adm. Noel A. M. Gayler, USN, Commander in Chief, Pacific Command.

Around 9:00 A.M., April 12, a USAF HH–53 Super Jolly Green Giant helicopter landed on the field, designated Landing Zone Hotel, with a four-man combat control team. In the next few minutes, U.S. Marine Corps CH–53 Sea Stallion helicopters from the USS *Okinawa*, an amphibious assault ship eight miles off the Cambodian coast, began landing with a ground-security force under the command of Col. Sydney H. Batchelder Jr., USMC. This force, from the 31st Marine Amphibious Unit, quickly deployed around the soccer field to protect the landing zone, but the Cambodians who gathered to

Landing Zone "Hotel" in Phnom Penh, Cambodia.

watch the helicopters posed no danger. There was no panic or chaotic rush to escape. While the first helicopters were landing, ground vehicles carried Americans, selected Cambodians, and others from the embassy to the soccer field.

As soon as each CH–53 helicopter discharged its marines, it loaded evacuees and took off to make room for the next helicopter. The landing zone was big enough to accommodate three of the big choppers simultaneously, if necessary. Ambassador Dean had expected as many as 780 evacuees. Less than 300 actually showed up, and almost all of them departed on the first wave of USMC helicopters. USAF CH–53s from the 56th Special Operations Wing that hovered over the area waiting their turn to load passengers were not needed. A pair of USAF HH–53s from the 40th Aerospace Rescue and Recovery Squadron evacuated the last of the ground-security force, seven late passengers, and the combat control team. As the last helicopters took off, Khmer Rouge rockets and mortars

HH–53 crews prepare in Thailand for Operation EAGLE PULL.

began to zero in on the soccer field. A helicopter was hit by ground fire and suffered minor damage. There were no U.S. casualties and no aircraft lost. The whole operation took less than two and a half hours.

The Air Force played a greater role in EAGLE PULL than providing a few HH–53s and CH–53s. To cover the evacuation and escort the helicopters, F–4s, A–7s, and AC–130s from the 388th and 432d Tactical Fighter Wings flew twenty-six sorties, but they had to expend no ordnance. A pair of EC–130s from the 7th Airborne Command and Control Squadron provided General Burns with air traffic control and linked by radio the U.S. Embassy with the Joint Rescue Coordination Center in Thailand. KC–135s from the 307th Strategic Wing orbited for aerial refueling and radio-relay missions. OV–10s flew sixteen sorties, ready to provide forward air control if necessary, while RF–4s flew weather reconnaissance missions.

A total of 287 people left Phnom Penh by USMC and USAF helicopters on April 12. There were 173 Cambodians, 83 U.S. citizens, 30 third country nationals, and 1 U.S. citizen dependent. A few reporters, desiring to cover the fall of Phnom Penh, remained in the Cambodian capital. Most of the Cambodian evacuees had been U.S. government employees or their family members. They flew with the other evacuees first to the USS *Okinawa* and later on to Thailand.

Phnom Penh did not fall for another five days. During that time, Birdair C–130s continued airdrops over friendly enclaves and Pochentong Airport. They delivered 457 tons of rice and 371 tons of ammunition between April 13 and 17 on 55 flights. The airdrops ceased on April 17 when the Khmer Rouge took over Phnom Penh.

The Cambodian airlift was the largest sustained airlift operation between the Berlin Airlift of 1948–49 (Operation VITTLES) and the airlift to Bosnia (Operation PROVIDE PROMISE) of 1992–96. More than 5,400 missions to Pochentong delivered over 123,000 tons of food, ammunition, fuel, and other cargo in 2 years. In addition to that, more than 3,000 air-drop missions transported almost 39,000 tons of cargo to surrounded enclaves around Cambodia during the same time. That was better than three times the cargo air-dropped to Khe Sanh in 1968. More than 8,400 air-land and air-drop missions delivered 162,000 tons of cargo to Cambodia. Civilian aircrews or airlines delivered about 60,000 tons of this on some flights.

The Cambodian airlift taught several valuable lessons. Like Operation VITTLES, it proved airlift can feed and supply a city surrounded by enemy forces. Between early February and mid-April 1975, Phnom Penh depended on airlift alone for food and military supplies. The airlift ultimately failed, however, because the United States refused to finance the increasing level of supplies needed and because enemy ground forces were able to close Pochentong. Operators of the C–130s and DC–8s delivering supplies to Phnom Penh used the airport long after it came under enemy artillery fire by altering flying and taxiing patterns, moving off-load areas, and temporarily suspending flights. No airlift aircraft were lost, and only eight were damaged.

For the first time in USAF history, civilian-contract aircrews flew airlift missions into an airfield under enemy fire. The Cambodian airlift proved that contracting between the Military Airlift Command and private airlines could work. The Birdair flights represented a truly combined effort of civilian aircrews, military aircraft, and military maintenance crews. USAF supervision of the DC–8 airlift flights revealed advantages and disadvantages. Contracting saved money, but civilian airlines did not offer the same flexibility and responsiveness of a purely "blue suit" operation.

The final evacuation of Phnom Penh also taught some valuable lessons. Planning for Operation EAGLE PULL began years in advance of its execution, and the preparations paid off. Careful selection of the landing zone and provision for enough resources, in combination with the element of surprise, enabled the operation to proceed without the panic and chaos that attended the previous evacuation of Da Nang in neighboring South Vietnam. Both loyalist Cambodians and Khmer Rouge expected the final evacuation to take place with fixed-wing aircraft at Pochentong Airport, not by helicopters from a soccer field.

If anything, Operation EAGLE PULL committed too many resources to the evacuation. No one could tell in advance the degree of opposition the aerial evacuation would encounter. Fighters and gunships flew missions without expending any ordnance. Embassy officials overestimated the number of evacuees, forcing helicopters to return to their home bases or ships without passengers. The helicopters flew holding patterns concentrated in a single area, risking damage from enemy antiaircraft weapons.

On the other hand, the evacuation of Phnom Penh demonstrated interservice cooperation. USMC and USAF helicopter crews worked well with those of USN ships and USAF aircraft under a single operational commander. Unfortunately, not all of the operation participants agreed on the meaning of terms. For example, to some "L-Hour" meant the time the USMC helicopters launched from the USS *Okinawa*, while to others it meant the time they landed in Phnom Penh. The use of ultrahigh-frequency radio networks would have improved communication between the helicopters and the controlling EC–130s. The HH–53 helicopters proved superior in some respects to the CH–53s in the operation. Unlike the CH–53s, the HH–53s were air-refuelable by HC–130 aircraft, which allowed them to have longer ranges and to hover and circle longer.

The aerial evacuation of Phnom Penh provided both the Air Force and the Navy practice for the larger evacuation of Saigon at the end of the month, but the earlier operation in fact went much smoother. The final evacuation of Americans from South Vietnam precipitated a rush of refugees desperately attempting to flee the country, because they had seen what happened after the fall of Cambodia. Not long after the Khmer Rouge took Phnom Penh on April 17, the Communists forced all of the city's residents to move into the countryside and began a series of mass executions that eventually left as many as two million people dead. The Khmer Rouge tortured and enslaved many of the survivors. The Cambodian airlift and Operation EAGLE PULL delayed the coming of this dark age and allowed some of its potential victims to escape to freedom.

Crisis in Southeast Asia: Mayaguez Rescue

Daniel L. Haulman

DATES: May 12–15, 1975

LOCATIONS: Cambodia and Gulf of Thailand

OVERSEAS BASES USED: U-Tapao Royal Thai Air Force Base (RTAFB), Thailand; Cubi Point and Clark Air Base (AB), Philippines; Kadena AB, Okinawa

AIR FORCE ORGANIZATIONS:

WINGS:	SQUADRONS:
41st Aerospace Rescue and Recovery	7th Airborne Command and Control
56th Special Operations	16th Special Operations
60th Military Airlift	
62d Military Airlift	
307th Strategic	
314th Tactical Airlift	
347th Tactical Fighter	
374th Tactical Airlift	
388th Tactical Fighter	
432d Tactical Fighter	
437th Military Airlift	

AIR FORCE AIRCRAFT: CH–53, HH–53, A–7, F–4, F–111, AC–130, C–130, HC–130, KC–135, OV–10, C–141, RF–4, U–2, C–9, C–5

Operations

On May 12, 1975, as the American civilian merchant ship SS *Mayaguez* on a voyage from Hong Kong to Thailand passed about sixty miles off the Cambodian mainland, a gunboat pulled alongside, and armed Khmer Rouge soldiers climbed aboard. They quickly seized the vessel and its forty-man crew, but not before one of the crewmen sent a "mayday" distress message.

When U.S. President Gerald Ford learned that an American ship had been seized in international waters, he responded

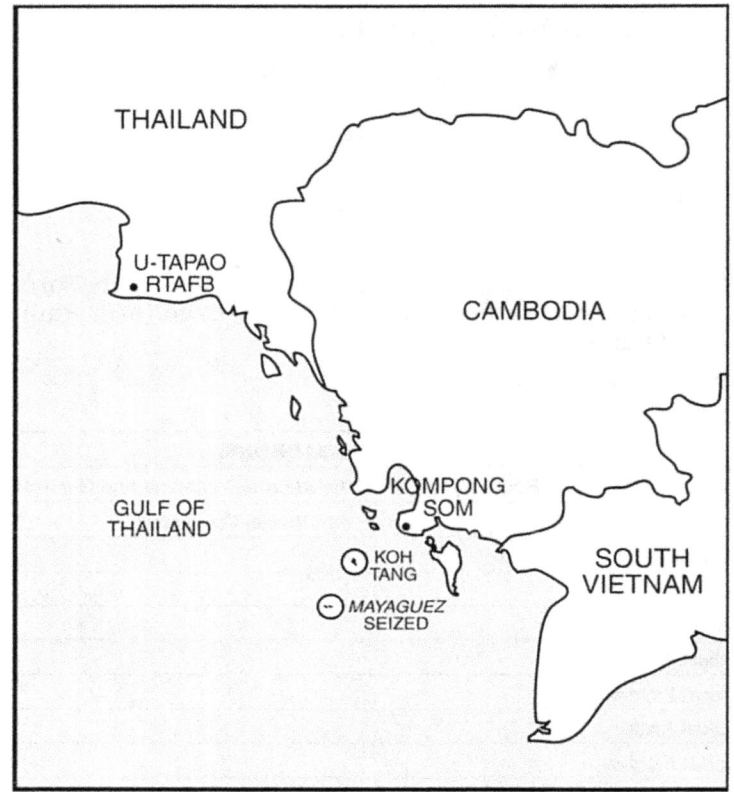

Area of USAF Operations during Mayaguez Crisis

immediately. He remembered that North Koreans had seized the U.S. Navy ship *Pueblo* in 1968 and held its crew for a year, not releasing them until the United States had issued an apology. Just a month before the *Mayaguez* seizure, Cambodia and South Vietnam had fallen to Communist forces, suggesting that the United States was a "paper tiger." President Ford sought a quick solution to the crisis through diplomacy, but that option faded quickly. Since the collapse of the Phnom Penh government a month earlier, the United States had no formal diplomatic ties with Cambodia. Ford tried negotiating through China and the United Nations, but neither produced any immediate results. He turned from the state to the defense department.

Marines board a CH–53 helicopter bound for Koh Tang.

President Ford ordered military aircraft to search the Gulf of Thailand for the *Mayaguez*. USAF F–111s from Thailand located the ship near Koh Tang (Tang Island), about thirty-four miles southwest of the mainland city of Kompong Som. Reconnaissance flights suggested that the Cambodians were holding the *Mayaguez* crew on the tiny island. The President hoped to rescue the American hostages before they were taken to the Cambodian mainland.

At the time, the United States still maintained powerful military forces in Thailand and the Philippines. Lt. Gen. John J. Burns, USAF, Commander, Seventh Air Force, and the U.S. Military Advisory Group in Thailand assumed local command of the rescue operation, reporting to Adm. Noel A. M. Gayler, USN, Commander in Chief, Pacific Command. USAF F–4s, A–7s, F–111s, and AC–130s from Thai bases kept watch over the *Mayaguez* and Koh Tang, prevented the ship from being taken elsewhere, and stopped virtually all shipping between the island and the Cambodian mainland. They sank or damaged seven Cambodian gunboats, but they could not prevent a fishing boat from voyaging from Koh Tang to Kompong Som on the mainland, despite their use of rockets and riot control agents. Reconnaissance flights showed that the boat might contain some of the *Mayaguez* crew. Actually, all of the captured Americans were aboard the fishing boat, but Burns believed that most of them remained either on the ship or on Koh Tang.

U.S. air and ground forces concentrated at U-Tapao, the nearest Thai base to the scene. Among them were USAF CH–53 Knife helicopters from the 56th Special Operations Wing and HH–53 Super Jolly Green Giant choppers from the 40th Aerospace Rescue and Recovery Squadron. Both helicopter types bore armor plating and machine guns, and the HH–53s could refuel in the air. One of the CH–53s, loaded with air policemen, crashed on the way to U-Tapao, killing all twenty-three men aboard. Meanwhile, 16 Military Airlift Command C–141s carried more than 1,100 U.S. Marines from Kadena AB in Okinawa and Cubi Point in the Philippines to the Thai base. The movement took twenty-two hours. At the same time, a flotilla of U.S. Navy ships, including the aircraft carrier USS *Coral Sea* and the destroyers USS *Henry B. Wilson* and USS *Harold E. Holt,* voyaged toward the Gulf of Thailand.

General Burns and his staff planned to use about 230 marines to board the *Mayaguez* and assault Koh Tang simultaneously, hoping to find the *Mayaguez* crew members on either the ship or the island. Pacific Command intelligence sources estimated as few as 19 enemy soldiers on the island, although the Defense Intelligence Agency warned that there could be 200 or more. Lt. Col. Randall W. Austin, USMC, Commander of the Marines destined for Koh Tang, reconnoitered the island in a USAF aircraft on May 14 and expected little opposition. Normal amphibious procedure called for a three to one numerical superiority for an attack and a preliminary bombardment. Burns refused preparatory air strikes on Koh Tang because he did not want to hit the *Mayaguez* crewmen he believed to be there.

Early on May 15, the rescue operation began. Three USAF helicopters transported forty-eight Marines to the *Holt*. As the *Holt* sailed toward the *Mayaguez,* USAF A–7s dropped tear gas cartridges on the decks of the merchant ship to immobilize any enemy who might be aboard. Shortly afterwards, the *Holt* pulled alongside the *Mayaguez,* and Marines with gas masks boarded the ship. They found it empty. The Navy personnel could not start the old merchant ship's engines, so the *Holt* attached a line and began towing the ship away from the vicinity of Koh Tang. At this point, the Cambodian government broadcast a message that it was going to release the *Mayaguez*. The message contained no reference to the crew members, who were still in an unknown location. Since General Burns reported that the *Mayaguez* crewmen were probably on Koh Tang, President Ford directed that military operations continue.

Eight USAF helicopters loaded with about 180 Marines attempted to land on the northern side of Koh Tang. Disaster followed. An entire entrenched enemy battalion heavily armed with automatic weapons, rocket launchers, mortars, heavy-caliber machine guns, and grenades opened fire on the big helicopters as they approached. Three went down, including one with most of the Marines' forward air control radio equipment. Four other helicopters suffered severe damage, one of them returning to Thailand without unloading its men. Only one escaped heavy damage. The helicopters delivered about 130 Marines to Koh Tang in the first assault wave.

The Cambodian soldiers outnumbered and outgunned the U.S. Marines, who were fragmented into three groups. They needed air support, but it was slow in coming. A USAF forward air control A–7 flew overhead to direct air strikes but had difficulty communicating with the Marines on Koh Tang. Some of the ground forces contacted the airplane with survival radios. Flying high and fast, the A–7 could not determine the exact location of friendly or enemy forces on the island and refused to direct heavy fire into areas that might contain Americans. General Burns had ordered that supporting fire from the air be limited to small-caliber gunfire or riot-control gas to prevent casualties among possible *Mayaguez* crewmen.

While the fighting on Koh Tang continued, reconnaissance aircraft spotted the *Mayaguez* crewmen in a fishing boat in the Gulf of Thailand. The *Wilson* intercepted the boat and took on the liberated Americans. Now both the *Mayaguez* and its crew were free, but the fighting on Koh Tang continued. Austin needed reinforcements to allow him to fight off the enemy until he could unite his scattered troops and withdraw safely. Burns' superiors debated the need for putting more

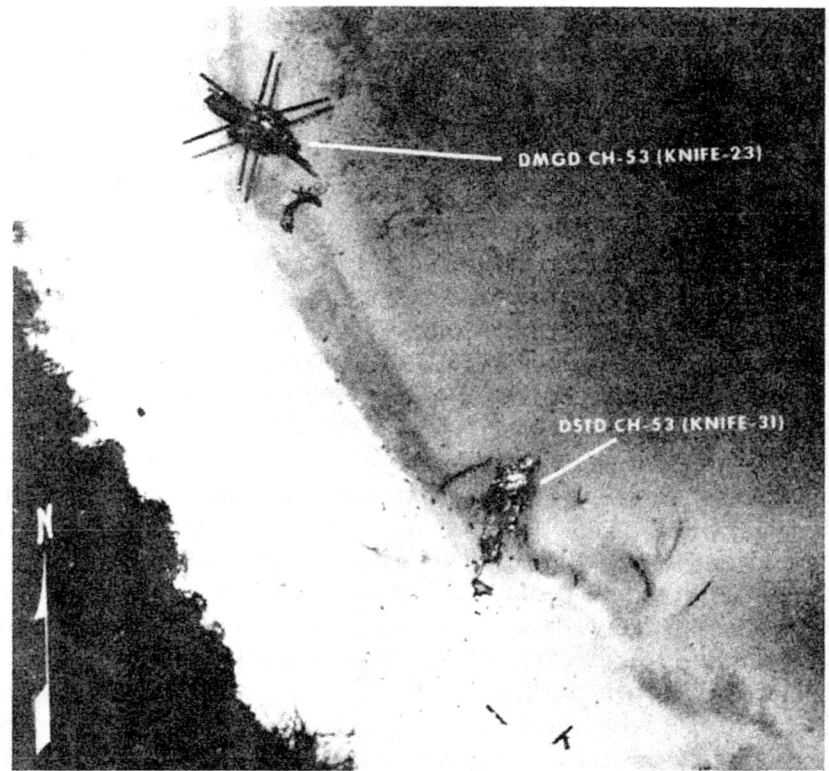
Wreckage of U.S. helicopters on Koh Tang.

Marines on an island from which they were to withdraw but eventually decided a second assault wave was necessary, even with seven of the helicopters destroyed or severely damaged. Four surviving helicopters landed Marine reinforcements on Koh Tang around noon, bringing the number of Americans on the island to about 220. A fifth helicopter was hit repeatedly and had to turn back without unloading its troops.

Once General Burns learned that the *Mayaguez* crewmen were not on Koh Tang, he directed heavier air bombardment of the island. A series of F–4, A–7, and AC–130 air strikes reduced enemy fire. American strafing increased, first with 20- and 40-millimeter ammunition and later with 105-millimeter ordnance from the AC–130 gunships. In the late afternoon, Maj. Robert W. Undorf, USAF, arrived in an OV–10 Bronco aircraft to act as forward air controller. The OV-10, which could fly lower and slower than the A-7, allowed Undorf to pinpoint the positions of the Marines and to direct more accurate gunfire from the USAF fighters and gunships. At about the same time, the two groups of Marines on the western side of the island established a combined perimeter, while a search and rescue HH-53 helicopter evacuated twenty-five Marines isolated on the eastern side of the island. KC-135s and HC-130s orbiting over the Gulf of Thailand refueled the fighters and helicopters. To disrupt the enemy defenders psychologically, a C-130 dropped a huge 15,000-pound BLU-82 bomb, the largest non-nuclear explosive in the American arsenal, on the southern part of the island. It fell far enough away not to injure any Marines, leaving a crater the size of a football field. By then, the aircraft carrier USS *Coral Sea* had arrived, but it used its fighters to hit targets near Kompong Som on the Cambodian mainland in order to prevent their intervention in the island fighting. Other U.S. Navy ships bombarded Koh Tang to support the Marines.

As darkness approached, Burns had very few USAF helicopters left for the extraction of the almost 200 troops remaining on Koh Tang. During the insertions and search and rescue attempts, eleven helicopters had been destroyed or damaged. Only three USAF helicopters accomplished the final extractions, two of them making repeated trips. Picking up the last of the Marines was extremely dangerous, not only because the enemy continued to challenge the helicopters and soldiers with heavy fire, but also because of almost total darkness. Air Force fighters and gunships, directed by additional OV-10s, provided air support for the final extractions. The helicopters took the Marines to the *Coral Sea* and the *Holt*, each equipped with a small helicopter deck. The troops had been on Koh Tang a total of fourteen hours.

The *Mayaguez* rescue operation was a qualified success. The primary purpose of the mission, the rescue of the forty-man *Mayaguez* crew and the return of their ship, had been accomplished. The United States had demonstrated that it would not tolerate the seizure of its ships in international waters and discouraged Khmer Rouge piracy, which had threatened other ships in the Gulf of Thailand. The action restored, to some extent, the confidence of U.S. allies in the willingness and ability of the administration to respond to Communist challenges, a confidence that had fractured after the fall of the Cambodian and South Vietnamese governments.

The *Mayaguez* operation, on the other hand, aroused a great deal of negative criticism. Counting the helicopter that crashed in preliminary movements in Thailand, the U.S. Air Force lost four CH–53 helicopters. Enemy fire badly damaged eight others. More important than the loss of aircraft was the loss of life. In the assault on Koh Tang, the United States lost eighteen lives, most of them in one destroyed helicopter. The helicopter crash in Thailand took the lives of another twenty-three USAF personnel. In the contingency as a whole, the United States suffered ninety-one casualties, including forty-one dead and fifty wounded, to save the lives of forty men who might have been released without military action. Viewed as a whole, the operation cost more lives that it saved.

Of all the lessons learned in the *Mayaguez* incident, the first was that inadequate intelligence leads to disastrous results. American intelligence failed to locate the *Mayaguez* crewmen, leading planners to think that they were either still on the ship or on nearby Koh Tang, when in fact they were in neither place. American intelligence also failed to predict accurately the strength of the enemy on Koh Tang. Observers, including the USMC commander, who had flown over the island the day before the assault, expected only token resistance. The USAF helicopter crews and Marines flew into an ambush. They should have known better. The USAF and USN aircraft that kept watch over the *Mayaguez* and Koh Tang on May 14 had attracted considerable antiaircraft gunfire from the island. Given the short suspense, the scanty intelligence is more understandable.

Should American aircraft have bombarded Koh Tang before the Marines attempted to land there? After all, preliminary bombardment was a traditional part of Marine Corps amphibious doctrine. But General Burns believed that *Mayaguez* crewmen were on the tiny island and did not want to endanger them. If he had thought the crew was not on Koh Tang, there would have been no reason for the assault.

Air support for the Marines was initially poor. This was not because the EC–130 airborne command and control center was too far from the scene of action, as some critics have charged. Operation commanders did not want to endanger the *Mayaguez* crewmen they believed to be on Koh Tang, the enemy destroyed a helicopter that contained most of the Marines' forward air control radio equipment, and the fast and high-flying A–7 could not pinpoint the location of friendly or enemy positions. The OV–10 proved to be a more effective forward air control aircraft than the faster and higher-flying A–7. The poor selection of landing sites also contributed to the inadequate initial air support, because it placed friendly and enemy troops in such close proximity that heavy air strikes would have resulted in fratricide.

The Cambodians abandoned the *Mayaguez* and released its crew at the same time the costly assault on Koh Tang was beginning, suggesting that military action was premature and unnecessary. There was no previously prepared operational plan to build on or consult. The crisis began on May 12, and President Ford sent American men into battle three days later. He could have allowed more time for diplomacy to work, but he wanted to rescue the *Mayaguez* crewmen before they could be taken to the mainland. Even if the United States had had diplomatic relations with the new Cambodian regime, there was no assurance that it exercised full control over the Khmer Rouge forces on Koh Tang and at Kompong Som.

Riot-control gas, used extensively in the *Mayaguez* operation, was not very effective as a military instrument. It did not prevent the fishing boat with the *Mayaguez* crew from leaving Koh Tang and reaching the Cambodian mainland on May 14. Gas played no useful part in the retaking of the *Mayaguez*, because the ship was empty when it was boarded. A change in the wind made the gas useless on Koh Tang during the fighting there, blowing it out to sea.

The BLU–82 "daisy-cutter" bomb had little effect on the battle on Koh Tang. It was dropped far enough from the Marines to avoid injuring them, but it was also far enough from the battle line to make little difference there. It had been designed to clear helicopter landing zones in the jungles of Southeast Asia and had been very effective for that purpose, but that was not how it was used on Koh Tang. Dropped late in the fighting, the big bomb had little more than a psychological effect during the operation, although the football-field size area it cleared might have also contained some enemy troops and weapons. More effective were the air strikes of A-7s, F-4s, and AC-130s.

Although the initial U.S. air attacks from the *Coral Sea* on the Cambodian mainland occurred just before President Ford learned that the *Mayaguez* crew was free, they continued afterwards. Some critics have suggested that the subsequent air strikes were useless bluster, because the purpose of the operation had already been achieved. The air raids were designed not to free the crew but to prevent hostile Cambodian forces on the mainland from joining in the battle on Koh Tang, which was not yet over.

The United States suffered strained relations with Thailand as a result of the *Mayaguez* operation. Anxious to avoid confrontations with its new Communist neighbors, the Thai government officially protested the use of its territory to stage U.S. attacks against Cambodia. For diplomatic reasons, one C-5 and thirteen C-141s transported all remaining U.S. Marines in Thailand back to Okinawa and the Philippines within twenty-four hours of the assault on Koh Tang. The Thai government expelled all U.S. military forces from Thailand within a year, but that decision had been made in March of 1975. The *Mayaguez* affair was the last major American military operation in Southeast Asia.

Crisis in Tropical Africa: Operations ZAIRE I and II

Daniel L. Haulman

DATES: May 16–June 16, 1978

LOCATION: Zaire

OVERSEAS BASES USED: Rhein-Main Air Base (AB), Bitburg AB, Ramstein AB, Germany; Torrejon AB, Rota AB, Spain; Royal Air Force (RAF) Mildenhall, United Kingdom; Brussels (Melsbroek), Belgium; Solenzara (Corsica), Colmar, Avord, France; Pisa (Camp Darby), Italy; Geneva, Switzerland; Ascension Island; Roberts Field (Monrovia), Liberia; Dakar, Senegal; Kinshasa, Kamina, Lubumbashi, Zaire; Agadir, Morocco; Abidjan, Ivory Coast; Libreville, Gabon; Lome, Togo

AIR FORCE ORGANIZATIONS:

WINGS:
60th Military Airlift
62d Military Airlift
63d Military Airlift
349th Military Airlift Wing (Associate)
436th Military Airlift
437th Military Airlift
438th Military Airlift
443d Military Airlift Wing, Training
445th Military Airlift Wing (Associate)
514th Military Airlift Wing (Associate)

AIR FORCE AIRCRAFT: C–141, C–5

Operations

After Congo President Mobutu Sese Seko replaced Moise Tshombe of Katanga in 1965, he developed a dictatorship that was especially unpopular in Katanga, where rich copper mines and cobalt resources attracted European and American miners and engineers. Mobutu renamed the country Zaire and Katanga

Province, Shaba. Katangan rebels who had fled to neighboring Angola invaded Shaba Province in May of 1978, hoping to drive Mobutu from power, or at least liberate the province from his control. The rebels captured the provincial capital of Kolwezi and the city of Mutshatsa. The fighting and rebel-led mass executions trapped and endangered almost 3,000 Belgian, French, and American mining and engineering workers.

Area of USAF Operations during ZAIRE I and II

Belgium, France, and the United States, all members of the North Atlantic Treaty Organization, considered intervention. They had more to fear than the threat to the lives of their citizens in Zaire. Cuba had some 43,000 troops in at least 14 African nations, including newly independent Angola, from which the rebels had struck. Western nations relied more on Zaire than any other nation for scarce cobalt, which came primarily from Shaba Province. If Zaire became a Communist state like Angola and Cuba, the Soviet Union might be able to deprive the West of one of its most valuable resources in the Cold War. There were other reasons for intervention. The

United States had long supported operations in Zaire designed to prevent the country's dissolution, and as dictatorial as Mobutu was, he seemed to be a lesser evil than a divided or Marxist Zaire. In 1978, Belgium still had thousands of citizens and a billion-dollar investment in Zaire.

Western leaders considered launching a rescue operation similar to DRAGON ROUGE in 1964 in which Belgian paratroopers dropping into the Congo from American transports had saved the lives of many foreigners. A French airdrop of Moroccan paratroops in 1977 had driven the Katangans back into Angola. The USAF Military Airlift Command (MAC) prepared to airlift elements of the 82d Airborne Division from North Carolina to central Africa, marshaling C–141 Starlifters and C–130 Hercules aircraft for the operation.

When U.S. President James (Jimmy) E. Carter learned that most U.S. citizens in Shaba had been able to leave, he refused to commit ground troops after all. Just a few years earlier, he had witnessed the collapse of South Vietnam after the loss of tens of thousands of American lives. Carter decided instead to support logistically a Belgian and French paratroop operation in Shaba by airlifting fuel, ammunition, equipment, and supplies from Europe and the United States to Zaire. He scrupulously consulted Congress and followed the guidelines of the International Security Assistance Act of 1977. The operation might have involved newly trained female Air Force pilots, and Congress had not yet approved their participation in combat. President Carter decided that American cargo airplanes flying to Zaire would avoid the combat zone in Shaba.

To coordinate the various routes for the complicated airlift, MAC set up airlift control elements (ALCE) at various locations in Europe and Africa. During the first phase of the operation, ALCE personnel operated from Solenzara (Corsica), France; Dakar, Senegal; Brussels, Belgium; and Kinshasa and Lubumbashi, Zaire. Later, MAC set up other ALCEs at Agadir, Morocco; Lome, Togo; Abidjan, Ivory Coast; and Libreville, Gabon. Mission-support teams deployed at Roberts Field (Monrovia), Liberia; Kamina, Zaire; Colmar, France; and Geneva, Switzerland. Ground personnel to operate these ALCEs and mission-support teams came from the U.S. Air Forces in Europe (USAFE) and some of MAC's C–130 units.

Moroccan troops prepare to board a C–141 after service in Zaire.

In mid-May 1978, Belgium and France chartered airliners and military airplanes, including C–130s and C–160s, to airlift paratroops from Europe to central Africa. About 1,300 Belgian paratroops took off from Brussels, while 600 members of the French Foreign Legion flew from Corsica to Zaire. On the morning of May 20, Belgian troops aboard C–130s landed at Kolwezi's airport and began moving into the rebel-held city. At the same time, French paratroops secured major sections of the city, interrupting a mass execution. No major battle followed. The rebels retreated, allowing the Belgian and French troops to gather the European workers who survived the rebel invasion and executions. Flown to other parts of Zaire, the refugees boarded commercial airliners to Europe. By May 21, about 2,100 refugees had flown to Brussels or Paris. The next day, as more European civilians headed from Africa to Europe, Belgian and French troops began withdrawing from Kolwezi.

U.S. airlifters supported the Belgian and French combat operation, providing crucial fuel, ammunition, vehicles, and other equipment and supplies. Between May 16 and 27, MAC cargo aircraft transported 931 tons of cargo and 124 passengers to Zaire on 42 C–141 and 1 C–5 missions. Twenty-eight of the C–141s in what was called ZAIRE I came from the 437th and 438th Military Airlift Wings in South Carolina and New Jersey, while the C–5 came from the 436th Military Airlift Wing in Delaware. Loading at bases in Germany, Belgium, France, Italy, and Spain, the cargo aircraft landed for replacement crews and refueling at Roberts Field in Liberia and at Dakar in Senegal. Using these staging bases on the west coast of Africa allowed the MAC airplanes to fly over the Atlantic Ocean instead of over potentially hostile territory. In Zaire, they landed at Kinshasa, the capital, and at Kamina and Lubumbashi near the combat zone.

Ten C–141 missions from Brussels, capital of Belgium, to Kamina transported more than one hundred tons of cargo. At first, the Starlifters staged at Roberts Field, but a shortage of fuel there forced them to switch to Dakar. Other C–141s transported forty-two tons of aircraft bulk-fuel bladder systems from Camp Darby near Pisa, Italy, to Kinshasa. Four bladder-configured Starlifters then shuttled 352 tons of fuel from the Zairian capital to Kamina in 12 missions. Belgian C–130s flying troops and refugees between Kamina and Kolwezi were thus able to refuel.

French troops who flew from Zaire to Corsica observe a C–5.

For the French, American C-141s and a C-5 transported 437 tons of military cargo and 120 passengers from Solenzara to Lubumbashi, staging through Dakar. The C-5, then the largest airplane in the world, carried a fuel truck that was too large for the Starlifters or any of the French and Belgian airplanes. C-141s also shuttled between Dakar and Lubumbashi carrying military vehicles, supplies, and fuel.

The second phase of the airlift was called ZAIRE II. Between May 31 and June 16, 1978, American air transports helped the Belgian and French soldiers to withdraw from Zaire to Europe and replaced them with black African troops. Sixty-one C-141 Starlifter missions and 11 C-5 Galaxy missions moved 1,619 tons of cargo and 1,225 passengers during this phase. To improve inadequate communications between ALCEs along the air routes, American C-141s transported satellite equipment from Europe to Africa. Fourteen missions airlifted 809 French troops and 225 tons of cargo from Lubumbashi to Corsica. Most of the Belgian troops and refugees flew from Zaire to Europe on Belgian military and chartered aircraft, but the United States devoted 6 Starlifter missions to move 129 tons of cargo in support of the Belgian withdrawal.

Fifty C-141 and C-5 missions moved 1,214 tons of cargo as well as 416 troops from Morocco, Ivory Coast, Gabon, Senegal, and Togo to Zaire to replace the Belgian and French forces. The aircraft carried jeeps, trucks, ammunition, communication gear, small arms, mobile kitchens, and medical supplies. Replacement of white Europeans with black Africans during the Zaire contingency stifled propaganda from Communist nations that the operation was another example of white European oppression of black Africa. The U.S Air Force airlifted supplies and vehicles from Avord and Colmar to Lubumbashi for the African troops. A relief airlift also contributed to favorable world public opinion. Two C-141 missions transported fifty-one tons of International Red Cross food and medical supplies from Geneva to Lubumbashi and Kinshasa to combat hunger and disease in Zaire.

MAC aircrews and aircraft that took part in the Zaire contingency in 1978 came from seven wings of the Twenty-First and Twenty-Second Air Forces. A third of USAF participants in the operation were members of the Air Force Reserve assigned to three associate wings that used aircraft and resources of the active wings with which they were associated. Among the participating Reservists was Lt. Kathleen R. Cosand, one of the first female Air Force pilots who completed training in September 1977. Various tactical airlift wings provided ground personnel for the ALCEs and mission-support teams, but USAF C-130 aircraft did not participate in the contingency flights.

The experience of ZAIRE I and II in 1978 taught the Military Airlift Command and the Air Force some valuable lessons. Inadequate communications at first endangered the success of the operation. If American combat troops had deployed by air from the United States to central Africa, as originally planned, very good but very bulky and heavy communication gear would have accompanied them. When those flights were cancelled, MAC decided to scale back flights of communication equipment. The gear subsequently deployed and set up at Corsica, Kinshasa, Kamina, and Lubumbashi was not adequate, because it lacked sufficient power to span the enormous distances between some of the ALCEs. At the start of ZAIRE II, the Joint Chiefs of Staff authorized the deployment of satellite terminals to solve the problem. Terminals set up in Corsica, Morocco, Senegal, Togo, and two bases in Zaire allowed almost simultaneous command and control communications. At the conclusion of the Zaire contingency in 1978, MAC recommended that quick-reaction communication packages, including satellite terminals, be available to the Air Force for similar operations. MAC also recommended other communication improvements, such as equipment and software to allow encoding of transmitted weather data. The command further advised that every deployed ALCE should have access to the Defense Communications System's voice telephone network.

As in previous operations to the Congo (Zaire) in the early 1960s, many airfields in Africa lacked adequate infrastructure or supplies to support extensive or sustained airlift operations. Shortages of fuel, support facilities, communication equipment, potable water, food, shelter, and ground transportation complicated the airlift. For example, lack of aircraft fuel at Roberts Field in Monrovia forced some flights to go to Dakar instead. At Kinshasa, lack of shelter at the airport forced crews to stay over twenty miles away, resulting in poor communications between the crew quarters and the airfield. The Military Airlift Command had to send large amounts of equipment and supplies to allow the African bases to support the deployment of large numbers of U.S. military personnel, including rotating aircrews, ground crews, ALCEs, refuelers, and communications technicians. Enough bases provided refueling support for the C-141s on the ground, but ZAIRE I and II demonstrated the need to continue modification of the Starlifters for in-flight fueling capability.

ZAIRE I demonstrated the necessity to deploy the ALCEs before the arrival of the first cargo airplanes. Sometimes the ALCEs did not arrive at an airfield until after aircrews, who needed points of contact at each base to give them information such as airfield fuel supplies, aircraft parking space, and personnel support facilities. They also required more information on Africa, including current aeronautical charts on the area. ZAIRE I and II also confirmed the need for more prepositioning of equipment and supplies to allow a sequenced flow of aircraft along the MAC worldwide routes and to reduce overconcentration of resources at any one base prior to the actual flights.

Some of the problems to surface were organizational. Various commands confused MAC with overlapping airlift requests. The command identified a need for one Joint Chiefs of Staff agency to consolidate and validate airlift requirements during a contingency. MAC also concluded that more staff, support personnel, and time should be devoted to planning for such a contingency and that staff functions had to be more clearly defined. The redundant requests for information inundated the ALCEs. A central point of contact for data would protect subordinate airlift agencies from extraneous requests for information that would interfere with their ability to accomplish the missions.

Various computer systems were available for the Zaire airlift in 1978, including the Joint Operational Planning System, the World-Wide Military Communications Control System Intercomputer Network, and the Integrated Military Airlift Planning System, but users demanded more computer support. For example, no software existed to provide required force-deployment information at short notice.

One important lesson from ZAIRE I and II was that, among the nations of the Free World and possibly in the world at large, only the United States had the capacity for massive airlift operations involving the transportation of large quantities of fuel and bulk cargo. At the time, only the United States had an aircraft like the C-5, able to handle oversized cargo. MAC's large fleet of C-141 heavy-cargo airplanes was unmatched by any other nation. Using these tremendous capabilities, the United States provided the Belgian-French paratroop operation with its logistical foundation and replaced the European troops with soldiers of sub-Saharan African nations.

Of all the U.S. military services, the Air Force proved to be the most useful instrument for the ZAIRE contingency in 1978. The need for a quick response over a long distance to a country in the interior of a continent called more for airlift than sea lift. The U.S. Army would have played a larger role if the President had decided to deploy American combat troops, but he did not.

There were few diplomatic problems. Spanish officials denied the use of Torrejon AB as a staging base when third country nationals such as French or Belgians were aboard. Still, the State Department was able to secure blanket clearances to fly over and land in most countries, with waivers of requirements to list aircraft tail numbers, aircraft commanders, and loads. The 1978 ZAIRE operation attracted far more international support than the similar 1964 DRAGON ROUGE operation to the same country. Many sub-Saharan nations had grown suspicious of the large contingent of Soviet-supplied Cuban troops in Africa and were more concerned about Soviet imperialism than a return to European or American colonialism. French diplomacy in the French-speaking countries of sub-Saharan Africa contributed to the suspicious attitude toward the Soviet Union.

ZAIRE I and II accomplished important foreign policy goals of the United States. ZAIRE I saved the lives of thousands of people, most of whom were citizens of nations allied with the United States. ZAIRE II transported black African troops to replace the white soldiers from Europe, thus avoiding the perception of renewed European imperialism. Both ZAIRE I and II helped preserve the unity of Zaire, which might have suffered the secession of Shaba Province and a resultant civil war. The operation also prevented a Marxist government from coming to power in Zaire, which could have led to a larger number of Soviet-supplied Cuban troops in Africa. Finally, ZAIRE I and II demonstrated the ability of the United States and its Air Force to transport by air extraordinary amounts of crucial cargo over long distances in short periods of time, an ability that is crucial in a world of proliferating contingencies.

Crisis in Iran: Operation EAGLE CLAW

Edward T. Russell

DATES: December 8, 1978–April 25, 1980

LOCATION: Iran

OVERSEAS BASES USED: Hellenikon Air Base (AB), Athens, Greece; Masirah Island, Oman; Mehrabad Airport, Tehran, Iran

AIR FORCE ORGANIZATIONS:

NUMBERED AIR FORCE:	WINGS:
Twenty-First	1st Special Operations
	436th Military Airlift
DIVISION:	437th Military Airlift
322d Airlift	438th Military Airlift

AIR FORCE AIRCRAFT: C–5, C–141, EC–130, MC–130

Operations

In the mid-1970s, Islamic fundamentalists, urged on by the exiled Ayatollah Ruhollah Khomeini, grew more and more dissatisfied with the leadership, reforms, and government of Iran, under Mohammed Reza Shah Pahlavi. In August 1978, approximately 44,000 Americans, including 700 military members, 250 defense department employees, and 8,000 defense-related contractor personnel lived in Iran. In early December, when antigovernment demonstrations in Iran began to threaten the well-being of U.S. military dependents in the country, the Joint Chiefs of Staff (JCS) directed the Military Airlift Command (MAC) to fly out dependents wishing to leave Iran. Consequently, on December 8–9, the Twenty-First Air Force flew 2 C–5 and 9 C–141 special assignment airlift missions carrying 903 persons from Mehrabad Airport in Tehran, the capital of Iran, to bases in the United States and Germany. Throughout the remainder of the month, violence and disorder mounted, leading the U.S. Department of State to recommend that all American dependents leave the country. By the end of December, the JCS, at the request of the Secretary of State, directed MAC to provide space-available seating on scheduled MAC flights from Iran to dependents of American citizens. In response, MAC increased the number of regularly scheduled missions to Tehran to two a day. C–5s and C–141s flew these missions equipped with the maximum number of seats. The airlift continued throughout January 1979 amidst further demonstrations, strikes, and general turmoil.

The Shah fled the country on January 16 and Khomeini triumphantly returned on February 1. He appointed a government four days later and began to transform Iran into a theocratically ruled Islamic state. In addition to draconian domestic measures, he completely abandoned the Shah's pro-Western orientation and adopted a foreign policy of absolute hostility toward the United States and the Union of Soviet Socialist Republics. In February, an estimated 1 million people demonstrated in Tehran, and at least 500 died in a clash between factions.

As a result of this turmoil, the U.S. Department of State ordered increased efforts to evacuate all American dependents and nonessential industrial and military personnel from Iran. On February 8, MAC added more missions to the scheduled flights from Tehran. On February 10, the Iranians closed Mehrabad Airport, forcing suspension of airlift operations. Altogether, between December 9, 1978, and February 10, 1979, 34 C–5 and 87 C–141 flights airlifted 5,732 passengers, 687 tons of cargo, and 169 pets from Tehran. On February 11, in anticipation of a possible requirement to provide additional U.S. military support for evacuation operations in Iran, the JCS ordered MAC's Aerospace Rescue and Recovery Service (ARRS) to deploy six HH–53 helicopters and five HC–130 tankers from Royal Air Force Woodbridge, United Kingdom, to Incirlik AB, Turkey. The JCS also tasked the Commander in Chief, Atlantic Command, to deploy to Incirlik AB one combat-equipped Marine infantry detachment that could reinforce the U.S. Embassy compound in Tehran during an evacuation. Furthermore, in case an immediate evacuation became necessary, MAC ordered six C–141 aircraft at Athens, Greece, on alert.

On February 13, the JCS ordered the Marine detachment to stay at Lajes AB, Azores, on alert, prepared for further deployment within three hours following notification. The JCS also directed the ARRS task force to remain at Sigonella, Italy, pending further guidance. The next morning, armed guerrillas stormed the U.S. Embassy compound in Tehran and seized 102 Americans hostage until Khomeini security forces, responding to U.S. requests for assistance, returned the embassy to U.S. control. After this action, the JCS directed the ARRS task force to leave Italy and proceed to Incirlik. The government of Turkey, however, stipulated that the aircraft arrive with no weapons or military equipment aboard, that the helicopters depart for Iran with the permission of the Iranian government, and that the helicopters be used to evacuate only U.S. personnel and their families. The JCS did not order the emergency evacuation force to Iran. On February 17, the Iranian government reopened Mehrabad Airport, and MAC flew its final evacuation mission—a C-141 that airlifted sixty-nine passengers to Athens. Between February 17 and 26, 13 commercial Boeing 747 missions chartered by the state department airlifted 4,099 more passengers from Tehran to cities in Europe and the continental United States. By March 1, the United States decided to airlift out of Tehran all but skeletal staffs at the embassy and at some corporate headquarters.

The tension continued to mount. Hardly a day passed without some manifestation of anti-American sentiment. News broadcasts, demonstrations, speeches in Parliament, and venomous pronunciations from the Ayatollah reflected this attitude. Khomeini blamed the United States and the "great Satan," U.S. President James E. Carter, for Iran's troubles. In May 1979, a crowd of 150,000 gathered at the U.S. Embassy chanting "death to Carter." Despite this activity, President Carter, in an effort to maintain contact with Iran, did not recall American Foreign Service personnel. Meanwhile, the Shah, diagnosed with cancer, requested treatment in the United States. Acting against the advice of almost all of his advisors, President Carter allowed the Shah to enter the United States for surgery and radiation treatment at the New York-Cornell Medical Center. The deleterious effect of this decision became painfully clear on November 4, 1979, when the

Iranians seized the American embassy and took fifty-three U.S. diplomatic personnel hostage. For the remainder of his presidency, Carter worked to free these citizens. The United States tried diplomatic initiatives, the seizure of Iranian assets, economic sanctions, and passive military air and naval deployments—all failed.

From the first day of the crisis, the National Security Council discussed military options such as the seizure of Iranian oilfields, retaliatory bombing, mining of harbors, total blockade, various covert operations, and a rescue attempt. President Carter eventually decided to go with the rescue attempt. This decision caught the JCS by surprise. The United States lacked bases and other resources in the area. Intelligence sources in Iran had disappeared after the revolution. Operationally, the United States did not have a force to conduct the rescue or contingency plans for it. After five months of intensive preparation, a complicated operational rescue plan emerged. It involved eleven groups of men drawn from the U.S. Army, Navy, Air Force, Marine Corps, and Central Intelligence Agency (CIA). The President and his military advisors approved the plan and ordered its execution.

The operation, known as EAGLE CLAW, called for 3 MC–130s to carry an assault force of 118 troops from the island of

MC–130 flying low over a desert.

Masirah, off the coast of Oman, to Iran, landing 200 miles southeast of Tehran at a desolate, uninhabited location called Desert One. Unfortunately, this site was very close to a highway. Accompanying the MC–130s would be three fuel-bearing EC–130s. After landing in the desert, they would wait for the eight RH–53D helicopters from the carrier USS *Nimitz*, located in the Gulf of Oman. These would arrive approximately thirty minutes after the last C–130 had landed. The commanders and planners agreed that a minimum of six helicopters would be required to carry out the mission. They sent eight helicopters so that if anything went wrong with two, they would still have the minimum number. The helicopters would then refuel from the EC–130s and load the assault force. The C–130s would return to Masirah while the RH–53s proceeded to the assault force's hiding site. The helicopters would unload the troops, then proceed to a separate site fifteen miles to the north in the hills, where they would hide during daylight.

Meanwhile, two agents, who would have been placed in Iran several days before, would rendezvous with the assault force and lead the troopers five miles overland to a remote wadi sixty-five miles southeast of Tehran. There they would hide until dark. The agents would then leave, obtain a pickup truck and a passenger van, return to the site, and transport six drivers and six translators to a warehouse in Tehran where six enclosed Mercedes trucks were stored. The drivers and translators would pick up the Mercedes trucks, return to the hiding site, pick up the assault force, and enter Tehran. While the main assault force drove through Tehran to the embassy compound, a thirteen-man assault team, using the van, would rescue three hostages being held in the Foreign Ministry Building. Upon arriving at the embassy, the assault force, divided into three elements, would neutralize the outside guards, scale the embassy wall, enter the compound, neutralize the interior guards, locate and secure the hostages, and determine if helicopters could land within the embassy grounds. If no obstacles existed, one helicopter would land, pick up the hostages, and fly them to Manzariyeh, an airport approximately thirty-five miles south of Tehran. The rest of the helicopters would then pick up the assault force. If obstacles existed and could not be removed, the assault force would blow a hole in the embassy wall, and lead the hostages

Iran and Persian Gulf during Hostage Rescue Attempt

to a nearby soccer stadium where the helicopters could accomplish the airlift.

While the assault force conducted the rescue operations in Tehran, a U.S. Army Ranger contingent would fly in, take, and secure the airfield at Manzariyeh. They would hold the field until the helicopters arrived from Tehran. Once everyone arrived at Manzariyeh, all of the hostages, drivers, translators,

MC–130 of the type used in the rescue attempt.

helicopter crews, agents, Special Forces personnel, and the assault force would be airlifted out of Iran on C–141 aircraft. The Rangers would then destroy any American equipment left on the field and fly out.

On April 24, 1979, the first MC–130 launched from the island of Masirah. It carried the ground and air commanders, a team tasked to block the highway, and one of the assault elements. The other five C–130s would follow one hour later. As the first MC–130 crossed the Iranian coast, it dropped to 400 feet to avoid enemy radar. At approximately the halfway point, the air commander received word that the eight helicopters had launched from the *Nimitz*. After landing successfully at Desert One, team members unloaded the equipment. Before they could block the highway, a bus approached the landing zone. The blocking force fired on the bus, stopped it, and detained forty-five Iranians. Before this incident ended, an Iranian gasoline-tanker truck came down the road. When it did not stop, the troopers launched an M72 LAW (light antitank weapon), igniting the truck. Finally, when a small pickup truck approached, the driver evidently sensed the danger, turned around, and fled. The U.S. ground commander decided to continue the mission, and the first MC–130 took off to return to Masirah.

The second MC–130 landed shortly afterward. The burning tanker truck served to light the area, while the troopers unloaded this aircraft. It then taxied onto the rough airstrip and took off for the return flight to Masirah. In short order, one more MC–130 and the three EC–130s landed in the desert and took their positions with engines idling to wait for the helicopters.

At first, the helicopter mission bordered on normal, but approximately two hours after take-off, one crew received cockpit indications of an impending rotor-blade failure. The crew landed, verified the malfunction, and abandoned their aircraft. A companion aircraft landed, picked up the crew, and continued the mission. Approximately one hour later, the pilots saw what appeared to be a fog bank several miles ahead. However, it turned out to be the first of several large layers of desert dust and sand. When the RH–53s flew into this mess, they encountered a cyclonic dust storm. Intense winds buffeted the aircraft, and visibility dropped so that the pilots could not see the ground from as low as seventy-five feet, nor could they see the other aircraft. The helicopters immediately separated and proceeded individually to Desert One. The pilots described the experience as flying in a darkened milk bowl. With no visual references, the pilots, wearing night-vision goggles, flew on instruments, at low-level, in the dark, through the turbulent winds. Several experienced vertigo but successfully kept their aircraft in the air. As the flight continued, another helicopter experiencing navigation and flight-instrument problems, decided to abort and return to the *Nimitz*. This left six helicopters proceeding to Desert One. During the long flight across the desert, a third helicopter experienced hydraulic problems, continued the mission, hoping the problem could be fixed on landing.

Meanwhile, at Desert One, the ground forces waited impatiently. They needed to refuel the helicopters, board them, and fly to the hiding site before daylight, and time was running out. Finally, an hour to an hour and a half late, the helicopters began arriving. The ground commander realized that part of the mission would have to be flown in daylight; still he decided to continue. He ordered the assault force to board the helicopters. Simultaneously, the Americans began loading the detained Iranians on board the MC–130 for evacuation to the Manzariyeh Airport. While the assault force boarded the RH–53s, the pilot of the helicopter with hydraulic problems conferred with the helicopter commander. They concluded that the aircraft could not be fixed at Desert One and would have to be abandoned. This decision left five mission-ready helicopters. These were not enough. When notified that he had only five helicopters, the ground commander decided to cancel the rescue mission. He notified his commander in Egypt, who in turn forwarded the recommendation through the chain of command to President Carter, who reluctantly approved.

At Desert One, noise, dust, and confusion prevailed. The commanders decided to refuel the helicopters so that they could return to the *Nimitz* and load the assault force on the C–130s to return them to Masirah Island. The desert floor rocked from the roaring engines of four C–130 and five RH–53 aircraft, and dust and sand flew everywhere. While the burning tanker truck cast an eerie glow, the assault force began loading onto the C–130s for evacuation. The helicopters had moved near the EC–130s to refuel when suddenly disaster struck. Evidently, a rotary blade on one of the helicopters struck an EC–130. The resultant explosion destroyed both aircraft and endangered the other nearby aircraft. Eight men died. The commanders decided to load everyone on the remaining C–130s and abandon the four functional helicopters. As quickly as possible, the troopers and helicopter crews boarded the Hercules, which took off for Masirah. The mission had tragically failed. Although President Carter continued to work to free the hostages, the Iranians held them captive until January 20, 1981.

When the news broke, critics attacked everything from the plan to the maintenance of the helicopters, but the major factors contributing to the failure were the unexpected dust storm and the lack of backup helicopters. However, even in those areas, there were extenuating circumstances. The United States had no way to insert meteorologists into the

Iranian desert to predict or warn about dust storms. The *Nimitz* could not carry any more helicopters in its hangar nor could any be carried on the deck for fear that Soviet satellites would detect them and the Iranians would be warned. Perhaps the most significant result of the Iranian operation was the eventual formation of the U.S. Special Operations Command and its USAF component, the Air Force Special Operations Command. The military had learned that especially in operations of this type, where personnel were drawn from the Army, Navy, Air Force, and Marine Corps, joint planning and joint training were crucial. The U.S. Special Operations Command provides the forum and structure for continuous planning and training.

Crisis in Grenada: Operation URGENT FURY

Daniel L. Haulman

DATES: October 24–November 3, 1983

LOCATION: Grenada

OVERSEAS BASES USED: Roosevelt Roads Naval Air Station, Puerto Rico; Grantley Adams International Airport, Barbados; Point Salines, Pearls, Grenada

AIR FORCE ORGANIZATIONS:

DIVISION:	WINGS: (con't.)
552d Airborne Warning and Control	380th Bombardment
	384th Air Refueling
WINGS:	410th Bombardment
1st Special Operations	412th Military Airlift Wing (Associate)
2d Bombardment	436th Military Airlift
7th Bombardment	437th Military Airlift
9th Strategic Reconnaissance	438th Military Airlift
19th Air Refueling	452d Air Refueling Wing, Heavy
22d Air Refueling	459th Tactical Airlift
23d Tactical Fighter	463d Tactical Airlift
33d Tactical Fighter	512th Military Airlift Wing (Associate)
55th Strategic Reconnaissance	514th Military Airlift Wing (Associate)
60th Military Airlift	
62d Military Airlift	**GROUPS:**
63d Military Airlift	68th Air Refueling
67th Tactical Reconnaissance	134th Air Refueling
97th Bombardment	159th Air Refueling
305th Air Refueling	193d Electronic Combat
314th Tactical Airlift	913th Tactical Airlift Group (Associate)
315th Military Airlift Wing (Associate)	932d Aeromedical Airlift
317th Tactical Airlift	
375th Aeromedical Airlift	**SQUADRON:**
379th Bombardment	7th Airborne Command and Control

AIR FORCE AIRCRAFT: AC–130, EC–130, MC–130, C–130, C–141, C–9, C–5, KC–10, KC–135, E–3, F–15, A–10, SR–71, U–2, RF–4, RC–135

Operations

In October 1983, a military coup on the tiny Caribbean island nation of Grenada aroused U.S. attention. Coup leaders Bernard Coard and Gen. Hudson Austin arrested and then assassinated Prime Minister Maurice Bishop, imposed a twenty-four-hour shoot-on-sight curfew, and closed the airport at Pearls on the east coast, about twelve miles from the capital, St. George's, located on the opposite side of the island. U.S. President Ronald W. Reagan, who did not want a repetition of the Iranian hostage crisis a few years earlier, considered military intervention in order to rescue hundreds of U.S. citizens attending medical school on the island. Adm. Wesley L. McDonald, USN, Commander in Chief, Atlantic Command, began planning an evacuation.

After attaining independence from Great Britain in 1974, Grenada belonged to both the British Commonwealth and the Organization of Eastern Caribbean States (OECS). On October 21, Sir Paul Scoon, Grenada's governor-general, who represented the Commonwealth, asked the OECS for help in restoring order to the island. On October 22, the OECS requested that Barbados, Jamaica, and the United States intervene militarily in Grenada.

Bishop, who had taken power in a 1979 coup, had allowed hundreds of Cubans into Grenada to construct a new airfield with a 9,000-foot runway at Point Salines on the island's southwestern tip. The new air base could serve as a springboard for Cuban military operations in Africa and South America or allow the Soviet Union to disrupt U.S. supply lines that crossed the Caribbean Sea. Hence President Reagan decided to invade the island, not only to rescue U.S. citizens, but also to restore democracy and eliminate a growing Cuban military presence.

The Department of Defense called the invasion Operation URGENT FURY. Vice Adm. Joseph Metcalf III, USN, Commander, Second Fleet, took command of the URGENT FURY joint task force, which included elements of all the military services. The Pentagon assigned Maj. Gen. H. Norman Schwarzkopf,

USA, Commander, 24th Mechanized Infantry Division, to advise Metcalf on the employment of ground forces. Brig. Gen. Richard L. Meyer, USAF, Vice Commander, Twelfth Air Force, directed some of URGENT FURY's strategic and tactical airpower missions, while Maj. Gen. Robert B. Patterson, USAF, Vice Commander, Twenty-First Air Force, supervised the operation's airlift forces. Admiral Metcalf divided Grenada into two zones. His plan called for U.S. Marines from a naval task force to assault Pearls and Grenville in the northeast, while U.S. Army forces, airlifted by the Air Force, attacked Point Salines some five miles southwest of St. George's.

Military movements began before the invasion, which was set for October 25. U.S. Marine and Navy forces on the way to the Mediterranean Sea diverted toward Grenada, while the U.S. Air Force deployed E-3 Airborne Warning and Control System

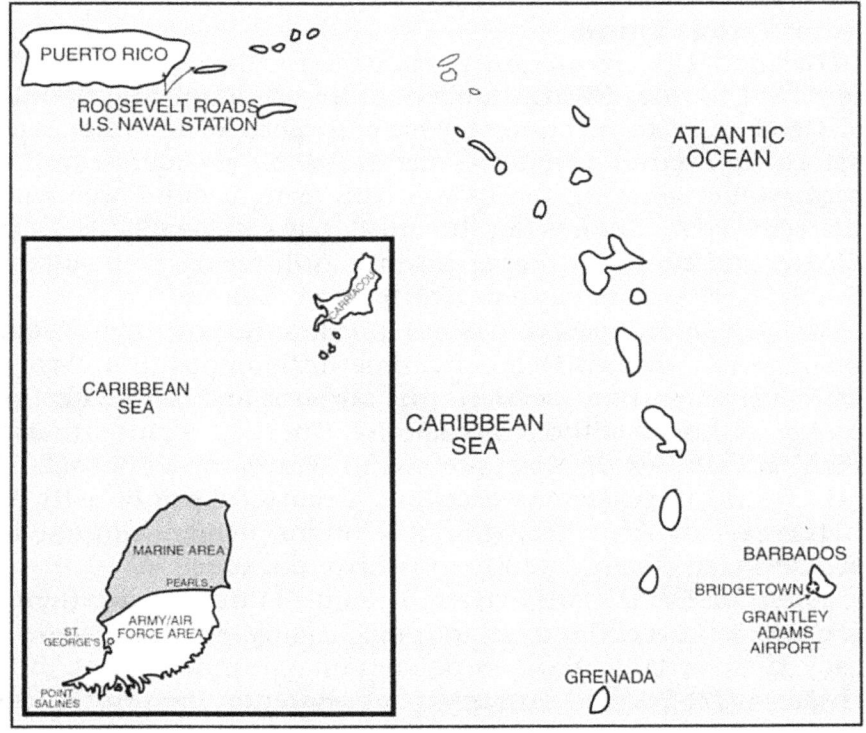

Area of USAF Operations during URGENT FURY
Inset: Areas of Operational Responsibilities on Grenada

(AWACS) aircraft and F–15 fighters to Roosevelt Roads Naval Air Station in Puerto Rico. Refueled by Strategic Air Command tankers, the airplanes patrolled the Caribbean Sea north and west of Grenada to detect and deter any air or sea movements from Cuba. At the same time, USAF strategic and tactical reconnaissance aircraft flew over Grenada to compile intelligence about the location of U.S. citizens and enemy forces.

Those enemy forces were larger and better equipped than the United States expected. Coup leader General Austin commanded the Grenadian army, recently equipped with a huge stockpile of weapons and ammunition from Communist countries. The armaments included more than 9,000 rifles and machine guns and over 5.5 million rounds of ammunition. The more than 600 Cuban construction workers at Point Salines and elsewhere on Grenada were military engineers who also served as soldiers under the command of Cuban Col. Pedro Tortola Comas.

The first U.S. troops on Grenada were Special Forces. One team of U.S. Navy SEALs landed on the island during the night of October 24 to reconnoiter Pearls Airport, while other teams set out to secure Governor-General Scoon's residence and the radio station near St. George's. A U.S. Army Delta Force reconnoitered Point Salines for the next day's invasion. Both the SEALs and the Delta Force ran into stiff enemy opposition in the St. George's area and at nearby Point Salines.

The U.S. Marines who assaulted Pearls Airport by helicopter just before dawn on October 25 met little opposition. Arriving with surprise, they secured the airport and Grenville in a couple of hours without a casualty. The U.S. Army attack at Point Salines was not as successful. Waves of USAF MC–130 and C–130 transports, which had departed Georgia with two battalions of Army Rangers the night before, approached southwestern Grenada in the predawn darkness. AC–130 gunships from Florida had arrived at Point Salines before them to provide air cover for the landings. Using low-light sensors, they discovered Cuban construction equipment and other obstacles blocking the runway. Consequently, the first wave of transports prepared to drop their troops instead of landing. At this point, inertial navigation equipment on the two lead MC–130s malfunctioned, forcing the crews to delay their drops. As one MC–130 dropped the first Rangers, enemy searchlights illuminated it, and antiaircraft batteries opened up. Although the antiaircraft fire damaged the aircraft, its pilot skillfully maneuvered out of range. The other transports in the first wave diverted until an AC–130 could quell the enemy fire. By the time the aircraft returned to complete the drops, dawn had arrived. Attacking more than one-half hour after the U.S. Marines, the Army troops met a completely prepared enemy.

The AC–130s attacking the batteries noted the hilltop antiaircraft guns could not depress their barrels to fire low. To avoid being hit, the MC–130s and C–130s dropped the first battalion of Rangers with parachutes from an altitude of only 500 feet. Some of the 700 air-dropped Army troops hot-wired a bulldozer to clear the runway so that transports could land a second battalion at Point Salines. They liberated 138 American students at a campus near the airfield but soon learned that hundreds more students remained behind enemy lines at Grand Anse four miles to the north.

Heavily armed Cubans and Grenadians put up stiff resistance as the Rangers moved north toward Grand Anse and St. George's. To reinforce the Rangers, USAF C–141 Starlifters transported two battalions of the 82d Airborne Division from North Carolina to Point Salines. The limited airfields on Grenada forced the U.S. Air Force to rely heavily on staging bases between the United States and Grenada. USAF airplanes already crowded the ramps and runways at Roosevelt Roads, forcing the United States to depend on Grantley Adams International Airport in Barbados. From there, C–130s shuttled thousands of tons of war materiel to Grenada. Sniper fire at Point Salines sometimes prevented use of the entire runway, of which only 5,000 feet was complete anyway, and at first there was room for only 1 C–141 on the ground at a time. The Pearls runway was too short for Starlifters. Extremely large C–5 Galaxies, which could not land on either of the Grenadian airfields, unloaded their URGENT FURY passengers and cargo, including some helicopters, in Barbados for later flights to Point Salines and Pearls.

The heavy fighting just north of Point Salines convinced Metcalf and Schwarzkopf to send U.S. Marines on an amphibious

C-130 unloading at Point Salines with engines running.

assault at Grand Mal in western Grenada just north of St. George's. Armed with tanks, the U.S. Marines drove into the capital and rescued the Navy SEALs, who had been surrounded at the governor-general's residence and the radio station. Further south, Army Rangers used USMC helicopters to rescue about 224 U.S. medical students trapped at Grand Anse while naval bombardment, air strikes, and AC–130s kept enemy troops at bay.

While the Marines captured St. George's and moved south, the Army Rangers and airborne troops advanced methodically to the north and east. They met heavy opposition at Fort Rupert, Fort Frederick, Richmond Hill Prison, and Calivigny Barracks but prevailed with the close air support of AC–130 gunships, carrier aircraft from the USS *Independence*, and bombardment from U.S. Navy ships. At the end of October, U.S. Marines, supported by USAF A–10 attack aircraft, assaulted the island of Carriacou just north of Grenada to capture a suspected guerrilla base. By early November, U.S. forces on Grenada had achieved most military objectives. They captured coup leaders Austin and Coard along with almost 700 Grenadian and Cuban troops. When the Marines deployed to their assigned destination in the Mediterranean, the Military Airlift Command (MAC) transported additional battalions of U.S. Army airborne troops to Grenada. These troops and Caribbean forces protected Governor-General Scoon and an interim government until a democratic government could be established.

To transport about 164 wounded U.S. soldiers from Grenada to Barbados, Puerto Rico, and the United States, the USAF employed C-141 Starlifters, C-130 Hercules, and C-9 Nightingales. Some of the rescued U.S. medical students treated wounded American soldiers. MAC moved the dead to a Department of Defense mortuary at Dover, Delaware. In Operation URGENT FURY, the United States lost nineteen people. Enemy casualties were at least 45 killed and almost 400 wounded.

A primary purpose of the invasion had been to evacuate endangered citizens from Grenada. Between October 26 and 30, 1983, the U.S. Air Force transported about 700 noncombatant passengers from Grenada. The evacuation took sixteen C-141, one C-5, and two C-130 flights. Hundreds of medical students flew to Charleston Air Force Base, South Carolina. MAC also evacuated about 200 third country nationals from Grenada. Twenty C-130 missions transported 755 Cubans from Grenada to Barbados for repatriation.

Reconnaissance, close air support, delivery of troops, transportation of cargo, movement of casualties, evacuation of citizens, and movement of prisoners were not all the U.S. Air Force accomplished in URGENT FURY. KC-135s and KC-10s provided air refueling for the transports, gunships, and fighters. Air National Guard EC-130s flew psychological warfare missions. Other EC-130s and E-3s provided communications and air control. When the island government became stable enough to allow U.S. Army occupation troops to leave, MAC returned at least 6,000 to the United States on C-141s and C-130s.

URGENT FURY was at once a combined and a joint operation. Troops of Barbados, Jamaica, and other Caribbean states joined U.S. forces in a combined task force. A 300- to 400-man Caribbean Peacekeeping Force under Brigadier Rudyard Lewis of Barbados deployed to Point Salines early in the operation, first to guard Cuban prisoners and later to support the establishment of an interim government. The branches of the U.S. military interacted and cooperated, and

Army Rangers board a C-141 to return from Grenada to the United States.

Reserve and National Guard forces contributed significantly to the successful invasion.

With overwhelming military power, the United States took two full days to subdue an island only twenty-one miles long and twelve miles wide. Despite the overall success of the operation, the U.S. Air Force and the other services learned important lessons as a result of the Grenada invasion. Foremost among these was the need for adequate airfields and staging bases. Pearls Airport on Grenada was too small for either C-5s or C-141s, and Point Salines at first lacked enough space for more than one C-141 on the ground at a time. Ramp saturation prevented Roosevelt Roads Naval Air Station from serving as the primary staging base, forcing the United States to rely on the international airport at Barbados. Only skillful management of aircraft flights prevented Barbados' airport from becoming saturated as well. The Grenada invasion encouraged the U.S. Air Force to continue the development of the C-17, a transport aircraft that would combine the capacity, range, and speed of a strategic airlifter with the C-130's ability to land and take off on short runways. With such an airplane, staging bases would be less necessary.

This operation revealed other inadequacies in the USAF C-130 fleet. Most Hercules aircraft lacked precision navigation equipment, forcing them to rely on lead aircraft for night operations. Malfunctions of lead aircraft systems caused costly delays and upset the sequence of airdrops at Point Salines. Each C-130 also required improved radio equipment so that information could be transmitted securely. Finally, the C-130s lacked upgraded defenses against antiaircraft weapons.

The operation confirmed the value of the AC-130 in the close air support role. Maj. Gen. Edwin Trobaugh, USA, Commander, 82d Airborne Division, preferred the gunships to naval bombardments, helicopters, and land artillery because of their speed, accuracy, and versatility. The AC-130s repeatedly silenced and destroyed enemy artillery batteries and armored personnel carriers.

The invasion of Grenada revealed the shortcomings of intelligence. Without a political or military presence on the island, the United States lacked tactical intelligence about the exact location of the U.S. medical students, the strength of Cuban forces, the number of enemy antiaircraft artillery batteries at Point Salines, and runway obstructions. An extremely short planning time contributed to the shortage of intelligence. More planning time would have allowed U.S. Atlantic Command to incorporate the advice of more ground, air, logistical, and public relations experts. A decision to exclude the press from Grenada until the third day antagonized U.S. news organizations and deprived the operation of possibly positive publicity. The Pentagon decided to include a pool of reporters in future operations.

URGENT FURY repeated the lesson that air superiority is a prerequisite for airlift success. Lacking the element of surprise that benefited the USMC helicopters at Pearls, the USAF transports that carried Army Rangers to Point Salines required AC-130 gunships to suppress hostile enemy antiaircraft fire before they could complete their drops. Fortunately, Grenada lacked an air force that might have neutralized the AC-130s. Only after the dropped Rangers cleared the airfield of obstacles were the other C-130s able to land with more troops.

The experience of URGENT FURY encouraged the Department of Defense to pay more attention to the routing of airlift requests. Many of these did not go through proper channels for validation. The Twenty-First Air Force and the Military Airlift Command received some requests directly. Without going to the supported command, such requests caused delays and confusion.

The various branches of the U.S. armed forces used incompatible radio equipment and procedures that resulted in poor communication during the invasion. Ground, air, and sea forces could have supported each other more effectively if their communications had been more standard. URGENT FURY convinced defense department planners to standardize communication equipment and procedures among the services so that they could act symbiotically.

The operation uncovered flaws in joint command structures that contributed to the failure of the various services to work together as one team. Leaders of several commands acted without clear concepts of the limits of their authority, and the Chairman of the Joint Chiefs of Staff often intervened in the operation. The Military Airlift Command controlled airlift and the Strategic Air Command retained operational control of the URGENT FURY strategic reconnaissance and air refueling missions. The experience of the Grenada invasion encouraged Congress to reorganize the defense department with passage of the Goldwater-Nichols Department of Defense Reorganization Act of 1986, which established a more "purple" or joint Pentagon, with one command in charge of one operation.

Despite mistakes from which the defense department and the Air Force learned valuable lessons, URGENT FURY was unquestionably a success. The invasion of Grenada accomplished much more than its triple mission of rescuing U.S. citizens, restoring democracy to the island, and eliminating a hostile Cuban/Soviet base in the Caribbean. It was the first clear U.S. military victory since the war in Southeast Asia, restoring pride in the United States and its armed forces that had declined in the wake of setbacks in Vietnam, Cambodia, Iran, and Lebanon. URGENT FURY provided military leaders such as General Schwarzkopf valuable experience in joint combat operations that they were able to use in the far larger Southwest Asia War. The many missions that air power performed in URGENT FURY proved its indispensability in a future of joint contingency operations.

Raid on Libya:
Operation ELDORADO CANYON

Judy G. Endicott

DATES: April 14–15, 1986

LOCATION: Libya

OVERSEAS BASES USED: Royal Air Force (RAF) Fairford, RAF Lakenheath, RAF Mildenhall, RAF Upper Heyford, United Kingdom

AIR FORCE ORGANIZATIONS:

WINGS:	GROUP:
48th Tactical Fighter	11th Strategic
306th Strategic	
	SQUADRON:
	42d Electronic Combat

AIR FORCE AIRCRAFT: F–111, EF–111, KC–10, KC–135

Operations

In 1969, a group of junior military officers led by Muammar Qadhafi overthrew the pro-Western Libyan Arab monarchy. Since then, Qadhafi's relations with the United States, and most Western European nations, as well as moderate Arab nations, have been confrontational. By the mid-1980s, Libya was one of the leading sponsors of worldwide terrorism. In addition to subversion or direct military intervention against other African nations and global assassinations of anti-Qadhafi Libyan exiles and other "state enemies," Qadhafi has sponsored terrorist training camps within Libya and supplied funds, weapons, logistical support, and safe havens for numerous terrorist groups.

As a presidential candidate, Ronald W. Reagan criticized President James (Jimmy) E. Carter's approach to the Iranian hostage crisis, saying that, if elected, his policy would be one of "swift and effective retribution" against international terrorists. Between January 1981 when President Reagan took office and

April 1986, terrorists worldwide killed over 300 Americans and injured hundreds more. With National Security Decision Directive 138 signed on April 3, 1984, President Reagan established in principle a U.S. policy of preemptive and retaliatory strikes against terrorists. But the very nature of terrorism has usually made impossible the assignment of certain guilt to any one government. By the mid-1980s, Americans had grown angry and frustrated with elected officials' inability to stem the increasing tide of terrorism.

On December 27, 1985, terrorists attacked passengers in the Rome and Vienna airport terminals, killing nineteen (including five Americans) and injuring over one hundred. The terrorists possessed passports confiscated from Tunisian guest workers in Libya and grenades from the stocks of the Libyan Arab army. In addition, intelligence sources claimed that Qadhafi had paid the terrorist Abu Nidal a bonus of five to six million dollars for the operation. Despite the strong evidence that connected Libya to the incident, the U.S. administration officials determined that they did not have sufficient proof to order retaliatory strikes against Libya at that time. President Reagan imposed economic and other sanctions against Libya, publicly denounced Qadhafi for sponsoring the operation, and sent the Sixth Fleet to exercise off the coast of Libya.

Contrary to international law, Qadhafi had proclaimed 32° 30' N, including the entire Gulf of Sidra, to be the northern boundary of Libya. To dispute this claim, the U. S. Navy periodically staged freedom of navigation exercises in or near the Gulf of Sidra. During the 1986 exercises, a naval surface action group crossed on March 24 below the disputed latitude, which Qadhafi dramatically called the "Line of Death." Soon afterward, a Libyan missile battery near Sirte fired two SA-5 missiles at the F-14s flying combat air patrol. The F-14s, aided by naval EA-6B electronic jammers, evaded the missiles, as they did on two other occasions that evening, but the Navy's restraint had ceased. Before the exercise ended on March 27, naval forces sank at least two Libyan antiship-missile vessels racing toward the surface action group and damaged another. In addition, carrier-based aircraft damaged the radar at the Sirte air defense facility (one of Qadhafi's most sophisticated) after it had again locked onto naval aircraft.

OPERATION ELDORADO CANYON

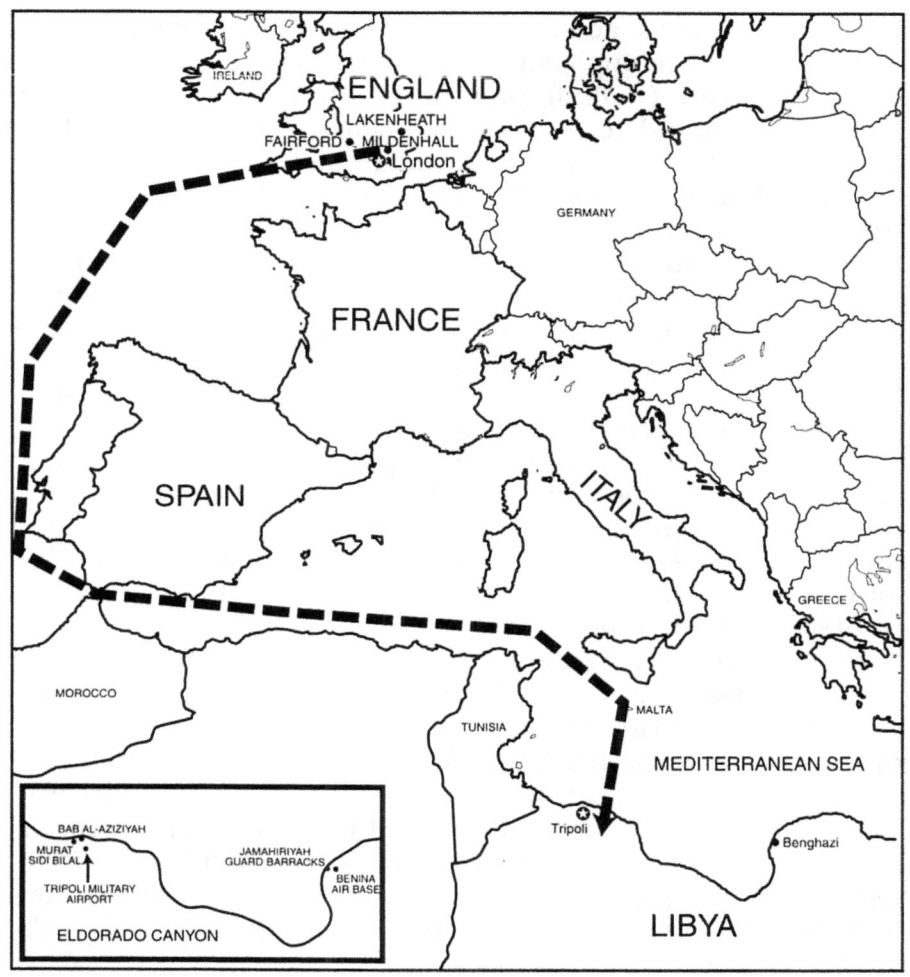

USAF Strike Force Route for ELDORADO CANYON
Inset: Operation ELDORADO CANYON Targets

However, if the Reagan administration thought that evidence of Libya's military weakness and vulnerability might encourage Qadhafi to give up his support for terrorist activities, it was mistaken.

On April 2, plastic explosives detonated aboard a TWA flight bound for Athens, killing four Americans. Although a caller in Beirut claimed the bombing constituted a response to the recent U.S. Navy's actions against Libya, the few physical traces of the bombing pointed to involvement by Syria, not Libya. However, Qadhafi praised the terrorists as freedom fighters and vowed to escalate the violence against U.S. targets, civilian and noncivilian, throughout the world. Then, in the early hours of April 5, in Berlin a large bomb gutted LaBelle Club, a discotheque popular with U.S. servicemen. The explosion immediately killed an American infantryman and his girlfriend and injured over 200 others, including more than 75 Americans. This time, electronic surveillance intercepted two messages to Qadhafi from the East Berlin Libyan People's Bureau that definitely linked Qadhafi to the bombing. A few hours prior to the detonation, the People's Bureau had told Qadhafi that something being planned would make him happy. Following the bombing, they sent notification in general terms, stating the precise time of the discotheque explosion. President Reagan now had the evidence he sought. On April 9, he authorized an air strike against Libya and attempted to obtain support from European allies.

Armed with the evidence against Qadhafi, Vernon Walters, U.S. Ambassador to the United Nations, pressed the governments of Italy, Germany, England, France, and Spain for more severe sanctions against Libya. With the last three nations he also discussed support for a raid against Libya. Margaret Thatcher, Prime Minister of Great Britain, gave permission for the U.S. Air Force to launch its portion of the raid from British bases. The governments of France and Spain denied permission to fly over their countries, thereby increasing the Air Force's round-trip to almost 6,000 miles.

Military planning for a possible operation against Libya had begun shortly after the December attacks in Rome and Vienna. The U.S. President ordered the joint U.S. European Command (USEUCOM) to prepare contingency plans for possible targets in Libya. U.S. Air Forces in Europe (USAFE) military planners identified possible targets, along with planning on how those targets could be attacked, assuming that the British government would allow the United States to stage operations from British bases. General Bernard W. Rogers, USA, Commander, USEUCOM, designated Vice Adm. Frank B. Kelso, USN, Commander, Sixth Fleet, to be overall commander of the joint service operation, code-named Operation ELDORADO CANYON. Planners determined that a nighttime attack provided the best chance of evading Libya's formidable air defense network. Considering the proximity of possible targets to civilian population centers, use of aircraft that provided the most precise targeting available would afford the least possibility for collateral damage in civilian areas.

USAF planners chose the 48th Tactical Fighter Wing, based at RAF Lakenheath, to perform the Air Force portion of the attack. Col. Sam W. Westbrook III, USAF, a former Oxford Rhodes scholar and Southeast Asia combat veteran, commanded the 48th, USAFE's only F–111F wing. Its aircrews regularly trained for nighttime-precision missions. While it had its systems reliability problems, the F–111F (nicknamed Aardvark) provided the long-range, nighttime, all-weather, and precision-strike capabilities required. Using terrain-following radar, the F–111F could avoid enemy radar and ground obstacles, while flying as low as 200 feet above the ground; its Pave Tack laser-targeting system guided ordnance to the target.

Navy and Air Force liaison officers coordinated strike planning that incorporated President Reagan's desire to avoid damage to Libya's economic infrastructure or the death of innocent civilians. From the list of possible targets, the National Security Council, with President Reagan's approval, selected five; four were linked to Qadhafi's terrorist-training infrastructure and the fifth dealt with the enemy defensive threat. The Bab al-Aziziyah barracks in Tripoli was the command center of the Libyan terrorist network. The complex included a billeting area for Qadhafi's personal Jamahiriyah guards and, at times, Qadhafi's own residential compound. The Murat Sidi Bilal training camp, near Tripoli, trained naval commandos and terrorist frogmen. The military side of the Tripoli Airport held Soviet-built IL–76 Candid aircraft that had been used in support of terrorist activities. The Benghazi Jamahiriyah military barracks served as an alternate terrorist command center and included a storage and assembly facility for MiG aircraft. The fifth target, Benghazi's Benina fighter base, housed night-capable MiG–23 Flogger E interceptors that posed a threat to the attacking force.

A 48th TFW F–111F bomber based at Lakenheath, England.

Admiral Kelso assigned the three targets in and around Tripoli to the 48th Tactical Fighter Wing, while assigning to the Sixth Fleet the two targets at Benghazi, as well as responsibilities for combat air patrol and suppression of enemy air defenses. EF–111A Ravens (also nicknamed Sparkvarks) from the 42d Electronic Combat Squadron, based at RAF Upper Heyford, would accompany the F–111Fs to help the Sixth Fleet's Marine EA–6B Prowlers jam enemy radar systems. The plan called for striking all targets simultaneously and limited each aircraft to a single pass at its target to lessen the time that Libyan air defenses could react to the attack. Admiral Kelso imposed strict rules of engagement to avoid or reduce the possibility of civilian casualties in the congested urban area of Tripoli, while inflicting as much damage as possible on the targets. He insisted that each airplane should have positive identification of its assigned target on multiple systems and abort its attack if weapon-guidance or navigation systems were not fully functional.

At nearly the last moment, the strike force increased from six to eighteen F–111s, forcing the 48th to readjust the timing and flow of aircraft against each target, as well as identifying specific aiming points for the additional aircraft. Adding aircraft also necessitated gathering more Strategic Air Command tankers from far-flung locations. The strike force could not hit Libya and then return to its English base without aerial refueling en route. The European Tanker Task Force, a collection of KC–135s and KC–10s and aircrews on temporary duty from stateside wings, operated through the 306th Strategic Wing and 11th Strategic Group, located at RAF Mildenhall and Fairford, respectively, to refuel U.S. forces. In the two days before the Monday night strike, additional tankers streamed into the English bases, many of the aircrews not knowing their mission until they arrived. Col. Lynn T. Berringer, USAF, Commander, 306th Strategic Wing, and his staff planned the crucial refueling. Using the "mother-tanker" concept, each F–111 aircraft would remain with the same tanker during the long flight to Libya and rejoin that tanker following the attack.

By Monday, April 14th, all USAF forces were gathered and ready. At 5:13 P.M. Greenwich Mean Time, the tankers began launching in radio silence, with the F–111Fs and EF–111s beginning twenty-three minutes later, most of the force joining together over southern England. The aircraft flew and refueled entirely in radio silence to preserve tactical surprise. The nighttime silent air refueling was difficult for the strike force because few of the fighter crews had experience receiving fuel from the KC–10 tankers, which were relatively new in the European Theater. The F–111s flew with their electronic identification equipment turned off, hoping that inquisitive radar operators would see only a group of tankers on their screens. After the first refueling, six F–111 and one EF–111A airborne spares returned to their bases, leaving eighteen Aardvarks and five Ravens whose targeting, weapons delivery, and terrain-following radar were all fully functional at that point. From England, the aerial armada proceeded south, in flight cells, past Portugal and turned east through the Strait of Gibraltar into the Mediterranean Sea toward Libya, aiming for a simultaneous strike at 2:00 A.M. Libyan time. Those aboard the lead airborne command KC–10 included Colonel Westbrook, Colonel Berringer, and Maj. Gen. David W. Forgan, USAF, Headquarters USAFE Deputy Chief of Staff for Operations, who was the airborne mission commander for Operation ELDORADO CANYON.

A 48th TFW F–111F takes on fuel from a KC–135 Stratotanker.

At about the same time that the USAF task force took off from bases in England, the Navy's *Coral Sea* and *America* battle groups began a high-speed dash toward Libya in electronic silence, eluding Soviet surveillance. At 12:45 A.M., the Navy began launching its strike, surface-to-air missile (SAM) suppression, and support aircraft, also in electronic silence. After the F–111s finished their last refueling, they left their mother tankers in three attack groups: nine for Bab al-Aziziyah barracks; six for the Tripoli Airport; and three for Sidi Bilal.

At ten minutes before strike time, the EF–111As and the Navy's EA–6Bs began their electronic jamming against Libyan radar and communications, reputedly one of the most advanced air defense systems in the world. As the Libyan radars sprang into activity, trying to find and identify the airplanes, the Navy's A-7s and F/A-18s began firing missiles that rode the radar beams back to the sites, destroying more than a dozen before the raid was finished. An official from the tiny island of Malta notified Libya at least one-half hour before the raid began that unidentified aircraft were heading south toward Libya. Despite the warning, when the F-111Fs reached Tripoli, they found the streetlights on in the city below, cars driving with their headlights on, floodlights illuminating principal buildings, and airport runway lights shining. Libyan defenders launched unguided SAMs and directed intense antiaircraft fire at the Aardvarks, lighting up the night sky.

The Bab al-Aziziyah target, located in the densely populated city, was the most difficult of the Tripoli targets, because it did not show up well on radar. Mistakes and equipment failures especially hampered this attack. Of the nine F-111Fs (call signs Remit, Elton, and Karma) assigned to strike this target, one had flown the wrong direction after the final refueling, one aborted while still over the water, three aborted their attacks in the target area due to equipment malfunctions, and one (Karma 52) crashed into the ocean before reaching the target. Only three F-111s remained to drop their one-ton laser-guided bombs. Two of these attacks caused considerable damage to the compound, but the third F-111 crew misidentified its "offset aim point" on the radar screen, dropping the GBU-10s near the French embassy, one and one-half miles northeast of the intended target.

Three F-111s (call sign Jewel), also armed with laser-guided bombs, struck the Sidi Bilal naval commando training complex about fifteen miles west of Tripoli. All three dropped their bombs, despite the last being hampered by smoke from the preceding Paveways. The attacks severely damaged several buildings and destroyed a number of small training vessels at the docks.

The objective of the last six Aardvarks (call signs Puffy and Lujac) was the military side of the Tripoli Airport, with the specific objective of hitting the Soviet-made IL-76 jets used to transport terrorists and their weapons. Unlike the other two groups, which approached their targets from the sea, this group entered Libyan territory east of Tripoli and circled to attack the airport from the south, thus avoiding the main body of Libyan air defenses. One F-111 lost its terrain-following radar and aborted before reaching the target. The remaining 5 dropped their 500-pound Snakeye retarded-delivery bombs, which were equipped with parachutes to slow their descent so that the aircraft would not suffer damage from their own ordnance. Poststrike reconnaissance showed that the Snakeyes damaged several buildings, destroyed or severely damaged five IL–76s parked on the flight line, and touched off a number of fires and explosions.

Meanwhile, on the eastern side of the Gulf of Sidra, six A–6E Intruders from the carrier *America* struck the Benghazi Jamahiriyah military barracks, heavily damaging them and a nearby MiG–23 assembly facility. Another six A–6Es from the *Coral Sea* cratered the runway at Benghazi's Benina military airfield and destroyed or damaged numerous aircraft on the parking apron, including the MiGs that might have risen in opposition to the American forces.

By 2:13 A.M., all strike aircraft, except Karma 52, had safely crossed the Libyan coast, the A–6s heading toward the carriers and the F–111s toward the tankers waiting for them over the Mediterranean. Libyan antiaircraft guns and missile batteries continued to fire blindly into the sky for hours after the American aircraft had departed. Rattled Libyan gunners lit the skies for several nights following as well. All Navy aircraft had recovered on their carriers by 2:53 A.M., while the Air Force F–111s and EF–111s tried to locate their assigned tankers near Sicily, a task made more difficult because the F–111s were low on fuel. After the F–111s refueled, the Air Force armada remained in the area for an hour, hoping that the missing airplane would join up. The Navy continued the search for another twenty-four hours but found no trace of the plane or its crew. The survivors, as they made the long journey back to their English bases, mourned their two comrades, the pilot, Capt. Fernando Ribas-Dominicci, and the weapons system officer, Capt. Paul Lorence.

Politically, the raid against the terrorist state was extremely popular in the United States and almost universally condemned or "regretted" by our European allies, who feared that the raid would spawn more violence. The operation spurred Western European governments to increase their defenses against terrorism, and their intelligence agencies began to share information. Moderate Arab governments did not fall, nor did they rally behind Qadhafi; in fact, some (especially those who had suffered Qadhafi's interference) were quietly pleased. If the Reagan administration hoped the raid would create the internal conditions for Qadhafi's opponents to topple his reign, it was disappointed. However, Qadhafi's arrogance was shaken, and he retreated into the desert for many months afterwards.

The Air Force was saddened by the loss of the one F–111F crew, but the loss of one out of over a hundred aircraft used in the raid statistically was not a high toll. The high abort rate was disappointing, but made understandable by the severe rules of engagement under which the F–111Fs operated, coupled with the extreme length of the mission and the known fragility of some of the critical F–111 subsystems. Of the eleven crews that dropped their bombs, only one made a critical error that caused significant collateral damage. The U.S. government expressed regret for the loss of innocent lives but pointed out that unguided Libyan missiles and antiaircraft shells falling back to earth had caused much of the damage. Reconnaissance flights after the raid showed that all the targets had been severely damaged. Despite the disappointments, the Air Force could be proud that it successfully bombed three targets seen beforehand only in photographs, after a flight of over six hours, and in the face of strong enemy opposition.

Persian Gulf Crisis: Operation EARNEST WILL

William J. Allen

DATES: July 24, 1987–November 17, 1988

LOCATIONS: Saudi Arabia, Persian Gulf, Strait of Hormuz, Gulf of Oman

OVERSEAS BASES: Riyadh, Dhahran, Saudi Arabia; Diego Garcia

AIR FORCE ORGANIZATIONS:

NUMBERED AIR FORCES:	WINGS: (con't.)
Third	374th Tactical Airlift
Ninth Air Force/USCENTAF (Forward)	436th Military Airlift
Twenty-First	433d Military Airlift
Twenty-Second	463d Tactical Airlift
	552d Airborne Warning and Control
WINGS:	
9th Strategic	**GROUP:**
60th Military Airlift	11th Strategic
62d Military Airlift	
63d Military Airlift	**DETACHMENT:**
68th Air Refueling	Detachment 4, 4448th Mobility Support Squadron/European Liaison Force-One (ELF-ONE)
306th Strategic	

AIR FORCE AIRCRAFT: KC–10, KC–135, E–3, C–5, C–141

Operations

Until the late 1970s, American involvement in the Middle East hinged upon foreign policy based on two primary objectives: contain Soviet expansion and support Israel's freedom and territorial integrity. The Iran-Iraq War that started in 1980 threatened the peace and security of the region for nearly a decade and required new U.S. foreign policy objectives. President James E. (Jimmy) Carter set forth three principles as foreign policy for the Persian Gulf. These were to maintain the

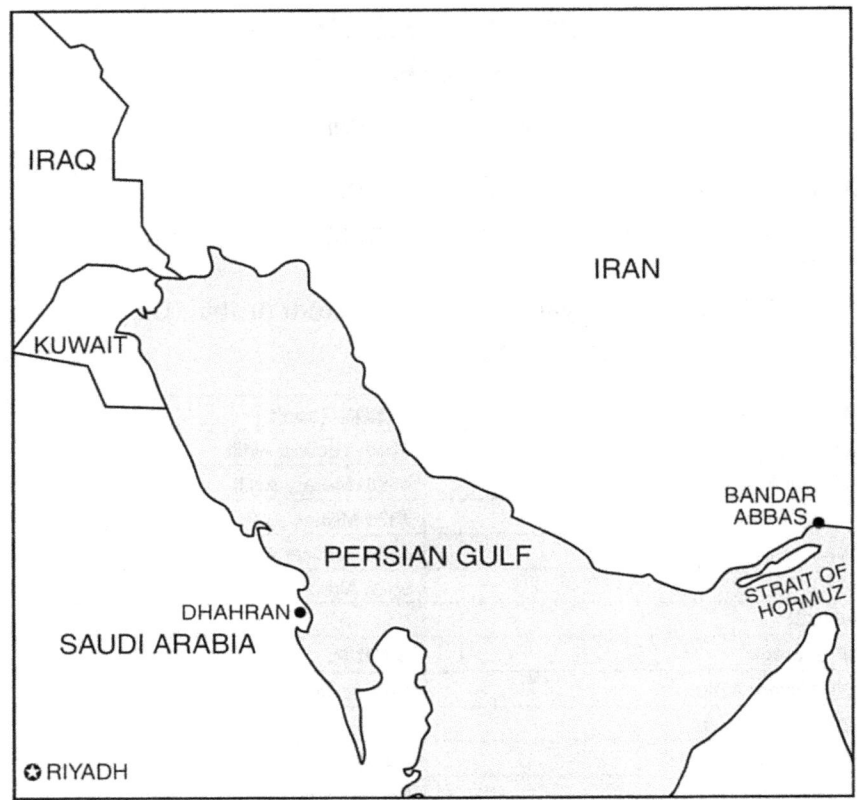

Persian Gulf Region during Operation EARNEST WILL

free flow of oil, deny the Soviets an opportunity to gain control of the region, and support the independence and stability of the Gulf States. U.S. Presidents Ronald W. Reagan and George H. W. Bush continued these objectives during their administrations.

By 1986, with the Iran-Iraq War still grinding on, the situation began to seriously threaten U.S. foreign interests in the region. The expanding war especially threatened U.S. objectives in the waters of the Persian Gulf, where the majority of the world's oil passed. Here, Iran, and to a lesser degree Iraq, increased the number of attacks on neutral shipping in the gulf. For example, in 1985 both countries attacked oil tankers in the gulf a total of fifty-three times. The next year, over 106 attacks on shipping occurred. During the same period, the Soviet Union increased its presence in the gulf diplomatically and conducted relatively benign minesweeping operations. The Kuwaiti government requested that the United States reflag eleven of their tankers under U.S. registry for protection, because they were increasingly the targets of Iranian attacks. Consequently, President Reagan ordered U.S. Central Command (USCENTCOM) to begin escorting American ships through the gulf—Operation EARNEST WILL.

Although a relatively small deployment of Air Force manpower and equipment, Operation EARNEST WILL, significantly, was the first joint contingency conducted under the guidelines of the 1986 Goldwater-Nichols Department of Defense Reorganization Act. Intended to integrate elements of all four services under one operational commander, the act recognized that none of the services could win a war on its own, but, through joint action, an enemy could be defeated. The new law gave Caspar W. Weinberger, U.S. Secretary of Defense, new authority to consolidate forces from all four services into a single operational entity under the commander of a unified command.

Prior to Operation EARNEST WILL, each service had its separate, but coordinating, operational chain of command in the gulf. For naval forces, the operational chain of command ran from Commander Middle East Forces to Commander Naval Forces, Central Command, to Commander in Chief, Central Command, to the Secretary of Defense. The operational control of the Middle East Forces commander only included the Persian Gulf waters to the Strait of Hormuz. The area south into the Arabian Sea fell under the operational control of the Commander, Pacific Fleet. The carrier group commander, steaming in the waters in or near the gulf, had an operational chain of command that ran from the Fleet Commander to the Commander of the Pacific Fleet to Commander in Chief, Pacific Command, to the Secretary of Defense.

Operational control of USAF aircraft was also a mixed affair. As early as 1980, the U.S. Air Force maintained a small presence in Saudi Arabia with the European Liaison Force-One (ELF-ONE) at Riyadh Royal Saudi Air Force (RSAF) Base. The detachment primarily provided air defense radar surveillance of the Persian Gulf for the Kingdom of Saudi Arabia. Central Command Air Forces (CENTAF) at Shaw Air Force Base (AFB), South Carolina, maintained operational control of ELF-ONE, which served as the linchpin of an air defense network that included RSAF and USAF forces.

Strategic Air Command (SAC) provided KC–135 and KC–10 tankers while Tactical Air Command (TAC) provided E–3 Airborne Warning and Control System (AWACS) for ELF-ONE, and both increased their presence during Operation EARNEST WILL. The 11th Strategic Group in England provided the deployed tankers while TAC's 552d Airborne Warning and Control Wing at Tinker AFB, Oklahoma, augmented command and control. Relying on the sophisticated sensors of the E–3A Sentry and other communications systems, deployed personnel from the wing passed air defense information to the Saudi air defense network. The RSAF employed its own F–15 and F–5 interceptors and surface-to-air missiles to defend the kingdom. By 1987, the U.S. commitment to Operation EARNEST WILL broadened ELF-ONE's mission.

As the Air Force agent to USCENTCOM, Headquarters Ninth Air Force had a dual role as a TAC numbered air force and CENTAF, which planned and directed aerial operations for the Southwest Asia theater. CENTAF deployed a headquarters contingent to Saudi Arabia to conduct land-based aerial operations for Operation EARNEST WILL. Known as CENTAF Forward, command and control personnel, planners, intelligence specialists, and other support personnel needed to provide twenty-four-hour operations arrived in June 1987. The ELF-ONE commander and staff provided CENTAF Forward in-country logistical support and liaison with their Saudi Arabian hosts.

Unlike typical Air Force contingency operations with massive airlift and movement of units to theaters, Operation EARNEST WILL did not see any additional airlift requirements beyond the weekly resupply flight levied upon Military Airlift Command (MAC). For the most part, the AWACS and tanker units at ELF-ONE deployed with their own people and equipment.

With operational control arrangements requiring massive coordination, the commander of Middle East Forces could only request naval air support through his carrier group commander, while his land-based air forces operated through

CENTAF. As a result of these command arrangements, forces were controlled piecemeal by CENTCOM, Pacific Command (USPACOM), and U.S. European Command. Secretary Weinberger was the first official in the chain of command with authority over all forces inside and outside the gulf.

On July 24, 1987, approximately twenty miles west of Farsi Island, the first of two reflagged Kuwaiti tankers, *Bridgeton*, hit a World War I vintage contact mine. Immediately at risk were the second tanker and a host of U.S. warships that included four frigates, three cruisers, and a destroyer. Overhead, USAF E-3 and KC-10 and USN A-6, E-2, and F/A-18 aircraft protected the vulnerable convoy from Iranian Silkworm missiles or other air attacks.

This event highlighted inadequate planning and poor use of intelligence information, leading Secretary Weinberger to change command arrangements in the gulf as provided by the Goldwater-Nichols Act. After consulting with the Joint Chiefs of Staff, Weinberger passed all operational control of forces supporting operations in the Persian Gulf to USCENTCOM and authorized the activation of Joint Task Force-Middle East, a joint staff to plan for the continued employment of forces in the gulf. A short, flexible chain of command that ran directly from the Middle East Forces to USCENTCOM, the Secretary of Defense, and the President permitted rapid decision making and allowed the theater commander to establish command arrangements based on his estimate of what the situation needed. The benefits gained with the new command arrangement would pay off handsomely during the course of the operation.

Only after *Bridgeton* hit the mine in the gulf was MAC called upon to fly special assignment airlift missions. The Twenty-Second Air Force managed these, delivering USN minesweeping specialists and equipment to the theater. The 10 missions flown by C-5 and C-141 aircraft carried approximately 380 passengers and 453 tons of equipment from the United States to Diego Garcia in the Indian Ocean. From there the equipment and people boarded USN vessels bound for the Persian Gulf. MAC also supplied additional Airlift Control Elements and Mission Support Teams at Clark Air Base, Philippines, and Diego Garcia to assist in this deployment.

During EARNEST WILL, AWACS crews flew the same routine mission profile as they did during normal ELF-ONE operations. The mission typically began with a premission briefing and aircraft checkout procedures lasting some forty-five minutes. Next came the takeoff and northeasterly flight of about twenty-five minutes to the prearranged orbit. After the E–3 climbed to at least 18,000 feet, the minimum altitude necessary for the outside air to cool the equipment, the radar was turned on. With radar and communication checks complete, the aircraft and crew were fully operational in about forty-five minutes after takeoff.

The E–3 could now relieve the AWACS aircraft already on station. It would fly a racetrack-surveillance pattern at about 31,000 feet for 6 hours, after which, the crew would fly to either a KC–135 or KC–10 tanker orbiting nearby for refueling. During refueling, the crew would turn off the aircraft's radar but maintain constant communications with controllers at Riyadh. An aerial refueling typically lasted fifteen to thirty minutes. With refueling complete, the AWACS needed approximately ten minutes to restore the radar to fully operational status. Returning to the racetrack orbit, the crew would normally fly for another six hours until relieved. With the exception of takeoffs, refuelings, and landings, the typical mission for AWACS flight crews was long and boring. However, during periods of heavy activity in the gulf, the flights could become extremely taxing for the mission crew members who manned the radar consoles, communication gear, and computers in the rear of the aircraft.

Flying the orbit was arduous duty for the five aircrews from the 552d Airborne Warning and Control Wing on temporary duty. Each crew remained in Saudi Arabia for approximately three weeks, flying a fourteen-hour mission every day and a half. Normally, crew members could expect to return to Saudi Arabia once more during their squadron's ninety-day rotation. That schedule was primarily driven by TAC's flying-hour restrictions limiting aircrews to 125 flying hours every 30 days and no more than 330 hours every 90 days. Each of the wing's three squadrons (963d, 964th, and 965th) spent two rotations in Saudi Arabia during Operation EARNEST WILL.

OPERATION EARNEST WILL

E-3 AWACs aircraft provided airborne surveillance and command, control, and communications functions during Operation EARNEST WILL.

The wing's maintenance specialists faced a schedule that was even more grueling than the rotation imposed on the aircrews. Some sixty to sixty-five people deployed with their respective squadrons for thirty days. Normally working twelve-hour shifts, most received one or two days off after two weeks. Working conditions in the ramp area were extremely challenging with temperatures reaching as high as 140 degrees Fahrenheit in the summer. With the help of contractors from Boeing, they provided a full range of flight-line maintenance services, including radar work, phased maintenance, and some engine repairs.

Over the course of Operation EARNEST WILL, SAC KC-135 and KC-10 aircraft flew more than 200 sorties, refueling over 900 aircraft. They also supported other operations in the gulf. For example, during Operation PRAYING MANTIS, a retaliation raid against Iranian oil platforms, April 18-24, 1988, the tankers delivered more than 2 million pounds of fuel to over 230 aircraft. The usual deployment of tankers at ELF-ONE included four KC-135 and two KC-10 aircraft and approximately fifty people.

At the height of operations, SAC deployed four KC-10 and four KC-135 aircraft with an additional thirty-seven members to maintain and fly them. An additional force of tankers deployed for a short while, July–October 1987, to Diego Garcia to support forces operating from the Arabian Sea.

Temporary duty periods for the SAC contingent varied. Each tanker detachment commander, deploying from RAF Fairford in the United Kingdom, spent about four weeks in the theater. Aircrews and crew chiefs accompanied their own aircraft and also spent four weeks. However, additional maintenance and support technicians drawn from throughout SAC generally spent only two or three weeks in the Persian Gulf area.

While providing AWACS and tanker support for Operation EARNEST WILL missions, USAF members also participated in retaliatory combat operations. For example, on September 21, 1987, the Iranian ship *Iran Ajr* was captured in the act of laying mines in international waters. USN P-3 and USAF E-3 aircraft tracked the ship, which had been observed loaded with mines in port as it left Bandar Abbas, Iran, on September 18. During the night of September 21, two USA helicopters of

KC-135 refueling an F-16. The KC-135 is typical of the tankers used during Operation EARNEST WILL.

OPERATION EARNEST WILL

Task Force 160, U.S. Special Operations Command, observed the ship's crew laying six mines in the water. The Commander, Middle East Forces, decided to fire on the ship. After two rocket and machine-gun attacks, the Iranians stopped and abandoned ship. Navy SEALs boarded the ship and found more mines on deck. The captured ship was sunk, and its crew returned to Iran. The international press reported this incident, and the United States received considerable international support for the operation. The incident was not a result of chance, but a rather carefully timed and executed trap by Adm. William J. Crowe Jr., USN, Chairman, Joint Chiefs of Staff. He personally briefed helicopter crews in the gulf one week prior to the incident and provided them with clear rules of engagement and freedom to act.

Another example of American retaliation against continued Iranian mining came after the April 14, 1988 mine strike by USS *Samuel B. Roberts*. President Reagan approved a planned retaliation against three Iranian gas-oil-separating platforms and the Iranian frigate *Salaban* by USN Surface-Action Groups. These groups attacked and neutralized two of three platforms and damaged *Salaban*, which had long terrorized shipping in the gulf.

On April 19, during a day-long operation, Air Force E-3 AWACS assisted with the naval and air engagements against the Iranians. They directed USN A-6E Intruders flying combat air patrol to the Mubarek oil field where Iranian patrol boats were attacking the SS *Willi Tide*, a U.S. vessel. The A-6s requested permission to attack the patrol boats. The request to attack the Iranians was relayed to the White House via satellite and approved in only three minutes. The A-6s armed with Mark 20 Rockeye Cluster bombs made short work of the three patrol boats.

Later, *Sahand* attacked Surface-Action Group D, whose mission was to find and neutralize *Salaban*. After an hour-long surface action, the naval group sank *Sahand*. During the engagement, USAF AWACS found and tracked *Salaban*. After watching its sister ship receive the full force of the group's attack, *Salaban* sailed to Bandar Abbas where it hid behind larger, commercial tankers. At 6:00 P.M., *Salaban* sailed into the gulf and fired surface-to-air missiles at A-6Es flying patrol and surface-to-surface missiles at USN vessels. An A–6E responded with a 500-pound laser-guided bomb, which reportedly went straight down the smoke funnel of the ship and exploded in the engine room. The U.S. attack was called off when the ship appeared to be sinking at the stern from the bomb's effects.

Command arrangements or rules of engagements cannot prevent accidents from occurring during any contingency, such as the case of USS *Vincennes* shooting down an Iranian civilian airliner on July 3, 1988. With the cease-fire between Iran and Iraq in effect in August 1988, CENTCOM ordered reduction of forces. The last of sixty-six escort missions during Operation EARNEST WILL ended on November 17, 1988.

As an integral part of the theater commander's combat forces, the Air Force provided daily command and control of the air, aerial refueling, and planning for joint air operations through CENTAF Forward. Simultaneously, the ELF-ONE contingent continued its mission of providing air defense early warning for Saudi Arabia. The successful outcome of Operation EARNEST WILL and subsequent retaliation operations could be directly tied to the premise of the Goldwater-Nichols Act. The theater commander had under his span of control USA special operations helicopters aboard USN ships, naval air cover, and USAF command and control and refueling aircraft. He also enjoyed a short, direct chain of command that ensured the orders issued and planning undertaken were not diluted by any competing service interest. In short, he was truly "in command."

Intervention in Panama: Operation JUST CAUSE

William J. Allen

DATES: December 17, 1989–February 14, 1990

LOCATION: Panama

OVERSEAS BASES USED: Howard Air Force Base (AFB), Omar Torrijos International Airport, Tocumen Airfield, Rio Hato Airfield, Panama

AIR FORCE ORGANIZATIONS:

NUMBERED AIR FORCES:	WINGS: (con't.)
Eighth	97th Bombardment
Ninth	118th Tactical Airlift
Fifteenth	136th Tactical Airlift
Twenty-First	137th Tactical Airlift
Twenty-Second	146th Tactical Airlift
	305th Air Refueling
WINGS:	314th Tactical Airlift
1st Special Operations	315th Military Airlift
2d Bombardment	317th Tactical Airlift
9th Strategic Reconnaissance	319th Bombardment
19th Air Refueling	340th Air Refueling
22d Air Refueling	349th Military Airlift
24th Composite	380th Bombardment
28th Bombardment	433d Military Airlift
33d Tactical Fighter	436th Military Airlift
37th Tactical Fighter	437th Military Airlift
42d Bombardment	438th Military Airlift
55th Strategic Reconnaissance	439th Military Airlift
60th Military Airlift	445th Military Airlift
62d Military Airlift	446th Military Airlift
63d Military Airlift	459th Military Airlift
68th Air Refueling	463d Tactical Airlift
96th Bombardment	512th Military Airlift

AIR FORCE ORGANIZATIONS: (con't.)

WINGS: (con't.)	GROUPS: (con't.)
552d Airborne Warning and Control	139th Tactical Airlift
1550th Combat Crew Training	180th Tactical Fighter
	193d Special Operations
GROUPS:	916th Air Refueling
105th Military Airlift	919th Special Operations
109th Tactical Airlift	1720th Special Tactics
125th Fighter-Interceptor	

AIR FORCE AIRCRAFT: C–130, AC–130, HC–130, MC–130, EC–130, C–5, C–141, MH–53, MH–60, F–117, F–15, F–16, EF–111, E–3, KC–135, OA–37, A–7

Operations

Since Panama's declaration of independence from Columbia in 1904, the United States has maintained a special interest in the small Central American country. The United States controlled and occupied the Panama Canal Zone, through which it built a forty-mile long canal over the next ten years to connect the Atlantic and Pacific Oceans. U.S. President Woodrow Wilson formally opened the canal on July 12, 1915, by proclamation. Political and domestic conditions in Panama remained fairly stable until 1968, when Brig. Gen. Omar Torrijos Herrera deposed President Arnulfo Arias Madrid. Through the efforts of U.S. President James (Jimmy) E. Carter and the U.S. Senate, a new Panama Canal Treaty took effect on October 1, 1979. The new treaty granted Panama complete control of the canal and withdrawal of U.S. military forces by January 1, 2000.

One of General Torrijos' sublieutenants in the Panamanian National Guard was Manuel Noriega. Noriega's rise to power began with an appointment to head the Panamanian military intelligence, where he became a key advisor and most trusted friend of Torrijos. After Torrijos's death on July 31, 1981, a struggle between leaders ensued, and in 1983, Noriega prevailed. He promoted himself to general and consolidated his air force, navy, and army into the Panamanian Defense Force (PDF). Noriega maintained ties with the U.S. intelligence community, furnishing

OPERATION JUST CAUSE

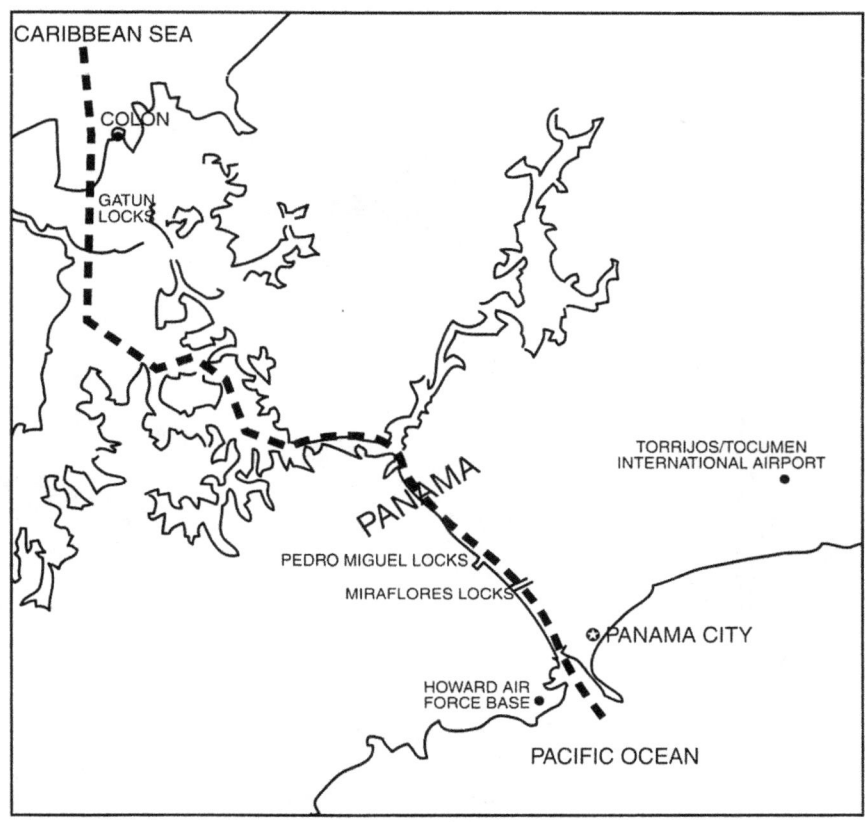

Panana Canal Zone during Operation JUST CAUSE

information on Latin American drug trafficking and money laundering, while at the same time engaged in such activities himself. By 1984, those opposing Noriega's regime openly criticized him and accused him of being a drug trafficker. By 1987, brutal repression of his people was enough for the U.S. Senate to issue a resolution calling for the Panamanians to oust him. Noriega in turn ordered his supporters to attack the U.S. Embassy, causing an end to U.S. military and economic aid. In 1988, a Miami federal grand jury indicted Noriega on drug-trafficking and money-laundering charges. However, he intensified his ruthless campaign against his own people and increased harassment of U.S. military personnel, their dependents, and other Americans.

U.S. Army personnel boarding C–5B in support of JUST CAUSE.

By 1989, U.S. President George H. W. Bush, concerned by the Panamanian government's harassment of U.S. military personnel and their dependents and the threat to U.S. national interests, decided to invade Panama. To oust the dictator, President Bush ordered the planning and execution of several contingencies setting the stage for an invasion from both within Panama and from the United States. During Operation NIMROD DANCER in May 1989, the Military Airlift Command (MAC) airlifted elements of the U.S. Army's 5th and 7th Infantry Divisions and the U.S. Marines' 2d Expeditionary Force to strengthen U.S. forces throughout Panama. By the time the operation ended, 34 C–5, 39 C–141, and 2 commercial L–1011 missions had airlifted 2,679 soldiers and Marines and over 2,950 tons of equipment into the country. Also in May, President Bush ordered U.S. forces in Panama to relocate dependents living off base to a secure military base. In most cases, on-base residents opened their homes to friends and coworkers until dependents could be airlifted back to the

United States. That airlift, Operation BLADE JEWEL, took place from May 16 to June 29, 1989. Commercial airlift, C–5s, and C–141s flew a total of 5,915 persons and 398 pets from Howard AFB to Charleston AFB, South Carolina. However, not all American citizens were evacuated from Panama during Operation BLADE JEWEL.

After Operation BLADE JEWEL, several key PDF officers attempted a coup against Noriega on October 3, 1989. They tried to take over PDF headquarters, known as the Commandancia, in Panama City. The rebels captured Noriega but, by chance, soldiers loyal to him were on a military exercise just outside the city. They returned, defeated the rebels, and freed Noriega. Shortly, the Panamanian government declared a "state of war" against the United States. The Bush administration, seemingly indifferent to an opportunity to overthrow Noriega, caused great concern to Congress and the media. But, President Bush had long anticipated the need to capture Noriega, and the recent troop buildup in Panama was part of a plan named PRAYER BOOK. This plan envisioned deployment of approximately five brigades and a corps headquarters within three weeks to Panama. However, the Joint Chiefs of Staff were concerned about the time needed to increase the U.S. military presence of about 13,000 people to nearly 26,000.

The U.S Southern Command oversaw what proved to be the largest U.S. military operation since the Vietnam War. Its commander, Lt. Gen. Maxwell R. Thurman, USA, delegated combat planning for the operation to the XVIII Airborne Corps at Fort Bragg, North Carolina. The corps headquarters, designated as Joint Task Force-South, devised the plans for Operation JUST CAUSE. Representatives from MAC, Strategic Air Command (SAC), and Tactical Air Command (TAC) worked with Joint Task Force-South and other headquarters to plan the aerial invasion and follow-on support. Meanwhile, General Thurman created the Joint Special Operations Task Force with personnel from Headquarters, Twenty-Third Air Force, who planned the special operations support for the ground forces.

By design, all four services participated as parts of several task forces. The ground forces were divided into Atlantic,

Semper Fi, Bayonet, and Pacific Task Forces. Task Force Atlantic, built around two brigades of the 7th Infantry Division, was to attack positions around the Caribbean end of the Panama Canal. Task Force Semper Fi would secure Howard AFB and the Bridge of the Americas. Assigned to attack the PDF headquarters and various installations in and around Panama City was Task Force Bayonet's 193d Infantry Brigade. Task Force Pacific's two brigades of the 82d Airborne Division would air-drop into both Torrijos International Airport and Tocumen Airfield, seizing these vital gateways for the arrival of reinforcements. Airborne Ranger brigades would lead the initial assaults on the airfields and also attack the PDF facilities at Rio Hato Airfield.

The units to invade Panama conducted numerous planning sessions and exercises that refined the assigned missions of USAF commands. MAC was responsible for the airlift of the assault forces and follow-on reinforcements. SAC was responsible for providing air refueling to USAF aircraft during the contingency. USAF special operations forces would fly special operations aircraft in support of the assault airlift and combat ground forces.

Continuing incidents between the PDF and off-duty U.S. military personnel and their dependents finally resulted in the death of a U.S. Marine and a sexual assault. President Bush's order on December 17, 1989, was simply "Let's do it." President Bush's stated objectives were to protect American citizens, support the democratically elected officials whom Noriega had ousted, keep the Panama Canal operational, and arrest Noriega to face his indictment. Operation JUST CAUSE was under way. Battle staffs and Crisis Action Teams all over the Air Force began mustering their respective forces in preparation for the pre-employment staging of airlift and air refueling forces. On December 18 and 19, MAC airlifters prepositioned assault personnel and equipment at several staging bases in the southeastern United States and at Howard AFB in Panama itself.

MAC originally planned to support the Army's air-drop and air-land missions with sixty-three C–141, twenty-one C–130, and two C–5 aircraft staging from the United States. During normal peacetime duty, these numbers would tax MAC's ability to provide enough airplanes and crews. Fortunately,

Peacekeepers patrolling the perimeter of Howard AFB, Panama.

the order for the invasion came during the Christmas season, when most aircrews and aircraft were at home. A disruption in plans occurred because the XVII Airborne Corps waited until the morning of the 19th to recall their troops. This late call reduced the time to load the 82d Airborne Division and caused many aircraft to descend on Pope AFB almost simultaneously, instead of in an orderly manner. Pope aircraft marshals found parking spaces for twelve more C-141s than the number planners believed the field could handle. In all, forty-five C-141s crowded Pope's ramps and taxiways. Twenty aircraft loaded 2,176 assault troops, and the others carried the division's equipment. As planned, the equipment-loaded C-141s flew to Charleston AFB, South Carolina, where they waited for the start of the airlift to Panama.

Adding to overcrowded conditions at Pope, the next disruption hit cold and hard for the loaders, crews, and troopers. Early on the 18th, weather forecasters warned that a severe ice storm would hit the base that afternoon. Considering all the planning that had gone into the operation, unforeseen ice could have easily frozen the invasion in place. The storm arrived on schedule with ice forming on the aircraft, causing serious delays. The normal climate being mild, Pope lacked equipment to deice so many aircraft. Airlift units from as far away as Dyess AFB, Texas, flew in deicing equipment and fluid. The extra deicing trucks and thousands of gallons of fluid arrived at Pope in time to limit further delays in launch times, but the postponements had a rippling effect for planned airflow and air refueling times.

As ground crews deiced the aircraft, loaders and paratroopers waited in miserable conditions, aerial-port technicians quickened the pace of loading the big transports to get the aircraft launched on time. But they needed help. Military retirees and Reservists from the local area heard that "something big" was up at Pope and Fort Bragg. Many volunteered to help in any way they could; some immediately went to work loading aircraft. The combined efforts of those in and out of uniform enabled the equipment-carrying C-141s to leave Pope for Charleston by 3:30 P.M. on the 19th. Most of the transports took off close to their scheduled departure times despite compressed loading times and hazardous weather.

While MAC airlifters staged airborne forces and equipment, SAC positioned KC-135 and KC-10 tanker crews at Seymour Johnson AFB, North Carolina, and Barksdale AFB, Louisiana. On the 19th, SAC tankers flew to their designated refueling tracks to refuel the airlift to Panama. The tankers also refueled TAC F-15s from Eglin flying a fighter cap near Cuba, E-3A AWACS aircraft providing command and control, and EF-111 radar-jamming aircraft protecting the airlift force. The delays due to deicing caused some tankers to remain in their refueling tracks near Panama too long. To remedy the situation, some KC-135s transferred their fuel to the larger KC-10s, which could stay longer to refuel aircraft. Overall, tankers from 23 squadrons pumped over 12 million pounds of fuel from December 20, 1989 to January 3, 1990 to aircraft supporting Operation JUST CAUSE.

The planned route of the air bridge to Panama required aircraft to fly through the "gap" between Mexico's Yucatan Peninsula and the western tip of Cuba. To avoid detection by Cuban radar, airlifters descended to the lowest possible safe altitudes. The C–141s dropped to 5,000 and the C–130s to 3,000 feet, based on factors such as the distance from Cuban radar and the curvature of the earth. To make matters more difficult, the crews flew to Panama under radio silence.

Four C–130s of the 317th Tactical Airlift Wing with equipment and troops of the 75th Ranger Regiment began the airlift from Hunter Army Airfield (AAF) at Savannah, Georgia, at 5:56 P.M. on December 19. Seven hours later, the Rangers made the first jumps at Torrijos/Tocumen. The aircraft that carried them were specially-equipped Special Operations Low-Level II C–130s. At 6:02 P.M., thirteen C–130s departed Lawson AAF at Fort Stewart, Georgia, with assault troops for Rio Hato, followed by C–130s carrying heavy equipment and two additional special operations Hercules aircraft.

Meanwhile, two C–5s loaded with forward area refueling equipment and an airlift control element left Hunter bound for Torrijos/Tocumen. Later, seven C–141s with troops of the 75th Rangers and five others carrying their equipment took off. At 10:30 P.M., thirty-one C–141s carrying heavy equipment and containers launched from Charleston AFB bound for the same destination. The C–141 aircraft carrying the 82d Airborne Division did not fly the planned single-wave, twenty-ship formation due to deicing delays. Instead, they departed Pope between 9:30 P.M. on December 19 and just after midnight in four waves.

Special tactics teams were the first USAF people on the ground at the Panamanian airfields prior to the designated "H-hour." They installed navigational beacons that guided the troop-laden aircraft to the drop zones. From the troop carriers, additional special tactics teams parachuted to the landing zones. Once on the ground, combat controllers hurriedly cleared the runways of parachutes, debris, and Panamanian-placed obstructions in preparation for the following air-land operations. Pararescuemen set up casualty collection points for triage and combat first aid for the wounded. The special tactics teams also provided air traffic control, command and control communications, assistance to gunship operations, refueling and rearming point management, air evacuation support, and emergency medical treatment.

Manuel Noriega in custody of DEA agents.

At three minutes past midnight on December 20, the first twelve C–141s dropped paratroopers and their equipment at Torrijos/Tocumen. The aircrews completed the drop using night-vision goggles to locate the darkened, blacked-out airfields. This marked the Air Force's first combat use of this highly valuable equipment. A minute later at Rio Hato, thirteen C–130s made their drop just after the combat debut of the F–117 Nighthawk, which dropped ordnance near the PDF barracks. Of the initial 111 aircraft involved in the assault, 84 flying at 500 feet dropped close to 5,000 troops in the largest nighttime airborne operation since World War II.

Providing a critical protective cover for assault troops, MAC's special operations aircraft suppressed ground threats, such as antiaircraft positions, and covered helicopters inserting Army Rangers. AC–130s of the 1st Special Operations Wing (SOW), from Hurlburt Field, Florida, and of the 919th Special Operations Group from Duke Field, Florida, provided close air and special sensor support. Other USAF special operations aircraft, MC–130Es, MH–53Js, HC–130Ps, and MH–60s, flew mostly at night in coordinated operations with Army and Navy Special Forces. In Panama, Air Force members at Howard AFB supported prepositioned U.S. forces. The Marines of Task Force Semper Fi launched their attack from Howard AFB. Under difficult "blacked-out" conditions on an aircraft-saturated airfield, Howard's people supported Army helicopter and AC–130 gunship operations. The assault C–130s also landed there to refuel, and several had to receive repairs for battle damage, before returning to the United States. Howard AFB also supported many other operations, including the follow-on airlift of reinforcements and the evacuation of the wounded to military hospitals in the United States.

Operation JUST CAUSE saw the U.S. Air Force undertake its largest and most complex air operation since the war in Southeast Asia. Over 250 aircraft took part in the invasion. Air Force special operations forces supported Army ground forces that eliminated organized PDF resistance by Christmas day. On January 3, 1990, Manuel Noriega surrendered to U.S. forces. A 1st SOW MC–130 flew him to Miami, Florida, for arraignment. By the end of hostilities, the PDF suffered casualties of over 300 killed, 124 wounded, and over 5,800 captured.

The experience gained by planners, crews, and ground personnel in building the air bridge to Panama during Operation JUST CAUSE proved invaluable. From December 20, 1989 to February 14, 1990, the Air Force flew almost 40,000 passengers and delivered over 20,650 tons of cargo. Included in the airlift were over 1.2 million pounds of food for displaced Panamanians. Air Force transports evacuated over 320 U.S. military casualties to hospitals in the United States and honorably returned 23 soldiers who died during the operation.

JUST CAUSE was the culmination of several operations during 1989 to fulfill President Bush's policy toward Panama. The more prominent achievements by U.S. military forces during this operation included the successful airborne invasion of Panama and capture of Panamanian dictator Manuel Noriega. The prepositioning of U.S. forces within the country, evacuation of military dependents, and the airborne invasion all contributed to a successful completion of Operation JUST CAUSE. However, as successful as the operation was, not everything went according to plan. For example, the North

Carolina ice storm delayed aircraft launches, causing tanker crews to adjust their refueling on-station time and some airlift crews to change flight plans while in-flight to arrive over the drop zone on time.

Despite these and other problems, Operation JUST CAUSE resulted in the return of democracy to Panama and secured the Panama Canal. In a mere eight months to come, some of these same airmen, soldiers, sailors, and marines would build and travel through another, larger air bridge during Operation DESERT SHIELD.

Crisis in Iraq: Operation PROVIDE COMFORT

Daniel L. Haulman

DATES: April 5, 1991–December 31, 1996

LOCATIONS: Southeastern Turkey and Northern Iraq

OVERSEAS BASES USED: Incirlik Air Base (AB), Adana, Antalya, Diyarbakir, Silopi, Batman, Turkey; Sirsenk, Iraq; Rhein-Main AB, Germany

AIR FORCE ORGANIZATIONS:

DIVISION:	WINGS: (con't.)	WINGS: (con't.)
322d Airlift	81st Tactical Fighter (later, 81st Fighter)	419th Fighter
	86th Tactical Fighter (later, 86th Wing, 86th Fighter)	435th Tactical Airlift
WINGS:	92d Air Refueling	436th Military Airlift
1st Fighter	100th Air Refueling	437th Military Airlift
3d Wing	131st Fighter	463d Tactical Airlift
16th Special Operations	132d Fighter	552d Airborne Warning and Control (later, 552d Air Control)
19th Air Refueling	138th Fighter	Composite Wing (Provisional), 7440th
20th Tactical Fighter (later, 20th Fighter)	140th Fighter	
22d Air Refueling	154th Composite	**GROUPS:**
27th Fighter	174th Fighter	1st Rescue
36th Tactical Fighter (later, 36th Fighter)	180th Fighter	10th Special Forces
39th Special Operations	192d Fighter	32d Fighter
39th Wing	302d Tactical Airlift	39th Tactical (later, 39th Operations)
48th Fighter	306th Strategic	43d Air Refueling
52d Tactical Fighter (later, 52d Fighter)	314th Tactical Airlift (later, 314th Airlift)	124th Fighter
57th Wing	317th Tactical Airlift	143d Tactical Airlift
60th Military Airlift	349th Military Airlift	154th Composite
66th Electronic Combat	366th Wing	159th Fighter

AIR FORCE ORGANIZATIONS: (con't.)

GROUPS: (con't.)	SQUADRONS:	SQUADRONS: (con't.)
185th Fighter	21st Special Operations	92d Air Refueling
187th Fighter	32d Fighter	93d Air Refueling
192d Fighter	43d Electronic Combat	114th Fighter
313th Tactical Airlilft	58th Military Airlift (later, 58th Airlift)	123d Tactical Reconnaissance
352d Special Operations	67th Special Operations	911th Air Refueling
944th Fighter	91st Air Refueling	

AIR FORCE AIRCRAFT: A–10, C–5, C–12, C–21, C–130, C–141, E–3, EC–130, EF–111, F–4, F–15, F–16, F–111, HC–130, KC–10, KC–135, MH–53, RC–135, RF–4

Operations

When an American-led international coalition bombed Iraq and drove the forces of Saddam Hussein from Kuwait in 1991, it weakened his power. Rebellious Kurds in northern Iraq, whom Hussein had brutally suppressed with chemical weapons three years earlier, launched a new uprising in early March. When Iraqi government troops defeated the rebellion a month later, threatening to repeat the massacres of the past, more than a million Kurds fled to Iran and Turkey. Hundreds of thousands more gathered on cold mountain slopes on the Iraqi-Turkish border. Lacking food, clean water, clothing, blankets, medical supplies and shelter, the refugees suffered enormous mortality rates.

On April 3, the United Nations Security Council authorized a humanitarian relief effort for the Iraqi Kurds. During the first week in April, the United States organized a combined task force for Operation PROVIDE COMFORT. Maj. Gen. James L. Jamerson, USAF, served as first commander. USAF C–130 cargo airplanes, which had deployed mostly from bases in Germany to Incirlik AB, Turkey, began air-dropping relief supplies directly to Kurdish refugees in the mountainous Iraqi border area on April 7. They delivered about 600 pallets of relief supplies per day, staging at Diyarbakir and Batman in southern and eastern Turkey. But airdrops alone proved to be inadequate. The refugees needed different quantities and types of cargo than those chosen for delivery, not enough cargo reached the people who needed it most, and some items actually landed on refugees, killing or injuring them. Moreover, the operation failed to address the root of the problem. The refugees could not stay where they were, and Turkey, faced with a restive Kurdish population of its own, refused to admit them in large numbers. PROVIDE COMFORT, therefore, evolved into a larger operation, with more than one phase, and the use of American ground troops.

On April 17, 1991, Lt. Gen. John M. Shalikashvili, USA, took command of the PROVIDE COMFORT Combined Task Force, and General Jamerson became commander of the air component. With United Nation's (UN) approval, Shalikashvili built temporary camps in northern Iraq and southeastern Turkey so that the refugees could come out from the mountains. He could better identify the needs of the refugees once they were in the camps. General Shalikashvili's next step was to enforce a security zone for the Kurds in northern Iraq so that they would feel safe enough to return to their homes. Once there, they would no longer need so many relief supplies. At first, such a security zone required extensive coalition ground and air forces. In a month, the Combined Task Force strength grew beyond 20,000 members. Over half of these were Americans, but the forces of twelve other countries participated in the operation.

Between mid-April and mid-July, General Shalikashvili and his task force were able to accomplish their immediate goals in the first phase of PROVIDE COMFORT. The Iraqi army withdrew from a security zone that eventually embraced the cities of Zakho, Al Amadiyah (Amadiya), Suri, and Dihok (Dahuk) and covered several thousand square miles. Shalikashvili met periodically with Iraqi military officials to avoid misunderstandings. USN sea-lift ships transported cargo to ports in Turkey for shipment by truck and helicopter to the Iraqi-Turkish border area. USAF cargo aircraft, including C–5 Galaxies and C–141 Starlifters, also moved thousands of tons of relief supplies from the United States to Turkey, flying via Germany to Incirlik, Adana, and Diyarbakir. During the first twenty days of PROVIDE COMFORT, C–5s and C–141s flew seventy-five missions from the United States and Europe to Turkey. C–5s

USAF enlisted men prepare to load a C–130 for Operation PROVIDE COMFORT.

also transported allied troops from Italy to eastern Turkey, and from there they moved overland to Zakho. The Air Force used C–130s to deliver cargo from eastern Turkey to Sirsenk Airfield in the security zone. By mid-July 1991, USAF airplanes had transported more than 7,000 tons of PROVIDE COMFORT relief supplies.

U.S. and coalition fighter aircraft provided air cover for the PROVIDE COMFORT ground forces in the security zone. The combination of air cover and ground forces, along with a promise of some degree of autonomy from Baghdad, persuaded most Kurdish refugees to return to their homes. By the end of May, only about 41,000 refugees remained in the camps. On June 7, the United Nations resolved to send forces to replace those of the American-led coalition, and by the middle of July, the PROVIDE COMFORT Combined Task Force withdrew from northern Iraq. A six-nation coalition ground force remained in southern Turkey, ready to enter Iraq again if necessary. Thus ended PROVIDE COMFORT I.

The second phase of PROVIDE COMFORT, which began in mid-July 1991, enforced the established security zone with U.S., British, French, and Turkish air power. All PROVIDE COMFORT II commanders, beginning with General Jamerson, were USAF generals. Coalition ground forces withdrew from

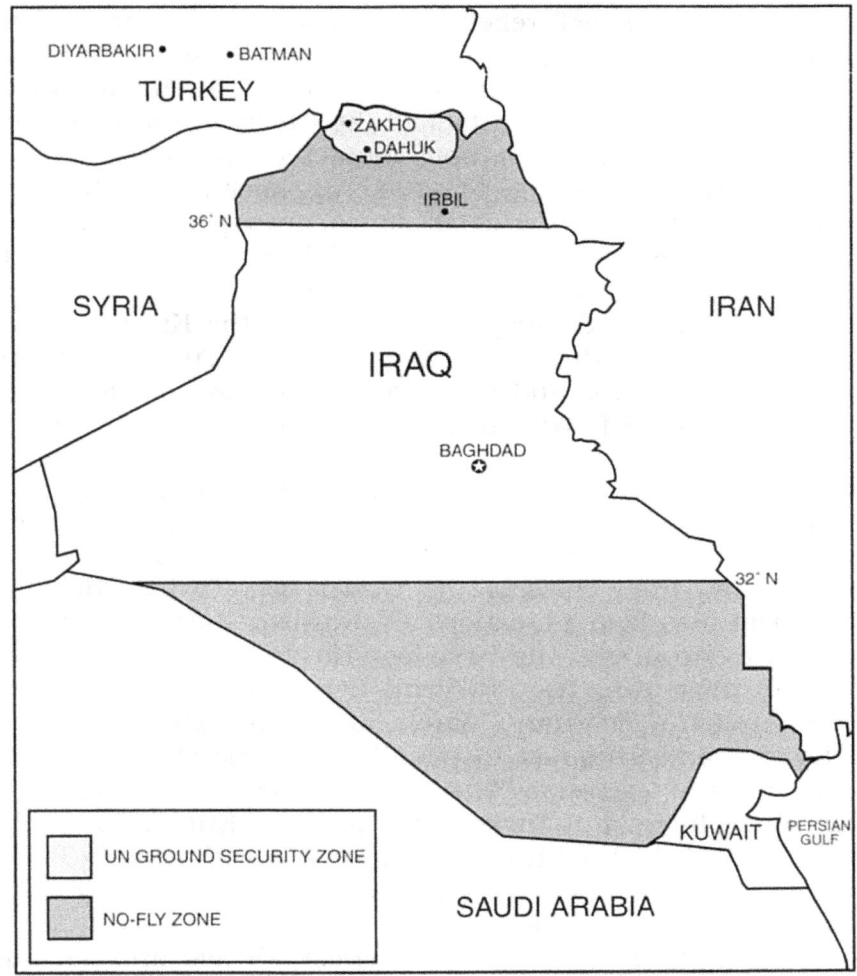

No-Fly Zones in Iraq during Operation PROVIDE COMFORT

southern Turkey at the end of September, increasing the burden on the remaining air units. By the end of the year, USAF members assigned to PROVIDE COMFORT still numbered more than a thousand, but the number of U.S. Army, Navy, and Marine Corps declined to less than 200. The coalition enforced a no-fly zone over northern Iraq, north of 36° N, from which Iraqi aircraft were forbidden. This no-fly zone covered more area than the UN security zone on the ground.

PROVIDE COMFORT relied increasingly on fighters as its primary missions evolved to enforcement of the no-fly zone, reconnaissance over the area, and readiness to retaliate if the forces of Saddam Hussein attacked the Kurds again. Humanitarian airlift, however, did not completely disappear. USAF C–5s, C–141s, C–130s, and KC–10s, supplemented with coalition aircraft and commercial airplanes, transported 119 tons of food and water and more than 4,000 bundles of clothing to the Iraqi Kurds during the winter of 1991–92.

Concerned that U.S. and UN support for the Kurds in Iraq might encourage Kurdish separatists in Turkey, Turkish military authorities demanded and received co-command of Operation PROVIDE COMFORT. With this arrangement, the Turks gained operational control over their own PROVIDE COMFORT troops. The Turkish government, which looked on the operation as a mixed blessing, allowed it to continue only by approving short-term extensions. The Turks wanted to discourage the Kurds of northern Iraq from crossing the border into Turkey, but the government also feared creation of a Kurdish state in Iraq that might have encouraged the 10 million Kurds in Turkey to create a state of their own. The PROVIDE COMFORT forces came to Turkey's relief in February, March, and April 1992, after avalanches and an earthquake inspired USAF humanitarian airlifts. In the long run, Operation PROVIDE COMFORT proved to be as much in the interest of Turkey as of the Iraqi Kurds. The coalition persuaded the Iraqi Kurds to refuse to cooperate with Turkish Kurds in separatist activities or to allow their territory to be used for cross-border raids.

In August 1992, the United States established another no-fly zone, this time in southern Iraq south of 32° N, to discourage renewed Iraqi military activity near Kuwait (Operation SOUTHERN WATCH). It complemented the PROVIDE COMFORT no-fly zone north of 36° N. Iraqi forces tested the no-fly zones in both south and north by sending fighters into them in December 1992 and January 1993. On December 27, 1992, F–16 pilot Lt. Col. Gary L. North, USAF, shot down an Iraqi MiG–25 in the southern zone. Less than a month later, on January 17, 1993, another F–16 pilot, Lt. Craig D. Stevenson, USAF, shot down an Iraqi MIG–29 in the north. Those were the only aerial victories of Operation PROVIDE COMFORT.

In January and June 1993, USN warships fired cruise missiles into Iraq to destroy a suspected nuclear facility and to punish Saddam Hussein for an attempt to assassinate former U.S. President George H. W. Bush. In January, April, June, July, and August 1993, USAF aircraft attacked Iraqi antiaircraft and radar sites in both the northern and southern no-fly zones after they fired at or locked onto coalition patrol aircraft. In 1994, Iraqi troops massed near Kuwait, prompting the United States to deploy more forces to Southwest Asia (Operation VIGILANT WARRIOR).

After 1993, Saddam Hussein did not often challenge coalition aircraft patrolling the no-fly zones, but U.S. units remained wary. On April 14, 1994, two American F–15s patrolling the northern no-fly zone accidentally shot down two USA UH–60 Black Hawk helicopters, killing twenty-six people, including fifteen Americans. Misidentifying the helicopters as hostile, the F–15 pilots failed to receive contrary information from either the helicopters or an orbiting E–3 aircraft. The "friendly fire" incident aroused negative public opinion and a demand for changes to prevent such accidents in the future.

The Iraqi Kurds did not maintain a united front against Saddam Hussein. One faction, eager to assert its power over another, invited the Iraqi army to help it take control of the city of Irbil in the American-protected no-fly zone. Iraqi tanks took the city in August 1996. Anxious to discourage Saddam Hussein from further military adventures, U.S. President William J. Clinton responded by expanding the southern no-fly zone to 33° N and clearing the additional territory of crucial air defenses by firing forty-four cruise missiles from USN ships and USAF B–52s (Operation DESERT STRIKE). During the same month, Iraqi forces fired a surface-to-air missile at a pair of F–16s patrolling the northern no-fly zone but activated the radar too briefly to score a hit or to reveal its location for an effective counterstrike.

Kurds of the defeated faction fled to the Turkish border. In Operations QUICK TRANSIT I, II, and III, the United States helped them move to safe areas in Turkey. Almost 7,000 refugees flew on to Andersen Air Force Base in Guam to be processed for eventual settlement in the United States (Operation PACIFIC HAVEN).

At the beginning of 1997, Operation NORTHERN WATCH replaced Operation PROVIDE COMFORT, which had ceased to be a predominantly humanitarian operation, to complement Operation SOUTHERN WATCH. The two security zones in northern and southern Iraq discouraged Saddam Hussein not only from acts of genocide against his people in those areas but also from invading Kuwait again.

Foremost among the lessons PROVIDE COMFORT taught was the need to avoid fratricide. The downing of the two USA helicopters generated a thorough investigation that led to changes in organization, procedures, training, and the rules of engagement. Maj. Gen. James Andrus, USAF, Commander, Third Air Force, led the initial investigation. Air Force Chief of Staff General Ronald R. Fogleman, who replaced General Merrill A. McPeak in October 1994, personally reviewed the cases of those involved to prevent such a situation from happening again.

The operation also revealed the limitations of airdrops alone. At first, U.S. transports dropped some food and clothing the Kurds refused to eat or wear, because planners did not realize what cargo was appropriate for the culture. The Air Force also had to reduce chances that air-dropped cargo would land on the very people it was designed to assist. More accurate intelligence assessments when the operation began could have precluded the extensive operational modifications that occurred later.

Operation PROVIDE COMFORT exposed some host-country problems. Distrustful of the Kurds in their own country, the Turks were reluctant to support an operation to help Kurds in Iraq. The Turkish government gave approval to the operation for only up to six months at a time and limited the number of coalition combat aircraft in the operation to forty-eight at a time. Turkey also waged a war against its own Kurds during PROVIDE COMFORT, which complicated the operation when Kurdish separatists sometimes mistook American aircraft for those of the Turks.

Friction among rival Kurdish factions in northern Iraq threatened PROVIDE COMFORT by giving Saddam Hussein an excuse to take the Kurdish city of Irbil in the no-fly zone. In future contingencies, the United States and its coalition partners should be more familiar with the divisions among the

A 52d Fighter Wing F–16 at Incirlik AB, Turkey, for Operation PROVIDE COMFORT duty.

people they are trying to assist, especially if such divisions could undermine the operation.

The need for alternative bases was another lesson to emerge from the PROVIDE COMFORT experience. Although fighters continued to operate from Incirlik throughout the operation, runway construction there forced larger aircraft such as E–3s, tankers, and strategic transports to use bases at Antalya, Adana, and elsewhere.

Operation PROVIDE COMFORT challenged the readiness of the U.S. Air Forces in Europe (USAFE). While USAFE personnel and aircraft decreased because of the post-Cold War reduction of forces, they were committed simultaneously in Turkey, Bosnia, and central Africa. The PROVIDE COMFORT patrols ate up flying hours that USAFE would have preferred to use for training. Command leaders, fearing that they were overextended, persuaded the U.S. Air Force to rotate more people and aircraft from other commands to serve in PROVIDE COMFORT.

The operation suffered from confusing definitions of territorial responsibility. The no-fly zone was larger than the security zone on the ground, which Iraqi troops were forbidden to enter. This allowed Iraqi troops to move antiaircraft weapons and radar into the territory below the no-fly zone, increasing the risk to coalition aircraft. The line between the areas for which the U.S. European Command and U.S. Central Command were responsible ran along the border between Turkey and Iraq. PROVIDE COMFORT bases were located in the U.S. European Command's area of responsibility, but the PROVIDE COMFORT no-fly zone was technically in the U.S. Central Command's zone. To solve the problem, Central Command allowed the European Command to patrol northern Iraq, while it concentrated on the southern no-fly zone.

One other problem that emerged from PROVIDE COMFORT was the absence of an exit policy. Strategists in Washington did not define a desired end state that would justify termination of the operation. No one knew exactly how long the no-fly zone over northern Iraq would have to be enforced, and PROVIDE COMFORT was eventually replaced by another operation with a different name but the same basic mission.

Despite mistakes and serious problems, Operation PROVIDE COMFORT succeeded in its purpose. It saved the lives of thousands of Kurdish refugees. By encouraging them to return to their homes in northern Iraq, it reduced hostile ethnic pressure on Turkey, a key North Atlantic Treaty Organization ally. It prevented Saddam Hussein from having a free hand in the northern part of his country, discouraging him from repeating genocidal incidents against the Kurdish minority. Operation PROVIDE COMFORT set a precedent for no-fly zones elsewhere, serving as a model for Operation SOUTHERN WATCH in southern Iraq and Operation DENY FLIGHT in Bosnia. Finally, PROVIDE COMFORT, in conjunction with SOUTHERN WATCH, discouraged Iraq from invading tiny Kuwait again. Saddam Hussein learned that his northern flank was as exposed as his southern to readily available airpower resources.

Crisis in Southern Iraq: Operation SOUTHERN WATCH

William J. Allen

DATES: August 2, 1992–To Be Determined

LOCATIONS: Saudi Arabia and southern Iraq

OVERSEAS BASES USED: Riyahd Air Base (AB), Dhahran AB, Al Kharj AB, Saudi Arabia; Shaikh Isa AB, Bahrain

AIR FORCE ORGANIZATIONS:

EXPEDITIONARY FORCES:	GROUPS:
4417th Air	4th Expeditionary Operations
4418th Air	49th Operations
	552d Operations
WINGS:	1681st Airlift
4th Air Expeditionary	1700th Operations
4401st Wing	4401st Operations
4404th Wing	4402d Operations
	4404th Operations
	4409th Operations (later, Air Base)

AIR FORCE AIRCRAFT: C–21, C–130, E–3, EC–135, EF–111, F–4, F–15, F–16, F–117, HC–130, HH–60, KC–10, KC–135, MC–130, MH–53, RC–135, U–2

Operations

On August 26, 1992, U.S. President George H. W. Bush announced a no-fly zone over southern Iraq in support of United Nations Security Council Resolution 688. Thus began Operation SOUTHERN WATCH, one of the longest contingency/deployment operations ever undertaken by the U.S. Air Force. The resolution protected Shiite Muslims under aerial attack from the Iraqi regime of Saddam Hussein in the aftermath of Operation DESERT STORM and enforced other United Nations (UN) sanctions against Iraq. Those sanctions included compliance with nuclear, biological, and chemical weapons inspection, plus dismantling, destruction, and import/export restrictions.

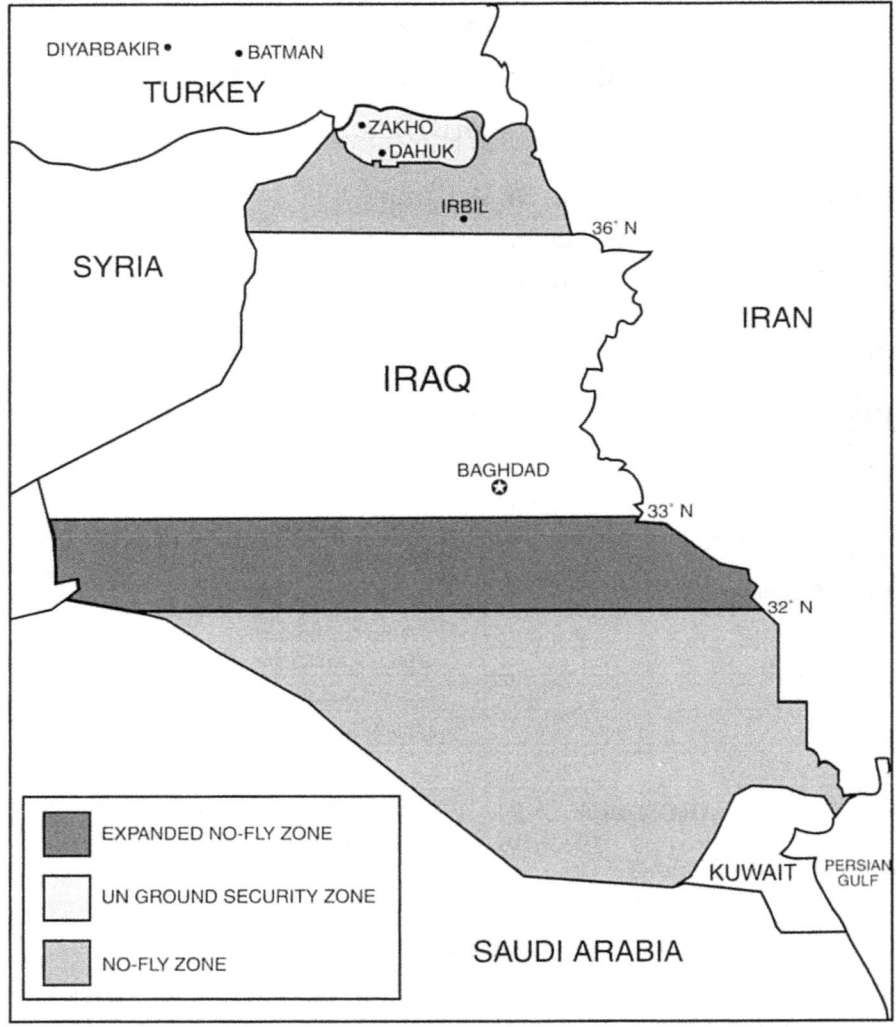

No-Fly Zones in Iraq during Operation SOUTHERN WATCH

Later UN resolutions included war reparations and Iraqi acceptance of the sovereignty of Kuwait.

The original no-fly zone (called "The Box" by SOUTHERN WATCH participants) encompassed all of southern Iraq south of 32° N. The Box excluded all Iraqi fixed- and rotary-winged aircraft. In the aftermath of an Iraqi massing of troops at the Kuwaiti border in October 1994, the United States declared it a no-fly, no-drive zone. Under the direction of U.S. Central Command, Air Force, Navy, and Army, as well as coalition (Saudi Arabia, Great Britain, France, and later, Kuwait) forces, combined to enforce the UN sanctions. The remaining U.S. forces in the Persian Gulf after DESERT STORM provided the forces for the newly organized Joint Task Force-Southwest Asia, which provided tactical command and operational planning for Operation SOUTHERN WATCH forces. On August 27, 1992, less than twenty-four hours after President Bush's announcement, these forces flew the first operational sortie.

Flying activities included fighter sweeps and patrols conducted against would-be targets in southern Iraq, reconnaissance, suppression of enemy air defense, air-to-air refueling, airborne warning and control system support, and other special missions. By February 1997, Operation SOUTHERN WATCH aircrews had flown more than 133,000 operational sorties, with over 86,000 being in The Box over southern Iraq.

The U.S. Air Force normally deployed personnel to Operation SOUTHERN WATCH on a ninety-day rotational basis. Operational flying squadrons deployed the necessary aircraft, personnel, and equipment needed to meet force-structure requirements, while support squadrons filled their ranks through individual tasking per occupational-specialty requirements. Once deployed, personnel were assigned to provisional units. From August 1992 to January 1997, Tactical Air Command, later replaced by Air Combat Command, activated eighty-one provisional flying squadrons, groups, and wings at various times to meet the manpower and force structure requirements of Operation SOUTHERN WATCH. Also, these commands activated an additional seventy-two provisional support units to support flying operations and meet changing requirements. At any given time, they deployed over 5,000 USAF members to support the operation. At times, such as the reinforcement of SOUTHERN WATCH during Operation VIGILANT WARRIOR, the ranks could swell to nearly 15,000 USAF people, plus additional Army, Navy, and Marine Corps personnel.

The Iraqi regime complied with the restrictions of the no-fly zone until December 27, 1992. Then the Iraqi air force sent two aircraft south of 32° N, threatening USAF patrol aircraft. A flight of F–16s attacked the intruders with missiles, shooting

This F–16 is still active at Eglin AFB, Fla., as a test aircraft. F–16s were used against MiG-25 intruders of the no-fly zone.

down a MiG–25 "Foxbat" aircraft. The American delegate to the UN delivered a demarché to the Iraqi delegate on January 6, 1993 over the violation of the southern no-fly zone and the threatening deployment of Iraqi surface-to-air missile systems to southern Iraq. Operation SOUTHERN WATCH forces subsequently met Iraq's refusal to remove the threatening missile systems by attacking both missile sites and the Zaafaraniyah Nuclear Fabrication Facility near Baghdad. On January 13–18, USAF aircraft struck missile sites in southern Iraq. Later, four USN warships launched forty-five Tomahawk land-attack missiles against the nuclear facility, followed by more USAF and coalition attacks against several missile and command and control sites in southern Iraq.

Again, on April 18, 1993, a USAF F–4G "Wild Weasel" aircraft fired on an Iraqi radar site that had threatened the aircraft. Later, on June 27, Operation SOUTHERN WATCH forces launched an attack on the Iraq Intelligence Service Headquarters in Baghdad in response to the April 1993 planned assassination attempt on former President Bush during his visit to Kuwait. Two days later, a Wild Weasel struck another hostile Iraqi radar site. On July 24, another Wild Weasel on a routine patrol over southern Iraq fired an antiradiation missile at an

Iraqi radar. As members of the Operation SOUTHERN WATCH team, two USN EA-6B "Prowler" aircraft fired missiles at another Iraqi radar site on July 29.

For much of 1994, the Iraqis seemed to accept daily patrolling by Operation SOUTHERN WATCH forces, since little Iraqi activity warranted retaliation or defensive protection by coalition aircraft. However, by October, Iraq had moved elements of its elite Republican Guard and regular army through southern Iraq to the border with Kuwait. This aggressive move led to the rapid reinforcement of Operation SOUTHERN WATCH forces during Operation VIGILANT WARRIOR. Troop strength in the theater swelled to over 25,000 U.S. personnel from all services. The number of available USAF aircraft grew temporarily to over 270 to meet the crisis.

In late 1995, Operation VIGILANT SENTINEL was launched to deter any Iraqi adventurism after several high-level Iraqis defected with their families to Jordan. Although a smaller reinforcement than Operation VIGILANT WARRIOR, this operation proved to the Iraqi leader the resolve of the United States and its coalition partners to keep Iraq out of Kuwait and Saudi Arabia.

Operation SOUTHERN WATCH became the USAF test for the Air Expeditionary Force (AEF) concept in October 1995, when a composite unit, designed to temporarily replace a USN Carrier Air Wing leaving the gulf area, arrived to support flying operations. The AEF provided forces with the same or greater capability than the units that they replaced. The first, AEF I, deployed with eighteen F-16 aircraft to Shaikh Isa AB, Bahrain, from October 28 to December 18. The AEF arrived fully armed and began flying within twelve hours of landing. The AEF concept proved sound, and since the first AEF deployment, several additional AEFs have deployed to support Operation SOUTHERN WATCH.

Following a terrorist attack against Saudi Arabian and U.S. forces in Riyadh in November 1995, Headquarters Joint Task Force-Southwest Asia implemented antiterrorism measures to deter further attacks against U.S. forces in the region. However, on June 25, 1996, a terrorist bombing killed nineteen USAF members at Dhahran AB, Saudi Arabia. The blast wounded another 547 people, including 250 Operation SOUTHERN WATCH personnel.

On September 3–4, USAF and USN aircraft hit targets in southern Iraq, a response to Iraqi military moves against Kurds in northern Iraq. In Operation DESERT STRIKE, B–52s and Navy ships launched forty-four cruise missiles against air defense batteries in southern Iraq. Then, in response to Iraqi aggression against Kurdish rebels in northern Iraq, U.S. President William J. Clinton expanded the no-fly zone to 33° N, just south of Baghdad. The expanded zone, combined with Operation PROVIDE COMFORT in northern Iraq, covered most of the airspace over Iraq.

In February 1998, President Clinton ordered U.S. forces to the Persian Gulf to deter Iraqi President Saddam Hussein from taking military action in the face of continued UN sanctions. Hussein refused to allow UN inspectors (specifically American inspectors) access to possible nuclear, biological, and chemical production sites located in or near his presidential palaces. The U.S. Air Force deployed additional F–117 stealth fighters, F–15s, and other aircraft and over 2,000 members. Although Hussein quickly relented and allowed the inspections, the U.S. forces did not redeploy until June 1998.

Since the beginning of Operation SOUTHERN WATCH in 1992, routine and emergency deployments have created several personnel and operational problems for the U.S. Air Force. Because of SOUTHERN WATCH and other deployments like Operations NORTHERN WATCH and DENY FLIGHT in Bosnia, USAF members faced multiple temporary-duty assignments within a given year. In the case of crews flying E–3 AWACS or EC–135 aircraft, the number of days deployed each year reached as high as 200 or more. While Operation SOUTHERN WATCH tested USAF pilots, aircrews, and support personnel in a near-combat situation, high deployment rates for some squadrons and individual mission-essential specialists created proficiency training, quality of life, and pilot retention problems. Because of the high deployment rates, the Air Force assessed its overall "Ops-Tempo" and took several measures that enhanced training and the quality of life for their members. These included limiting the number of days members deployed from their home base and cutting back the number of higher headquarters inspection visits, peacetime training exercises, and competitions.

Perhaps one of the most important improvements in both flying operations and the quality of life for USAF members resulted directly from the 1996 bombing at Khobar Towers, Dhahran AB. In the aftermath, the Air Force reviewed its entire security police, law enforcement, and force protection programs. The review resulted in a new security forces concept that proved to be more than just a change in specialty name. In 1998, the Air Force reorganized existing security police units into new security forces groups and squadrons that trained and specialized in all aspects of force protection, including terrorist activity and deployed force security.

By mid-1998, the Air Force continued routine deployments of personnel and aircraft to the desert, fulfilling its mission of patrolling the skies over southern Iraq and enforcing UN sanctions. General Ronald R. Fogleman, Air Force Chief of Staff, pointed out the significance of Operation SOUTHERN WATCH in July 1995. He stated, "What we have effectively done since 1992 is conduct an air occupation of a country. . .."

Crisis in Bosnia: Operation PROVIDE PROMISE

Frederick J. Shaw Jr.

DATES: July 2, 1992–January 9, 1996

LOCATION: Sarajevo, Bosnia-Herzegovina

OVERSEAS BASES USED: Rhein-Main Air Base (AB), Ramstein AB, Germany; Aviano AB, Falconara AB, Italy; Split Airport, Zagreb Airport, Croatia

AIR FORCE ORGANIZATIONS:

WINGS:	GROUPS:	SQUADRONS:
23d Wing	105th Airlift	2d Aeromedical Airlift
60th Airlift (later, Air Mobility)	123d Airlift	14th Airlift
62d Airlift	130th Airlift	16th Airlift
86th Airlift	135th Airlift	17th Airlift
94th Airlift	139th Airlift	37th Airlift
118th Airlift	143d Airlift	38th Airlift
123d Airlift	145th Airlift	40th Airlift
133d Airlift	153d Airlift	41st Airlift
136th Airlift	165th Airlift	55th Aeromedical Airlift
137th Airlift	166th Airlift	312th Airlift
146th Airlift	167th Airlift	
302d Airlift	176th Composite	
314th Airlift	179th Airlift	
315th Airlift	189th Airlift	
317th Airlift	908th Airlift	
349th Airlift	910th Airlift	
403d Airlift	911th Airlift	
435th Airlift	913th Airlift	
437th Airlift	914th Airlift	
440th Airlift	928th Airlift	
	934th Airlift	

AIR FORCE AIRCRAFT: C–130, C–141, C–5, C–9, C–17

Operations

By 1991, the collapse of Communism in Eastern Europe and the Soviet Union, coupled with the disintegration of the Soviet Union itself, had dissolved the political cement that bound ethnically diverse Yugoslavia into a single nation. Freed from the threat of external domination, Roman Catholic Slovenia and Croatia declared their independence from the Yugoslav Federation dominated by Eastern Orthodox Serbia. In early 1992, predominantly Moslem Bosnia-Herzegovina (Bosnia) also severed its ties to the Federation. Fearing their minority status, armed Serbs within Bosnia began forming their own ethnic state by seizing territory and, in the spring, besieging the Bosnian capital of Sarajevo.

In April 1992, the United States recognized Bosnia's independence and began airlifting relief supplies to Sarajevo. Early in May, Bosnian Serbs took control of the capital's airport, cutting off more than 300,000 people from food and other necessities. After negotiations with the warring parties, the United Nations (UN) organized an international relief effort, starting first with overland truck convoys from Croatia to Sarajevo. At the end of June, it took control of Sarajevo's airport, reopening it to international relief flights. On July 3, 1992, the UN airlift began when a French C–130 landed at Sarajevo with relief supplies. On the same day, U. S. Air Forces in Europe (USAFE) C–130s began delivering food and medical supplies.

The United States designated operations in support of the UN airlift PROVIDE PROMISE. It established a joint task force under U.S. European Command. Col. Patrick M. Henry, USAF, Vice Commander, 435th Airlift Wing (AW) at Rhein–Main AB in Germany, served as PROVIDE PROMISE's first mobility commander. The 37th Airlift Squadron (AS), a subordinate unit of the 435th AW, normally flew the PROVIDE PROMISE missions.

Most USAF transports took off from Rhein-Main, staged at Zagreb in Croatia or Aviano AB in Italy on the way to Sarajevo, or flew directly to the Bosnian capital. During a normal duty day, an aircraft might make several round-trips between Zagreb and Sarajevo before returning to Rhein-Main. The 435th

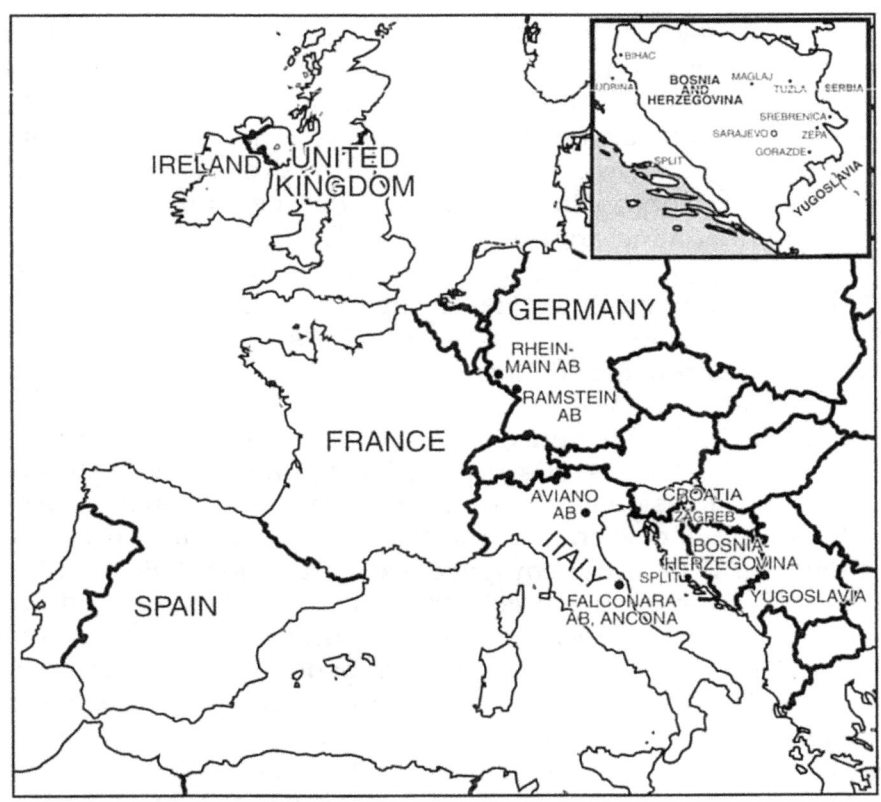

Europe during Operation PROVIDE PROMISE
Inset: Bosnia-Herzegovina

and 317th Airlift Wings provided the first C–130s, but Air Force Reserve (AFRES), Air National Guard (ANG), and regular USAF units began rotating aircraft to Europe for three-week deployments. Before long, about three C–130s were unloading at Sarajevo daily. Although the United States was only one of at least fifteen countries airlifting relief supplies to Sarajevo, by the end of 1992 its airplanes had delivered more than 5,400 tons of food and medical supplies. Despite gunfire around Sarajevo that shot down an Italian cargo airplane in September, U.S. airlifters avoided battle damage during 1992.

Shortly after the inauguration of U.S. President William J. Clinton in January 1993, PROVIDE PROMISE expanded dramatically. In February, Bosnian Serb mortars hit a market in central Sarajevo, killing sixty-eight people. Two American C-130s evacuated fifty wounded people from the Bosnian capital to Ramstein AB, Germany. During the same month, Bosnian Serbs blockaded Moslem enclaves in eastern Bosnia, preventing the arrival of UN truck convoys. At the end of February, President Clinton authorized American airdrops of food and medicine to the enclaves, including Tuzla, Srebrenica, Zepa, and Gorazde. Maj. Gen. James E. Chambers, USAF, Commander, Seventeenth Air Force, directed the effort, which began on February 28 with C-130s of the 435th Airlift Wing. Later, French and German aircraft would participate in the airdrops.

Profiting from experience acquired in northern Iraq (PROVIDE COMFORT), C-130s dropped thousands of leaflets explaining the mission's humanitarian nature and warning people to beware of descending bundles. During the first airdrops, regular USAF C-130s, equipped with the Global Positioning System (GPS) to ensure precision delivery, avoided ground fire by dropping their cargoes at night from altitudes in excess of 10,000 feet. Large parachutes and padded packages cushioned the fall of the first bundles, which sometimes weighed a ton. Lacking the GPS required for accurate nighttime deliveries, AFRES and ANG C-130s did not participate in the first airdrops. In later operations, they participated by flying in formations led by GPS-equipped aircraft.

To make possible the safe delivery of food to closely besieged population centers, members of the 352d Special Operations Group at Royal Air Force Alconbury, United Kingdom, developed a new tri-wall aerial delivery system (TRIADS). TRIADS's containers ripped open as they left the aircraft, scattering individual meals weighing only 2.2 pounds each. Deliveries by this method reduced the danger of injury or damage on the ground. By the middle of July 1993, PROVIDE PROMISE aircraft had dropped more than 7,000 packages of food and over 500 bundles of medical supplies.

The C-5, at that time the largest cargo aircraft in the Air Force, also participated in PROVIDE PROMISE. In April 1993, a C-5 from Travis Air Force Base (AFB) in California transported relief supplies from Massachusetts to Rhein-Main AB in Germany. At Rhein-Main, ground crews loaded the cargo aboard smaller airplanes for delivery to Bosnia. In August, a C–5 assigned to the 312th Airlift Squadron, 349th Airlift Wing, flew two water purification systems from Texas to Croatia. Each of the systems weighed in excess of eighteen tons. From Croatia, smaller C–130s ferried the water purification equipment to Sarajevo. During the same month, aircraft from the ANG's 105th Airlift Group delivered three more water purification systems to Europe for service in Sarajevo. Once assembled, the five systems afforded Bosnia's capital a clean water supply, reducing the chances of epidemics.

Aeromedical evacuation of Bosnian war casualties from Sarajevo continued in the summer of 1993 with a twist. Supplementing C–130 and C–9 flights from Bosnia to Germany, C–141 Starlifters began airlifting the wounded from Europe to the United States for medical treatment. The project was dubbed Operation SECOND CHANCE.

PROVIDE PROMISE passed a milestone on October 8, 1993 when it exceeded in duration the 1948–49 Berlin Airlift (Operation VITTLES). By then, American aircraft had transported more than 23,000 tons of relief cargo to Bosnia, with no major injuries or accidents. Surpassing this historic marker, the Bosnian airlift continued, as fighting waged on, claiming as many as 200,000 lives and leaving more than 2 million people homeless.

PROVIDE PROMISE airlifters embarked on a secondary operation in December 1993 called PROVIDE SANTA. Hercules aircraft dropped about fifty tons of toys and children's clothes and shoes over Bosnia. American military personnel stationed in Germany and German civilians donated the cargo. By early 1994, USAF transports from Rhein-Main also dropped thirty tons of mattresses, blankets, sleeping bags, candles, and beans over eastern Bosnia to enable the people on the ground to better cope with the winter.

The first damage to an USAF PROVIDE PROMISE aircraft occurred in early January 1994, when an exploding shell from artillery fire at the Sarajevo Airport hit a C–130. It was the sixth UN relief aircraft to suffer damage since July 1992. Despite the fact that there were no injuries and the damage was minor, the United Nations suspended PROVIDE PROMISE flights for about a week. When flights resumed, the C–130s employed proven tactics to reduce exposure to ground fire, approaching and departing the airport at steep angles and keeping their engines running during unloading. Fighting continued around Sarajevo with stray or deliberately aimed shots still causing casualties within the city. On February 5, mortars hit an open Sarajevan market, killing 68 people and wounding 200. The 2d Aeromedical Evacuation Squadron provided emergency treatment to the wounded, who were evacuated to Ramstein in four USAF C–130s and one International Red Cross aircraft.

In May 1994, a cease-fire provided USAFE with an opportunity to begin relocation of the 37th AS to Ramstein. The lull was also an opportunity to rebuild Sarajevo's food stocks by using larger C–141 Starlifters from the 315th and 437th Airlift Wings in place of the smaller, more maneuverable 435th Wing C–130s. As inevitably happened during the Bosnian civil war, the cease-fire broke down, and the approach to Sarajevo Airport once again became a shooting gallery. For protection from snipers and antiaircraft fire, aircrews, which often included female pilots technically banned from combat zones, wore helmets and flak vests. On July 21, one of the 437th Airlift Wing Starlifters, flown by Capt. Craig A. Breker, USAF, 62d Airlift Wing, drew ground fire in the vicinity of Sarajevo. Although twenty-five bullets hit the fuselage and several more struck both wings, damaging the hydraulic and fuel systems, Breker returned the plane safely to Rhein-Main. The incident marked the ninth time during PROVIDE PROMISE that USAF aircraft had been hit. Reacting to this and other incidents, the United Nations briefly suspended flights. At this time, the U.S. Air Force transferred the PROVIDE PROMISE C–141s to the Rwandan relief operations. During their three-month stint flying missions into Sarajevo, the large transports nearly tripled the amount of cargo delivered daily, quickly restoring the city's food supplies to adequate levels and building a surplus for distribution by ground convoy to surrounding Moslem enclaves.

PROVIDE PROMISE flights to Sarajevo resumed on August 9 with C–130s of the 37th AS employing steep angle approaches and deliveries to evade danger and deliver supplies. Numerous suspensions, prompted by fighting near the airport, harassing ground fire, or fear of Bosnian Serb reactions, interrupted deliveries. The final suspension of 1994 took place on December 31 when a fuel-laden UN aircraft skidded off the runway, creating a hazard that stopped flights until January 3, 1995.

Air-drop missions, primarily to Gorazde, Srebrenica, Zepa, Bjelimici, Tesanj, and Maglaj, continued through 1994. At the beginning of the year, the U.S. Air Force had expended more than 21,000 G–12 parachutes designed to drop a single 2,200-pound bundle from high altitudes at high velocities. Its inventory of G–12 parachutes nearly exhausted, the Air Force turned to the G–12D parachute, capable of 4,500-pound loads but designed for low-velocity deliveries at low altitude. Since low-altitude deliveries exposed aircraft and crews to danger, modifications were necessary. Working with Natick Laboratories, Rhein-Main parachute riggers adapted the G–12D parachutes for high altitudes primarily by reducing the area of the parachute (reefing) and dividing the cargo into two containers. Although early deliveries were not entirely on target, further modification and accumulated experience eventually resulted in accurate deliveries.

Seed for food and forage, which isolated Moslem communities needed to ensure their food supplies, continued to be among the most important cargoes delivered by parachute. Taking advantage of experience gained in 1993, PROVIDE PROMISE aircraft began dropping seeds in early rather than late spring to ensure adequate forage (red clover, alfalfa, bird grass, English grass) and food (beans, tomatoes, barley, and oats) in the encircled pockets. Except in the vicinity of Bjelimici and Zepa, where local officials failed to adequately secure the drop zones, the missions were largely successful, delivering 380 metric tons of seeds by May 9.

In June, air-drop missions slowed considerably as good weather and the cease-fire opened roads, allowing the distribution of food by convoy from Sarajevo. The respite ended in early August, when fighting resumed in the Bihac area, and UN officials requested airdrops to support the local population. Despite their vulnerability to surface-to-air missiles that ringed the area, UN transports, preceded by DENY FLIGHT fighters, flew missions over Bihac from August 11–18. These were the last PROVIDE PROMISE air-drop missions. Although Bosnian Serb forces continued periodically to blockade surrounded enclaves, they almost always permitted the entry of convoys before airdrops became necessary. In other situations the deteriorating military situation rendered airdrops too dangerous or futile.

In 1994, the U.S. Air Force accomplished a number of important organizational changes associated with PROVIDE PROMISE. On January 4, it activated the 38th Airlift Squadron to control deployed equipment, aircraft, and people assigned to the airlift. Squadron leadership rotated among Air National Guard, Air Force Reserves, and 23d Wing officers at ninety-day intervals. The May introduction of C–141 flights to Sarajevo permitted the 37th AS to begin a protracted transfer from Rhein-Main to Ramstein. In October 1994, the 86th Airlift Wing at Ramstein formally assumed operational control of PROVIDE PROMISE missions from the 435th AW at Rhein-Main. On December 20, the 37th completed its transfer to Ramstein and began flying missions from its new station.

A significant organizational change highlighted the beginning of 1995. All North Atlantic Treaty Organization (NATO) PROVIDE PROMISE missions other than those of the U.S. Air Force flew from Falconara AB, Ancona, Italy. To reduce operational costs, the UN High Commissioner for Refugees requested that the U.S. Air Force move its operations to Falconara as well. Accordingly, on January 13–15, the U.S. Tanker Airlift Control Element moved from Split, Croatia, to Falconara AB. Three C–130s of the 37th AS and maintenance technicians followed on January 16.

PROVIDE PROMISE flights into Sarajevo continued sporadically through March, disrupted by ground fire and other forms of harassment. On April 8, gunfire hit a 37th AS C–130 as it flared for a landing less than ten feet above Sarajevo's runway. More rounds struck while the aircraft was on the ground and as it took off. None of the six crew members, all of whom were wearing the flak jackets and helmets, were hit. One bullet, however, shattered the windscreen right in front of the pilot. Another severed a hydraulic line. Others struck an engine and a fuel tank. In all, twelve bullets penetrated the aircraft, which returned safely to Ancona.

Responding to this incident, UN officials suspended flights into Sarajevo indefinitely. Running from April 8 to September 15, this was the longest suspension of PROVIDE PROMISE missions. While the suspension was in effect, UN forces experienced a major humiliation at the hands of the Bosnian Serbs. In late May, NATO responded to the Bosnian Serb shelling of civilian targets near Sarajevo and the seizure of weapons from UN weapons-collection depots by bombing ammunition depots near Pale, the Bosnian Serb capital. In retaliation, the Bosnian Serb army seized more than 370 UN peacekeepers as hostages, forcing a cessation of the bombing.

Resolving to conduct future military operations without fear of reprisals, Britain, France, and the Netherlands formed a heavily armed and mobile UN Rapid Reaction Force to protect UN peacekeepers. Transportation of UN soldiers under PROVIDE PROMISE orders to Split, Croatia, designated Operation QUICK LIFT, began on July 8. By the end of the operation on August 11, 23 USAF C–141s and 35 C–5s had airlifted 4,500 British, Dutch, and German soldiers, 1,500 vehicles, and 1,500 trailers from bases in the United Kingdom, Germany, and the Netherlands to Croatia. From Split, the UN combat components traveled overland to Sarajevo, arriving in time to participate in the Bosnian civil war's final crisis. Its resolution would result in the termination of hostilities and the resumption of PROVIDE PROMISE missions to Sarajevo.

In July 1995, Bosnian Serb forces, emboldened by the United Nations irresolution during May, assaulted and captured Moslem "safe areas" in the vicinity of Srebrenica and Zepa. Atrocities against both combatants and noncombatants accompanied the fall of the two sanctuaries. On August 28, a mortar attack on a UN-designated safe area in Sarajevo killed thirty-seven civilians. After UN commanders determined that the attack came from a Serbian position, the United Nations authorized air strikes against Bosnian Serb targets. Beginning on August 29, the air strikes, in combination with a successful Croat ground offensive against Bosnian Serb forces in the north, brought the Bosnian Serbs to the negotiating table. On September 14, NATO halted the strikes after Bosnian Serb authorities promised unimpeded access to Sarajevo and the cessation of attacks on Moslem safe areas.

With the cease-fire and promise of permanent peace, PROVIDE PROMISE flights into Sarajevo resumed on September 16. Escorted by fighter aircraft, C–130s from the United

In December 1995, the Globemaster, assigned to 437th Airlift Wing, Charleston, South Carolina, began flights to Sarajevo in support of PROVIDE PROMISE.

States, Great Britain, and France and C–160 Transails from Spain delivered over 137 tons of cargo by September 17. Operations continued through October 9, when small-arms fire directed at an USAF C–130 during takeoff resulted in a brief suspension. The exhaustion of cargo stockpiled at Ancona, however, suspended PROVIDE PROMISE flights for three weeks, November 6–30.

PROVIDE PROMISE flights resumed on December 1 with five USAF and one French C–130 delivering sixty-five and a quarter metric tons of cargo, mostly peas, to the Bosnian capital. On December 8, the U.S. Air Force dramatically expanded its capacity to deliver cargo, introducing the C–17 Globemaster III on PROVIDE PROMISE missions. The C–17 was the largest USAF transport, and its sixty-four-metric-ton payload was four times that of the C–130 and over double that of the C–141. On December 8–11, 1995, five C–17s assigned to the Air Mobility Command's 437th AW at Charleston AFB, South Carolina, delivered 321 metric tons of gas heaters, pressed logs, flour, sugar, and chicken feed.

While the giant transports were making their last deliveries, a UN decision shortened the airlift. On December 10, the United Nations reduced the total tonnage of cargo to be delivered to Sarajevo by January 31, 1996, from 5,000 metric tons to 1,861 metric tons, exactly the size of the stockpile remaining at Ancona. In making this decision, the United Nations reasoned that the imminence of a permanent peace made unnecessary the accumulation of a larger reserve. On December 14, Bosnia's warring factions signed peace accords at Wright-Patterson AFB, Ohio. The formal cessation of hostilities, however, did not end the danger to USAF aircraft. On December 23, small-arms fire struck a 37th AS C–130 over Sarajevo. Only the Kevlar armor added as a precaution to squadron C–130s kept one round from reaching the flight deck. This was the last hostile fire incident affecting PROVIDE PROMISE airlifters. The last humanitarian air-land delivery into Sarajevo took place on January 4.

At its conclusion, the UN humanitarian airlift to Sarajevo was one of the longest airlifts in history. Flying into a besieged city, aircrews accomplished their missions at considerable risk. The approaches to Sarajevo Airport and isolated enclaves were war zones ringed by antiaircraft weaponry and often the location of bitterly fought battles. Ground fire, whether intentional or not, threatened allied aircraft 279 times during the entire airlift. In the worst incident, antiaircraft fire downed an Italian cargo aircraft in September 1992, killing four crewmen.

Despite the dangers, allied airmen accomplished their mission. Between July 2, 1992 and January 4, 1996, aircraft from 21 nations flew 12,886 sorties, delivering 159,622 metric tons of food, medicine, and supplies and evacuating 1,300 wounded. Responsible for approximately 95 percent of the humanitarian aid delivered to the city of 380,000 people, the airlift kept Sarajevo alive during its 3.5-year ordeal.

Canada, France, Germany, Great Britain and the United States were the principal participants, with the United States designating its portion of the airlift PROVIDE PROMISE. During PROVIDE PROMISE, the Air Force flew 4,553 C–130, C–141, and C–17 sorties, delivering 62,802 metric tons of cargo. The 37th AS was the main span of the allied air bridge, at times flying as many as six C–130 missions daily from Rhein-Main to Sarajevo. Later, at Ancona, the normal rate was three sorties per day. Additionally, USAF C–130s flew 2,222 sorties, dropping 28,748 Container Delivery System bundles and 1,185 TRIADS bundles.

On January 9, a formal ceremony marking the end of the airlift took place at Sarajevo. Ten minutes after the arrival of a USAF C–130 carrying visiting dignitaries, a French C–130 landed with a symbolic sack of flour. American, British, and French commanders then reported to UN officials that the airlift was officially over. The ceremony accurately captured the significance of the Sarajevan airlift. A large-scale multinational operation conducted under the auspices of the United Nations, the airlift owed its success to the military and diplomatic cooperation of many nations. For the United States and its NATO partners, the airlift was a tangible demonstration of their commitment to stability and peace in post-Cold War Europe.

Crisis in Somalia: Operations PROVIDE RELIEF and RESTORE HOPE

Daniel L. Haulman

DATES: August 14, 1992–March 25, 1994

LOCATION: Somalia

OVERSEAS BASES USED: Mogadishu, Kismayu, Baledogle, Belen Huen, Baidoa, Bardera, Oddur, Beledweyne, Somalia; Mombasa, Wajir, Kenya; Cairo West, Egypt; Jeddah New, Taif, Saudi Arabia; Djibouti, Djibouti; Addis Ababa, Ethiopia; Aden, Yemen; Lajes Field, Azores; Moron, Spain; Souda Bay, Greece; Royal Air Force Mildenhall, United Kingdom

AIR FORCE ORGANIZATIONS:

WINGS:	WINGS: (con't.)	GROUPS:
4th Wing	319th Air Refueling	98th Air Refueling
12th Airlift	349th Airlift	105th Airlift
16th Special Operations	380th Air Refueling	118th Airlift
19th Air Refueling	403d Wing	133d Airlift
22d Air Refueling	433d Airlift	135th Airlift
23d Wing	434th Wing	143d Airlift
43d Air Refueling	435th Airlift	145th Airlift
60th Airlift	436th Airlift	151st Air Refueling
62d Airlift	437th Airlift	157th Air Refueling
63d Airlift	438th Airlift	164th Airlift
100th Air Refueling	439th Airlift	170th Air Refueling
101st Air Refueling	445th Airlift	172d Airlift
108th Air Refueling	446th Airlift	176th Group
123d Tactical Airlilft	452d Air Refueling	179th Airlift
141st Air Refueling	459th Airlift	190th Air Refueling
146th Airlift	463d Airlift	352d Special Operations
171st Air Refueling	512th Airlift	453d Operations
302d Airlift	514th Airlift	457th Operations
305th Air Refueling	910th Airlift	906th Air Refueling
314th Airlift	914th Airlift	907th Airlift
315th Airlift		913th Airlift
317th Airlift		916th Air Refueling

AIR FORCE ORGANIZATIONS: (con't.)

GROUPS: (con't.)	SQUADRON:	
940th Air Refueling	16th Special Operations	
943d Airlift		

AIRCRAFT: C–5, C–141, C–130, KC–10, KC–135, AC–130

Operations

Civil unrest in the wake of a 2-year civil war contributed to a famine in Somalia that killed up to 350,000 people in 1992. As many as 800,000 refugees fled to neighboring countries, including Ethiopia, Kenya, Djibouti, and Yemen. Central and southern Somalia suffered most, because of the collapse of political and economic institutions there.

News broadcasts showing mass starvation stimulated an international relief effort. In July 1992, United Nations (UN) troops from Pakistan arrived to monitor a tenuous cease-fire that feuding factions had agreed to in March. In August, the United States launched Operation PROVIDE RELIEF, flying food on C–141 Starlifters from the United States and Europe to Kenya. Within Kenya, the Starlifters moved the relief cargo from Mombasa to Wajir, near the border with Somalia, where thousands of refugees camped. Workers cut trees at Wajir to make room for the large jet transports. The United States withdrew the Starlifters after initial deliveries but continued shuttling food in C–130s from Kenya to various locations in Somalia, where the airfields were too small to accommodate the C–141s. The airfields included Belen Huen, Baidoa, Bardera, Oddur, and Beledweyne. Unpaved and poorly maintained runways at some of these airfields forced USAF crews to replace tires frequently, and snipers occasionally interrupted deliveries. Despite these obstacles, PROVIDE RELIEF flights delivered more than 38 million pounds of food to Somalia and Kenya between August and December 1992. During the same period, ships from many nations delivered even more food to ports such as Mogadishu and Kismayu on the Somali coast.

Despite the large quantities of food that arrived, many people continued to starve because armed members of rival clans

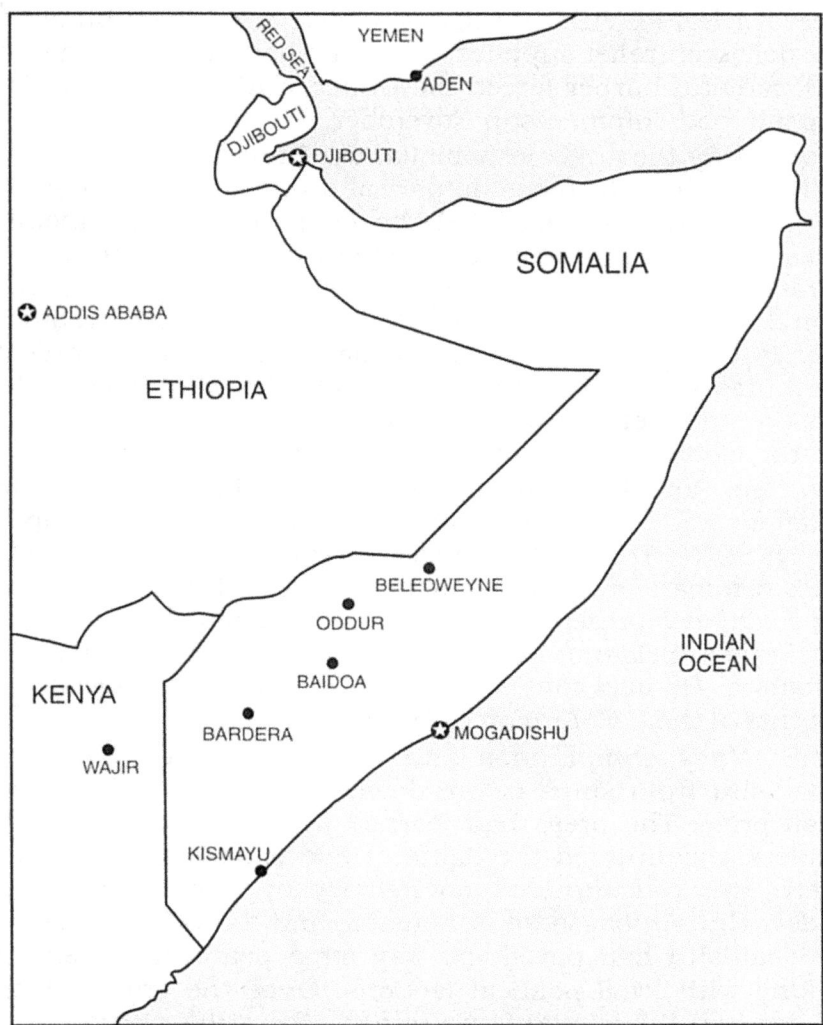

USAF Area of Operations during the Crisis in Somalia

intimidated relief workers and stole supplies from the warehouses and trucks of international relief agencies. In September 1992, the United States airlifted hundreds more UN troops from Pakistan to Somalia in Operation IMPRESSIVE LIFT. These soldiers escorted humanitarian supplies but were unable to stop the thefts and threats. In September and October, some of the PROVIDE RELIEF C–130s were hit by bullets as they delivered relief supplies, and the shelling of a cargo ship in Mogadishu harbor forced the United Nations to temporarily suspend food shipments in November.

To remedy the crisis in Somalia, the United States offered to send up to 40,000 troops as part of a multinational coalition. The United Nations accepted the offer, authorizing member states to establish a safe environment for humanitarian relief operations in Somalia. On December 4, President George H.W. Bush launched RESTORE HOPE, an operation to establish order in central and southern Somalia so that food could be distributed fairly. The RESTORE HOPE plan contained a clear mission statement with limited and measurable objectives so that the United States would not be drawn into a quagmire.

Lt. Gen. Robert B. Johnston, USMC, who had served as chief of staff for General H. Norman Schwarzkopf, USA, during Operation DESERT STORM the previous year, served as RESTORE HOPE commander. General Johnston led an international military coalition representing twenty-three nations, including Canada, France, Belgium, Sweden, Botswana, Nigeria, Tunisia, and Zimbabwe. He also commanded a joint task force consisting of elements of the U.S. Air Force, Army, Navy, and Marines.

U.S. Navy commandos and Marines coming ashore at Mogadishu from ships before dawn on December 9 achieved no surprise. The press had learned of the landings, and the invaders encountered the lights of television cameras. Fortunately, they encountered no military opposition. Robert B. Oakley, U.S. Ambassador to Somalia, and a U.S. Liaison Office in Mogadishu had paved the way for a peaceful invasion by working with local political factions. Once the ground forces had secured the capital city's airport, the airlift portion of the operation began.

The U.S. Air Force played a leading role in the first weeks of RESTORE HOPE, because the operation called for the rapid projection of U.S. forces at very long range. General Ronald R. Fogleman, USAF, dual-hatted commander of both Air Mobility Command (AMC) and U.S. Transportation Command, supported General Johnston with a new centralized organization of airlift and air refueling units. This organization was crucial given the post-Cold War scarcity of adequate staging bases. Brig. Gen.

A C–141 at Mogadishu, Somalia, in December 1992 participated in the strategic airlift phase of Operation RESTORE HOPE.

John W. Handy, USAF, commanded the AMC Tanker Airlift Control Center, which scheduled refuelings and flights for the complicated deployment.

Strategic airlift flights proceeded between the United States and Somalia through intermediate staging bases in Egypt (Cairo West), Saudi Arabia (Jeddah New and Taif), Ethiopia (Addis Ababa), Yemen (Aden), and Djibouti. Cargo airplanes such as C–5 Galaxies and C–141 Starlifters refueled over the Atlantic Ocean and Mediterranean Sea from KC–135 tankers based in the northeastern United States, at Lajes Field in the Azores, and at Moron Air Base, Spain. Saudi Arabia allowed a refueling track over the Red Sea supported by tankers from Operation SOUTHERN WATCH. On December 16, 1992, KC–135s from Souda Bay, Greece, began flying refueling missions for RESTORE HOPE. In addition to C–5 Galaxies and C–141 Starlifters, the Air Force eventually used KC–10 tankers as cargo planes for the long-range airlift. Commercial airliners also took part in the operation, as they had in the previous year's DESERT STORM. The airliners and cargo planes unloaded at Mogadishu, Baledogle, and Kismayu, with the vast majority going to the capital.

U.S. C–130s continued flying food from Kenya into Somalia as part of Operation PROVIDE RELIEF, and the two operations proceeded simultaneously until the end of February 1993. After the initial surge phase of RESTORE HOPE, Air Mobility Command connected its Pacific and Indian Oceans channel mission routes with Mombasa, Kenya, so that cargo could be delivered from there to Mogadishu. By mid-December 1992, RESTORE HOPE absorbed PROVIDE RELIEF administratively. When PROVIDE RELIEF ended on February 28, C–130s continued flying supply missions from Mombasa to Mogadishu.

RESTORE HOPE airlifted more than 32,000 U.S. and foreign troops to Somalia. Commercial airliners carried most of these, but U.S. military aircraft moved most of the 32,000 tons of cargo. KC–135 tankers flew more than 1,100 refueling missions, transferring more than 82 million pounds of fuel. The initial cargo went by air until ships could arrive. Once they did, sea lift quickly surpassed airlift in terms of tonnage delivered.

General Colin L. Powell, USA, Chairman, Joint Chiefs of Staff, urged the United States to turn over the mission of safeguarding the distribution of food in Somalia to the United Nations as soon as order was established and the food was flowing again. On March 26, the United Nations passed Security Resolution 814, which provided for a UN force to assume control of the operation. At the end of April, U.S. Secretary of State Warren M. Christopher notified UN Secretary-General Boutros Boutros-Ghali that the U.S.-led coalition had secured the area of operations and reversed the humanitarian crisis in southern and central Somalia. Operation RESTORE HOPE ended on May 4, 1993, when the United States turned over the mission to the UN organization in Somalia.

Redeployment airlift missions continued through the end of the month as U.S. forces began to leave Somalia. The subsequent Operation CONTINUE HOPE, that began on May 5, supported the United Nations with reduced U.S. forces, who served under Maj. Gen. Thomas Montgomery, USA. Less than 5,000 of the more than 25,000 U.S. troops who deployed in RESTORE HOPE remained in Somalia.

A C–5 unloads vehicles in Somalia during Operation RESTORE HOPE.

The UN operation went beyond RESTORE HOPE's clear mission of securing a safe environment for the distribution of humanitarian supplies. It attempted "nation building," or the construction of centralized political institutions in Somalia. This brought the United Nations into conflict with warlords, such as Mohammed Farah Aidid. On June 5, 1993, a battle between Aidid's forces and UN troops left two dozen Pakistani soldiers dead. The United Nations requested more U.S. troops, and General Montgomery appealed for more armor.

On October 3, a battle in Mogadishu between U.S. troops and Aidid's forces left eighteen Americans killed and eighty-four wounded. On October 7, U.S. President William J. Clinton announced that he was sending more troops and armored vehicles to Somalia. Their mission would be only to protect U.S. troops and bases; keep roads, ports, and communication lines open; and keep the warlords in check. He refused to commit the United States to nation building in Somalia and promised that the troops would be home by the end of March 1994. To send the reinforcements, the President had two options: twenty-one days by sea or eight days by air. He chose airlift.

There followed Operation RESTORE HOPE II, which between October 5 and 13, 1993 rapidly airlifted more U.S. troops, armor, and other military cargo from the United States to Somalia. Air Force C–5s transported most of the 1,700 deploying troops and 3,100 tons of cargo directly from Hunter Army Airfield near Fort Stewart, Georgia, and Griffiss Air Force Base near Fort Drum, New York, to Mogadishu. Only the C–5s could carry the eighteen heavy tanks and forty-four Bradley armored vehicles because of their weight and bulk. The nonstop flights from Georgia to Somalia took eighteen hours. After delivering the tanks, the C–5s staged at Cairo West, which took another four to five hours of flying. A crew could be together for as many as thirty hours (twenty-three hours of flying time). To cover the exhausting flights, operation leaders augmented crews with extra pilots and expanded the maximum number of hours allowed in a crew-duty day. As in the previous RESTORE HOPE operation, C–141 Starlifters also carried troops and their equipment from the United States to Mogadishu. Most of the Starlifters were grounded in mid-1993 because of wing cracks, and commercial airliners helped take up the slack during subsequent flights to sustain the troops.

By October 1993, Brig. Gen. John B. Sams Jr., USAF, had replaced General Handy as commander of the AMC Tanker Airlift Control Center. The Galaxies and Starlifters refueled from KC–10 Extenders and KC–135 Stratotankers 4 times on direct flights of 8,000 miles from the United States to Somalia—over the western Atlantic Ocean, the eastern Atlantic, the eastern Mediterranean Sea, and the Red Sea. The tankers came from bases in England, Spain, and Greece. During Operation RESTORE HOPE II, Stratotankers and Extenders transferred 17.2 million pounds of fuel. American AC–130 gunships also deployed from Europe and Florida to Africa. They operated over Somalia from Mombasa, Kenya. To support them, some C–5 flights carried gunship and support gear from three bases in the United States to Mombasa. At least eighteen airlift and air refueling wings from the Air Mobility Command, U.S. Air Forces in Europe, Air Force Reserve, and Air National Guard participated in RESTORE HOPE II. It was an echo of RESTORE HOPE and a reminder that such operations would be needed in the future. The last C–5 carrying American forces departed Mogadishu on March 25, 1994, and Joint Task Force-Somalia inactivated two days later. RESTORE HOPE II enabled U.S. forces to pull out of Somalia without more casualties, but the country was still left with anarchy and the threat of famine.

Ambassador Oakley, in a speech at the Federal Bureau of Investigation Academy on December 14, 1993, offered advice for future peacemaking operations. Echoing former Defense Secretary Caspar W. Weinberger and General Powell, Oakley recommended that such operations have an exit strategy, that forces move in quickly, that the efforts have the support of Congress and the American people, and that the position be modified for changing circumstances. The original Operation RESTORE HOPE, between December 1992 and May 1993, exhibited these qualities. Overwhelming force was deployed; there was nonconfrontational and constant dialogue among the factions and agencies involved; there was coordination among military, political, and relief agency leadership; and little question arose about command and control. After the United Nations took control of coalition military forces in Somalia on May 4, 1993, the Somalia effort began to slide toward a nation-building quagmire. RESTORE HOPE was unquestionably a successful operation. It was only after the conclusion of that operation that serious hostilities broke out.

RESTORE HOPE II was also a successful operation. It accomplished President Clinton's goal of rapidly projecting U.S. reinforcements to Somalia to prevent more U.S. deaths and to allow the United States to withdraw honorably from what began as a humanitarian operation. What failed were the poorly defined UN operations between the end of RESTORE HOPE in May 1993 and the beginning of RESTORE HOPE II in October.

The Somalia operations were milestones in USAF history that taught many lessons. They were AMC's first major airlifts and the most significant military operations since DESERT STORM. They tested the coordination of airlift and air refueling aircraft to compensate for a shortage of staging bases and proved the practicality of using strict flight scheduling in the post-Cold War environment of limited forward presence. The large C–5 Galaxies and C–141 Starlifters could not land at most of the airfields in Somalia, and at Mogadishu, they crowded runways and ramps. This experience demonstrated the need for either a network of better air bases or more aircraft such as the C–17. Shortages of C–5 and C–141 aircrews trained in aerial refueling threatened the efficiency of the operation, and shortages of spares reduced reliability rates for Galaxies and Starlifters to well below peacetime figures. While age sharply limited the use of C–141s, KC–10 aircraft proved to be good cargo-hauling substitutes. RESTORE HOPE also demonstrated the danger of extending crew-duty days, which inevitably led to personnel fatigue on long missions. The operation proved the practicality of new equipment, such as portable Global Positioning Systems for C–130 aircraft, which allowed them to determine their positions from satellite communications in a desert environment. Finally, the operations in Somalia revealed much about the probabilities of future humanitarian and contingency operations. Crises would continue to erupt in underdeveloped areas, and responses would be increasingly international in character, requiring communication and consensus among many coalition partners.

Resolution of Bosnian Crisis: Operation DENY FLIGHT

Daniel L. Haulman

DATES: April 12, 1993–December 20, 1995

LOCATION: Bosnia-Herzegovina (Bosnia)

OVERSEAS BASES USED: Aviano Air Base (AB), Brindisi, Pisa, Sigonella Naval Air Station, Malpensa, Genoa, Capodichino, Italy; Istres AB, France; Royal Air Force (RAF) Mildenhall, RAF Alconbury, RAF Fairford, Brize Norton, England; Hannover, Ramstein AB, Germany; Soesterberg, the Netherlands; Souda Bay, Greece; Split, Croatia

AIR FORCE ORGANIZATIONS:

WINGS:	WINGS: (con't.)	GROUPS:
1st Special Operations	100th Air Refueling	43d Air Refueling
3d Fighter	301st Fighter	103d Fighter
4th Wing	305th Air Mobility	104th Fighter
9th Reconnaissance	355th Wing	110th Fighter
16th Special Operations	401st Fighter	157th Air Refueling
19th Air Refueling	434th Fighter	175th Fighter
27th Fighter	442d Fighter	190th Air Refueling
31st Fighter	463d Airlift	930th Operations
36th Fighter	917th Fighter	944th Fighter
43d Air Refueling	924th Fighter	
48th Fighter	926th Fighter	**SQUADRONS:**
52d Fighter	7490th Wing (Provisional)	7th Airborne Command and Control
55th Wing		76th Airlift
60th Air Mobility		429th Electronic Combat
86th Wing (later, 86th Airlift)		555th Fighter

AIR FORCE AIRCRAFT: F–16, F–15, A–10, OA–10, RC–135, KC–135, KC–10, C–130, AC–130, MC–130, HC–130, EC–130, EF–111, MH–52, MH–53, U–2, C–21

Operations

When the Communist Party relaxed its political control over Yugoslavia in 1990, the country began to fracture along ethnic and religious lines. In 1991 and 1992, the provinces of Slovenia, Croatia, Bosnia-Herzegovina, and Macedonia seceded from Yugoslavia, which was dominated by Serbs under the leadership of Slobodan Milosevic. The large Serb minority in Croatia and Bosnia resisted the independence of those republics, hoping to forge a "greater Serbia" with the remainder of Yugoslavia. A devastating civil war resulted.

In early 1992, the United Nations (UN) sent a protection force to supervise a truce in Croatia, but a greater conflict within Bosnia-Herzegovina soon demanded the world body's attention. A plurality of Bosnia's population was Moslem, but large portions were Serbian or Croatian. Serbs under Radovan Karadzic and Gen. Ratko Mladic rejected the leadership of Bosnian President Alija Izetbegovic and seized large parts of the country. With huge quantities of arms from Yugoslavia, the Bosnian Serbs threatened to crush the infant republic and spread the war into other parts of the Balkans. The United Nations reacted by extending its forces to Bosnia and authorizing an international airlift of humanitarian supplies to Sarajevo, Bosnia's capital. Operation PROVIDE PROMISE began in July 1992 and continued for three and one-half years.

In September and October, the UN Security Council imposed a regional arms embargo and economic sanctions against Yugoslavia. European nations enforced the embargo and sanctions in an operation called SHARP GUARD. At about the same time, in an attempt to limit the war, the United Nations passed a resolution to ban military flights over Bosnia. The North Atlantic Treaty Organization (NATO) monitored the flights in Operation SKY WATCH but had no authority to enforce the ban. Aircraft from various factions in the war violated the "no-fly" zone over Bosnia routinely by the spring of 1993. On March 31, the UN Security Council passed Resolution 816, which authorized NATO to enforce the ban on military flights by shooting down violators. Another resolution set up six urban "safe areas" in Bosnia—Sarajevo, Bihac, Gorazde, Tuzla, Srebrenica, and Zepa. A third Security Council resolution demanded an end to hostilities in the safe areas.

NATO's Operation DENY FLIGHT attempted to enforce UN Security Council Resolution 816. The UN and NATO approached the operation with a "dual key" concept. Both international

USAF Area of Operations in DENY FLIGHT

organizations had to approve attacks before they could proceed. Adm. Jeremy M. Boorda, USN, replaced later by Adm. Leighton W. Smith, USN, served as commander of NATO's Allied Forces Southern Europe during the operation. Lt. Gen. Joseph W. Ashy, USAF, served as commander of Allied Air Forces Southern Europe until Lt. Gen. Michael E. Ryan, USAF, replaced him in late 1994. The only non-American in the NATO DENY FLIGHT command chain was the Italian commander of the 5th Allied Tactical Air Force, collocated at Vicenza, Italy,

A NATO AWACS aircraft over the Adriatic Sea during Operation DENY FLIGHT.

with a new Combined Air Operations Center, also under command of an American. Other nations that participated in DENY FLIGHT included the United Kingdom, France, the Netherlands, Spain, Turkey, and eventually, Germany and Italy. While France was not a military member of NATO, it willingly participated in the air operation because so many of the UN troops in Bosnia were French.

The 36th Wing at Bitburg AB in Germany flew initial DENY FLIGHT missions out of Aviano AB in Italy, which became the most important of the operation's bases. U.S. search and rescue aircraft operated from Brindisi, Italy, while USAF tankers flew from bases in other parts of Italy and from France. USAF reconnaissance aircraft operated from England. A USN carrier task force in the Mediterranean provided more fighters and electronic warfare aircraft, some of which refueled from USAF tankers orbiting over the Adriatic Sea.

DENY FLIGHT began on April 12, 1993, but at first there was little action. Most of the aircraft over Bosnia were either helicopters or PROVIDE PROMISE transports. NATO commanders could not easily determine whether the helicopters in

A USAF F–15 refuels from a KC–135 over the Adriatic Sea during Operation DENY FLIGHT.

the no-fly zone were flying humanitarian missions, especially since many of them, hostile or not, carried civilians or wore Red Cross symbols. Not wishing to cause an international incident, DENY FLIGHT ignored the helicopters.

In the summer of 1993, DENY FLIGHT assumed new roles. The UN Security Council authorized NATO close air support missions and offensive air strikes to protect UN forces. UN Secretary-General Boutros Boutros-Ghali gave his representative for the former Yugoslavia, Ambassador Yasushi Akashi, authority to veto NATO close air support missions. Boutros-Ghali himself retained the authority to veto retaliatory air strikes.

DENY FLIGHT enjoyed initial success. A Bosnian Serb mortar attack on Sarajevo's central market on February 5, 1994 killed or wounded more than 260 people. A few days later, NATO demanded removal of heavy weapons from around

Sarajevo, or they would be targeted. The mere threat of air strikes persuaded the Serbs to curtail their shelling and move their artillery back from the exclusion zone. On February 28, NATO aircraft scored their first aerial victories in the alliance's forty-five-year history. Two flights of F–16s from the 526th Fighter Squadron intercepted six Bosnian Serb jet aircraft over the no-fly zone and shot down four of them. One American F–16 pilot, Capt. Robert L. Wright, USAF, downed three of the violators. Ground strikes also demonstrated NATO's determination to enforce the UN resolutions. On April 10, 1994, two 512th Fighter Squadron F–16s struck a Bosnian Serb artillery command post involved in the shelling of Gorazde. This raid was the first NATO close air support mission. On August 5, two A–10s destroyed a Bosnian Serb armored vehicle after Serbs stole weapons from a UN-guarded collection point. The Serbs returned the weapons. In September, NATO launched other air strikes on Serbs who had attacked a French tank.

Despite these successes, Operation DENY FLIGHT was largely ineffective in quelling the war or stopping the advance of the Bosnian Serbs before August of 1995. Attacks on C–130s and C–141s flying humanitarian relief missions to Sarajevo sometimes forced temporary suspensions of PROVIDE PROMISE. Akashi was reluctant to approve NATO close air support missions because he feared the UN would appear to be taking sides against the Bosnian Serbs, who might retaliate against UN peacekeepers on the ground. He repeatedly refused to consent to requested air strikes or approved them too late to be effective.

The Bosnian Serbs regularly took UN hostages to stop NATO air strikes. After an air raid on a Bosnian Serb artillery position that was shelling Gorazde in April 1994, the Serbs took 200 UN hostages. As they expected, the UN suspended NATO air strikes. In November, NATO leaders convinced Boutros-Ghali to approve the largest alliance air raid yet against an airfield at Udbina, Croatia, from which Serb aircraft raided Bosnia. The Secretary-General sharply limited the targets that could be hit. Even so, the Serbs again seized UN hostages, and again the United Nations halted NATO air raids. In May 1995, the United Nations allowed NATO to strike a Serb ammunition depot at Pale near Sarajevo, but the Serbs took 370 UN hostages in retaliation, and the United Nations vetoed further NATO air strikes. To NATO's predominantly U.S. air commanders, such action apparently rewarded the Serbs for taking hostages, but then the United States had no troops on the ground in Bosnia to be taken hostage.

The next month, the emboldened Serbs shot down a USAF fighter, an F–16 flown by Capt. Scott O'Grady. He and Capt. Wright, who had shot down three Serb aircraft the previous year, were patrolling the skies near Udbina when the Serbs fired surface-to-air missiles at them. O'Grady was rescued a week later, but the Serbs had demonstrated their ability to down American fighter aircraft, which encouraged their further aggression.

In July, the Bosnian Serbs attacked the two UN safe areas of Srebrenica and Zepa. NATO requested air strikes, but UN approval came too late to prevent the fall of the cities. The conquerors killed thousands of Moslem men and expelled tens of thousands of refugees in an "ethnic cleansing" campaign to clear the area for Serb domination. The loss of one-third of the safe areas, and the genocide that followed, embarrassed both the United Nations and NATO. They appeared to be powerless in the face of Serb aggression, and participants in DENY FLIGHT realized it was time to either pull out or intensify the operation.

At meetings in July, NATO members decided to draw the line at Goradze, the most threatened of the four remaining safe areas. They warned that a Bosnian Serb attack on the city would result in the most severe retaliatory air strikes the war had yet known. NATO leaders persuaded Boutros-Ghali to let the UN Protection Force military commander, French Gen. Bernard Janvier, have the United Nations veto on NATO air strikes. In early August, the North Atlantic Council extended the Goradze ultimatum to the other safe areas, including Sarajevo. By mid-month, General Ryan briefed Admiral Smith and General Javier on a bold new air campaign plan, and before the end of the month, NATO was ready to launch an accelerated phase of DENY FLIGHT called Operation DELIBERATE FORCE.

To prevent the Serbs from taking hostages again and short-circuiting the air campaign, the UN force moved its personnel from vulnerable areas and accepted reinforcement from a new

Rapid Reaction Force composed of thousands of fresh combat troops from Britain, France, and the Netherlands. In an operation called QUICK LIFT in July and August, American cargo airplanes transported most of these troops from northwestern Europe to Split, Croatia, from which they moved overland into Bosnia's surviving safe areas.

Operation DELIBERATE FORCE began on August 30, 1995 shortly after a Bosnian Serb mortar attack on Sarajevo that killed thirty-seven and wounded eighty. As promised, the air campaign came swiftly and decisively, targeting Serb positions not just around Sarajevo and Gorazde but also all across Bosnia. According to General Ryan's plan, enemy air defenses were destroyed so that NATO aircraft could roam across the country at will. For the first time in airpower history, precision-guided munitions outweighed conventional bombs and missiles in a campaign. The air strikes ceased for a few days in early September to allow negotiations, but when the talks did not produce immediate Serb compliance with UN and NATO conditions, the remarkably accurate raids resumed until the Serbs signaled agreement on September 14. DELIBERATE FORCE participants stood ready to resume the intense air raids, but the Serbs showed evidence of compliance, and the operation officially ended on September 21.

Air power was only one reason for the Serb change of heart. In early August, a Croatian offensive lifted the siege of Bihac and drove as many as 200,000 Serbs from Croatia. In September, a combined Bosnian-Croatian offensive wrested huge regions of Bosnia from the Serbs. No doubt the DELIBERATE FORCE air strikes had helped cripple Mladic's military machine. By the time the operation ended, the Serbs were more willing to discuss a peace plan that gave them only 49 percent of Bosnia, because that was about all they had left. The Serbs also realized that they could no longer count on support from Belgrade. Milosevic encouraged Karadzic to come to terms so that UN sanctions against Yugoslavia (Serbia) would be lifted. In November, peace talks among the presidents of Bosnia, Croatia, and Serbia at Wright-Patterson AFB in Ohio produced an agreement to end the war in Bosnia. In December, as the peace accords were formally signed in Paris, Operation DENY FLIGHT ended, replaced by a new operation called JOINT ENDEAVOR to implement the agreements. The air aspect received the code name Operation DECISIVE ENDEAVOR.

Several strategic lessons emerged from the DENY FLIGHT experience. There was no precedent for a peace enforcement operation that demanded the cooperation of two international organizations, the United Nations and NATO. The lack of doctrine created inevitable friction, as the United States and NATO pressured the United Nations for permission to retaliate against the Bosnian Serbs while the United Nations sought to preserve impartiality in the Bosnian civil war and to protect its peacekeepers on the ground. The fall of Srebrenica and Zepa in July 1995 largely eliminated this conflict in goals and persuaded the United Nations to approve a more aggressive air campaign. The DELIBERATE FORCE phase of DENY FLIGHT worked better than earlier phases partly because restrictions were eased but also because the tide was turning on the ground. Conversely, Bosnian/Croatian ground offensives succeeded in part because air strikes crippled Serbian military forces.

The loss of Captain O'Grady's aircraft to enemy fire also taught some valuable tactical lessons. The U.S. Air Force learned to devote more attention to the suppression of enemy air defenses and react more sensitively to possible surface-to-air missile threats. It worked to improve communication between surveillance and combat aircrews and to reduce the vulnerability of combat air patrols by decreasing the predictability of flight patterns.

DENY FLIGHT taught some coalition and interservice lessons. Both the 5th Allied Tactical Air Force and the Combined Air Operations Center at first lacked enough high-level officers for this size operation, and NATO countries were reluctant to provide them. The objective wing concept produced personnel shortages, especially at the planning level. Internationally, France moved closer to resuming the full association with NATO she had rejected three decades earlier, and Germany deployed troops beyond its borders for the first time since World War II. Italy refused to allow the basing of F–117 stealth fighters at Aviano, and both Italy and France prohibited security police to carry weapons on their bases.

There were also technological lessons. The Combined Air Operations Center, 5th Allied Tactical Air Force headquarters, and the Allied Air Forces Southern Europe headquarters at first lacked the electronic and communications equipment needed for an intense air campaign across the Adriatic. The United States solved this problem by sending computer equipment, software, and skilled temporary-duty people for the successful DELIBERATE FORCE phase. The U.S. Air Force deployed a Contingency Theater Air Planning System at Vicenza and a new computer simulation system at Aviano that allowed aircrews to view the routes of future missions in three dimensions. DELIBERATE FORCE also demonstrated that precision-guided munitions produced enormous savings in lives, property, money, sorties, and aircraft. The Air Force successfully married the precision weapons with fighter-aircraft types that had never used them before in combat.

DENY FLIGHT taught air campaign planners to prepare bases large enough to accept contingency surges. NATO based as many as 140 aircraft at a time at Aviano, which normally accommodated 42. There was not enough ramp space. Living space was also a problem at Aviano, where as many as 2,400 personnel deployed at a time. The building of a tent city and the use of distant lodging provided a temporary solution. Fortunately, enough war materiel could be mustered from leftover Cold War stocks in Europe to furnish most of the needs of the primary DENY FLIGHT bases. Future contingency operations may not be as fortunate. DENY FLIGHT not only limited the Bosnian civil war, but also contributed, as much as any other factor, to its conclusion. It demonstrated the enormous potential of air power as a diplomatic instrument for the United Nations, NATO, and the United States.

Crisis in Haiti: Operation UPHOLD DEMOCRACY

William J. Allen

OPERATION DATES: September 9–October 12, 1994

LOCATION: Haiti

OVERSEAS BASES USED: Port-au-Prince International Airport, Cap Haitien Airport, Haiti; Roosevelt Roads Naval Air Station (NAS), Puerto Rico; Guantanamo Bay NAS, Cuba

AIR FORCE ORGANIZATIONS:

WINGS:	WINGS: (con't.)
4th Wing	314th Airlift
6th Air Base	355th Wing
7th Wing	436th Airlift
9th Reconnaissance	438th Airlift
16th Special Operations	552d Air Control
20th Fighter	
23d Wing	**GROUPS:**
33d Fighter	193d Special Operations
55th Wing	145th Airlift

AIR FORCE AIRCRAFT: C–130, AC–130, A/OA–10, E–3, EC–130, RC–135, EC–135, U–2, F–15, C–141, C–5, KC–135, KC–10

Operations

On September 18, 1994, U.S. President William J. Clinton signed the order that launched U.S. sea and air forces to the island nation of Haiti. Under the name Operation UPHOLD DEMOCRACY, the United States used its military forces to return democracy and the Haitian exiled president to a country whose people suffered under military dictatorship and corrupt government. USAF participation effectively ended October 12, when resupply of U.S. forces became routinely scheduled airlift missions and deployed aircraft and crews returned home. Three days later, Haitian President Jean-Bertrand Aristide and his entourage went back to Haiti in triumph, flying from Andrews Air Force Base (AFB), Maryland, aboard a USAF C–137 and a C–9.

Aristide, a leftist Roman Catholic priest, had been elected in December 1990 in a landslide victory as president of Haiti. He took office on February 7, 1991. He appointed as commander in chief of the Haitian armed forces Lt. Gen. Raoul Cedras, who on September 30, 1991 engineered a military coup that forced Aristide from power. With Cedras' regime came social and economic despair for most Haitians. Many attempted to find a better life in the United States by crossing the Atlantic Ocean by boat some 700 miles to Florida.

By January 1992, the number of Haitians the U.S. Coast Guard picked up at sea reached 14,000. The increasing flood of Haitians forced U.S. President George H. W. Bush to order those not eligible for political asylum returned directly to their home country. By May 1992, he had ordered the U.S. Coast Guard to repatriate all Haitian boat people without allowing them to apply for asylum. The flow of refugees slowed to a trickle.

On July 3, 1993, General Cedras and exiled President Aristide signed the Governor's Island Accord, which provided for Aristide's return by October 30, 1993. This agreement also called for the retirement of Cedras and other military leaders and the lifting of sanctions imposed by the United Nations and Organization of American States against Haiti. However, General Cedras ignored the agreement, and the flood of refugees began anew. By July 1994, thousands of refugees overwhelmed U.S. ability to send them back to Haiti. The United States detained the refugees at Guantanamo U.S. Naval Base, Cuba, and in other Caribbean countries. However, the situation in Haiti rapidly deteriorated until on September 8, 1994, when U.S. national leaders determined to intervene militarily.

The U.S. Atlantic Command (USACOM) developed Operation UPHOLD DEMOCRACY in two different plans, one a forcible entry and the other a passive entry plan. The first optioned for an airdrop of the U.S. Army's 82d Airborne Division, marshaled at Pope AFB, North Carolina, and special operations forces into Haiti's capital, Port-au-Prince, and other strategic drop zones. Initially, it called for sixty C–130 aircraft for the airdrop of heavy equipment and paratroopers at the International Airport in Port-au-Prince. Near the cities of Mirebalais,

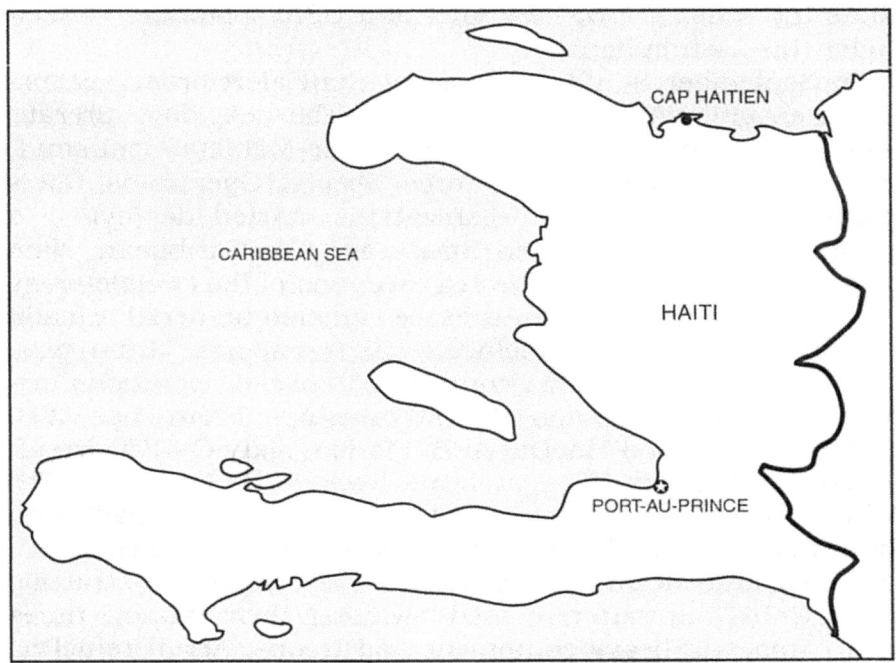

Haiti, Site of Operation UPHOLD DEMOCRACY

thirty miles northeast of Port-au-Prince, and Miragoane, fifty miles west of Port-au-Prince, forty-five C–141 aircraft would air-drop heavy equipment and paratroopers. Eight more C–141s would land troops at the International Airport in the capital city. Special operations teams required an additional seven C–141s to air-drop them into Port-au-Prince.

In the permissive-entry plan, if the Cedras government agreed to relinquish power peacefully, the U.S. Army's 10th Mountain Division from Fort Drum, New York, would land in Haiti by sea and airlift. The U.S. Air Force planned to airlift members of the 10th to Port-au-Prince and Cap Haitien, on the northern coast of Haiti. Further, armed forces from Jamaica, Trinidad, Tobago, Barbados, Antigua/Barbuda, Guyana, and Belize would also be airlifted into Haiti as part of the U.S.-led multinational force. USAF planners worked through evolving variations not knowing which of the two plans would be chosen at the last moment. USACOM planners looked to September

20 as the possible invasion date, and USAF planners worked under this assumption.

On September 8, 1994, the Joint Staff alert order authorized prepositioning of mobility forces. The next day, aircraft, crews, and support technicians from Air Mobility Command, Air Combat Command, Air Force Special Operations Command, and other USAF organizations started deploying to staging bases in the United States and the Caribbean. Nine days later, the Joint Staff directed execution of the forcible-entry plan. For the invasion, the Air Force gathered an aerial armada of over 200 aircraft that included 121 transports, 73 tankers, and several command and control and special operations aircraft like E–3 AWACS and AC–130 gunships. From Pope AFB, North Carolina, and MacDill AFB, Florida, sixty C–130 aircraft of the 314th Airlift Wing at Little Rock AFB, Arkansas, 7th Wing at Dyess AFB, Texas, and 23d Wing at Pope, departed on the initial wave on September 19. At Charleston AFB, South Carolina, and McGuire AFB, New Jersey, sixty-one strategic airlift C–141 aircraft remained awaiting their launch times with cargoes of heavy equipment and troops. Aerial refueling aircraft to support the armada came from Robins AFB, Georgia (twenty-eight KC–135s); Homestead AFB, Florida (eleven KC–135s); Roosevelt Roads Naval Air Station, Puerto Rico (nine KC–135s); Seymour Johnson AFB, North Carolina (twelve KC–10s); and Barksdale AFB, Louisiana (thirteen KC–10s).

From the start, the plan proceeded as scheduled, up to and including the launch of the second formation of troop-carrying C–130s. The lead assault wave, forty-six C–130s, consisted of eighteen aircraft loaded with paratroopers and twenty-eight carrying heavy equipment. The second wave of fourteen C–130s only carried paratroopers. All the heavy equipment aircraft left MacDill while the paratroop aircraft departed from Pope. As aircraft of the first wave flew to form up over the Atlantic Ocean, significant problems developed.

Flying from MacDill, the twenty-eight C–130s had good weather, took off as scheduled, formed up, and prepared to link up with the thirty-two aircraft from Pope. However, the C–130s from Pope experienced problems from the start. First, planners only allowed forty-five seconds between aircraft launches. Second,

C–130s staging at MacDill AFB during Operation UPHOLD DEMOCRACY, September 1994.

because of unusually heavy loads, they decided to use 700 feet of flight line, requiring aircraft to taxi to the far end of the runway, turn around, and then take off. This maneuver actually required between seventy and ninety seconds, resulting in excessive time between the first and last takeoffs. Additionally, the first aircraft launched was equipped with the master station-keeping equipment that allowed safe formation flying. With aircraft strung out over more than ten miles, the station-keeping aircraft became completely ineffective. To complicate matters more, Pope launched their aircraft during rain showers, and thunderstorms awaited the crews all along their flight to the south.

These problems created a stressful and uncertain situation for the Pope C–130 crews as they flew toward a rendezvous with the MacDill C–130s. Pope aircrews used speed adjustments to catch up with the lead C–130, an acceptable practice in small formations with minimum spacing but impractical for large formations spread over long distances. After all the C–130s from Pope were airborne and heading south, it was a formation only in name.

With the C–130s on their way to planned objectives, and the C–141s yet to launch, the Joint Staff ordered the invasion halted and the airborne forces to return to their respective launch bases for a twenty-four-hour period. At nearly the last minute, a diplomatic proposal that former U.S. President James (Jimmy) E. Carter offered General Cedras persuaded the junta leader to relinquish his control over Haiti. The unexpected decision caused a mission change from a military invasion to the insertion of a multinational peacekeeping force. When President Clinton and the Joint Staff thought that Cedras intended to cooperate fully, USACOM ordered on September 19 the cancellation of the forcible-entry plan. At the same time, the Joint Chiefs issued the execution order for the permissive-entry plan.

Transition between plans required a twenty-four-hour pause to reposition some aircraft now supporting the new plan. Those already in place for the deployment of the permissive-entry forces took off, carrying several U.S. Army units, and landed at Haitian airports as planned. These U.S. Army units delivered by the air and sea forces functioned as a military police force maintaining the peace. They also assisted in training a new police force for Haiti during the political transition period between the Cedras and Aristide governments.

On September 19, a C–5 carried members of the 436th Airlift Wing's Tactical Airlift Control Element from Dover AFB, Delaware, to Port-au-Prince to establish airlift control, aerial port, and other airfield support for aircraft bringing equipment and troops. Shortly thereafter, ground forces began arriving at Port-au-Prince on commercial and military aircraft. The permissive-entry plan required the deployed strategic airlift forces, C–5s and C–141s, waiting at Dover, McGuire AFB, New Jersey, and Griffiss AFB, New York, to fly to various locations for loading and then to Haiti before returning to their respective deployment bases. These large aircraft flew only to the capital city since no other airfields in Haiti could handle them. By September 26, USACOM had established requirements for twenty-five C–141 and ten C–5 daily inbound flights.

Although over 20,000 troops eventually arrived in Haiti, the initial execution of some portions of the permissive-entry plan was anything but smooth. For example, to move the 10th Mountain Division from its home at Fort Drum to Griffiss AFB, action officers coordinated ground and air transportation times. For its part, the division contracted with local school bus companies to move its troops. However, the troops did not always arrive at Griffiss on time to meet the scheduled aircraft launch. Thus, launch times slipped, resulting in the Tactical Airlift Control Element at Port-au-Prince sometimes not knowing exactly when or what type of aircraft would show up. This created problems when scheduling, unloading, and notifying Army soldiers when to expect arrival of equipment and troops at Port-au-Prince. Further, C–130s and USA helicopters distributing equipment and troops to airfields around the country had no firm scheduling times to pick up loads.

The C–141s, C–5s, and commercial aircraft delivered U.S. and foreign forces to Port-au-Prince, Roosevelt Roads NAS, Puerto Rico, and Guantanamo Bay Naval Air Base, Cuba. At these locations, the C–130s from MacDill AFB that originally supported the forcible-entry plan loaded troops and cargo and airlifted them to various airfields throughout Haiti. Later, on September 26, ten aircraft and crews from the 7th Wing redeployed from MacDill to Roosevelt Roads to conduct airlift operations to Haiti. USACOM also released the remaining MacDill C–130s and crews from participation in the crisis.

By September 30, USAF operations in Haiti became more or less routine as Air Mobility Command added supply airlift missions to point-to-point, or channel, mission scheduling. The airlifters of Operation UPHOLD DEMOCRACY helped deliver the peak military strength of the multinational forces of 20,931 by October 2. On October 10, General Cedras resigned and two days later left the country. After completing the movement of multinational forces from Roosevelt Roads, the remaining C–130s redeployed to their home station by October 12, ending USAF contingency flying operations for UPHOLD DEMOCRACY.

On October 15, 1994, Aristide returned to his country, the benefactor of a strong U.S. response to an oppressive dictator. General Cedras only agreed to leave after tough negotiations and perhaps the realization that he faced an approaching force similar to that of the airborne invasion of Panama in 1989. As in Panama, the Air Force brought to bear an overwhelming force of fighters, command and control aircraft, gunships and other special operations aircraft, reconnaissance airplanes, aerial refueling tankers, and thousands of troops aboard the airlift fleet of strategic and tactical aircraft. The successful adaptation to the last-minute change in mission, from military invasion force to airlifting peacekeeping troops, was a major indicator of the flexibility air power offers U.S. military and political leaders in fulfilling national foreign policy objectives.

Glossary

AAF. Army Airfield
AB. Air Base
AD. Air Division
AEF. Air Expeditionary Force
aeromedical evacuation. The sending of injured or ill patients by specially equipped aircraft from the contingency area to medical facilities, usually stateside, for further treatment. Trained medical personnel accompany patients on such flights.
AFB. Air Force Base
airborne. The capability to accomplish missions by airlift.
airborne alert. Having aircraft in the air, ready to undertake its mission.
Air Component Commander. The commander under the Joint Commander with responsibility for command and control of air assets in the theater of operations.
air-drop. To drop troops or materiel by parachute from aircraft in flight.
airland. To land troops or materiel by aircraft, as distinguished from air drop.
airlift. To transport personnel or cargo by aircraft.
alert. A state of readiness against impending danger or for immediate action.
ALCE. airlift control elements
ALTF. Airlift Task Force
AMC. Air Mobility Command
ANG. Air National Guard
ARRS. Aerospace Rescue and Recovery Service
AS. Airlift Squadron
AW. Air Wing
AWACS. airborne warning and control system

beddown. To survey and install at a base the facilities and other resources necessary to maintain and operate an aircraft system.

CALSU. Combat Airlift Support Unit
CASF. Composite Air Strike Force
CENTAF. Central Command Air Force. Air Force component of the U.S. Central Command.
CIA. Central Intelligence Agency
CINCCENT. Commander in Chief, Central Command
CINCPAC. Commander in Chief, Pacific Command
CINCPACFLT. Commander in Chief, Pacific Fleet
Cold War. The forty-year confrontation between the Union of Soviet Socialist Republics (USSR or Soviet Union) and the United States and its allies.
COMMIDEASTFOR. Commander, Middle East Forces
COMNAVCENT. Commander, Naval Forces, Central Command
Component Commander. In a joint force, the commander of a particular service component (e.g., the Air Component Commander). The Component Commander is subject to the commanding authority of the Joint Commander.
CONAD. Continental Air Defense Command

DAO. Defense Attaché Office
deploy. To send personnel, units, and aircraft to another location to accomplish a mission.
DOD. Department of Defense

FIS. Fighter-Interceptor Squadron

Group. The lowest headquarters organization of the U.S. Air Force, with squadrons and flights usually assigned to the headquarters.
GPS. Global Positioning System

IAF. Indian Air Force
IAPF. Inter-American Peace Force
ICBM. intercontinental ballistic missile
IRBM. intermediate-range ballistic missile

Joint Commander. The single commander authorized to exercise command authority or operational control over a joint force.

joint force. A military force made up of elements from two or more U.S. armed services and usually operating under a single Joint Commander.

joint operations. Military activities by a joint force.

Khmer Rouge. Communist rebel forces fighting against the legitimate government of Cambodia.

LAW. light antitank weapon

MAC. Military Airlift Command, predecessor of AMC
MATS. Military Air Transport Service, predecessor of MAC
MRBM. medium-range ballistic missile

NAS. Naval Air Station
NATO. North Atlantic Treaty Organization
no-fly zone. An area in which aircraft, usually military, are forbidden to fly. It is a type of exclusion zone, defined in doctrine as a zone established by a sanctioning body to prohibit specific activities in a specific geographic area. The purpose may be to persuade nations or groups to modify behavior to meet the desires of the sanctioning body. The sanctioning body may grant permission for specific flights (e.g., by aircraft of nations belonging to it).

OAS. Organization of American States
OECS. Organization of Eastern Caribbean States

PDF. Panamanian Defense Force
peace enforcement. Application of military force, or the threat of its use, normally pursuant to international authorization, to compel compliance with resolutions or sanctions designed to maintain or restore peace and order (Joint Publication 1-02, *DOD Dictionary of Military and Associated Terms*).
peacekeeping. Military operations undertaken with the consent of all major parties to a dispute, designed to monitor and facilitate implementation of an agreement (cease-fire, truce, or

other such agreement) and support diplomatic efforts to reach a long-term political settlement (Joint Publication 1-02).

peacemaking. Military operations intended to ameliorate suffering and facilitate a cease-fire and political settlement.

peace operations. A broad term that encompasses peacekeeping operations and peace enforcement operations conducted in support of diplomatic efforts to establish and maintain peace (Joint Publication 1-02).

PRIME BEEF. Base Engineer Emergency Force. A unit capable of deploying immediately to provide essential civil engineering support to a forward base and forces using that base.

rig. To prepare an aircraft's cargo for transport.
RAF. Royal Air Force
RSAF. Royal Saudi Air Force
RTAFB. Royal Thai Air Force Base

SAM. surface-to-air missile
SAC. Strategic Air Command
SEALs. sea, air, land. U.S. Navy special operations unit.
SECDEF. Secretary of Defense
sortie. A single flight by a single aircraft to accomplish a given mission.
SOW. Special Operations Wing
stage. Refers to use of an intermediate base between the origin and destination of the aircraft in order to refuel, perform maintenance, or rearm.
Squadron. A constituted and organized unit of the U.S. Air Force with no subordinate units assigned.

TAC. Tactical Air Command
TCW. Troop Carrier Wing
TFW. Tactical Fighter Wing
TRIADS. Tri-Wall Aerial Delivery System
TRW. Tactical Reconnaissance Wing

UHF. ultra-high frequency
UK. United Kingdom
UN. United Nations

unified command. A joint command made up of components of each armed service and responsible for command and control of military operations in a specific geographical area; for example, USEUCOM.

UNPROFOR. United Nations Protection Force

USA. United States Army

USACOM. United States Atlantic Command. The unified command responsible for contingency operations in the Atlantic Ocean, the Caribbean Sea, and the Gulf of Mexico. (USACOM lost responsibility for the Caribbean and the Gulf to USSOUTHCOM in June 1997.)

USAF. United States Air Force

USAFE. United States Air Forces in Europe

USCENTCOM. United States Central Command. The unified command responsible for contingency operations in East Africa and Southwest Asia.

USEUCOM. United States European Command. The unified command responsible for contingency operations in Europe and most of Africa.

USMC. United States Marine Corps

USN. United States Navy

USPACOM. United States Pacific Command. The unified command responsible for contingency operations in the Pacific Ocean, Far East, South Asia, and Indian Ocean regions.

USS. United States ship. A prefix to the name of a Navy vessel.

USSOUTHCOM. United States Southern Command. The unified command responsible for contingency operations in Central and South America. (Since June 1997, USSOUTHCOM has included the Caribbean Sea and the Gulf of Mexico, formerly part of USACOM.)

Viet Cong. Communist rebel forces fighting against the legitimate government of South Vietnam.

Wing. A headquarters organization of the U.S. Air Force: subordinate units, mostly groups but sometimes squadrons and flights, are assigned to the wing headquarters.

Bibliography

The USAF organizational histories on file at the Air Force Historical Research Agency provided much of the information summarized in the contingencies of this book. Often, these histories included supporting documents that contained primary sources. These unclassified histories, not cited here, are voluminous but may be easily retrieved by a search of the agency's computerized database.

Many recent documents are classified, and the writers could not use this information. They turned instead to current news sources, particularly, *Air Force Times* and the Air Force News Service E-mail bulletins as well as commercial newspapers and newsmagazines. These are readily available to the reader, as well, and database searches will yield the relevant articles.

The following citations should provide ample sources for students, scholars, and others interested in reading in greater depth concerning the contingencies. For most operations, these selections of published government documents, books, and articles provide significant information. All should be readily available from local libraries.

Government Documents

Acree, Cliff M. *The Iranian Hostage Rescue Mission: What Went Wrong?* Norfolk, Va.: Armed Forces Staff College, 1984.

American Force Information Service. *U.S. Forces in Haiti*. CD-ROM. Washington, D.C.: DOD Joint Combat Camera Center, 1995.

Balati, Frank E., Jr. *Military Intervention in Latin America*. Fort Leavenworth, Kans.: U.S. Army Command and General Staff College, 1983.

The Berlin Airlift: A Brief Chronology. Scott AFB, Ill.: Air Mobility Command History Office, May 1997.

Cole, Ronald H. *Operation Urgent Fury*. Washington, D.C.: Joint History Office, 1997.

Des Brisay, Thomas. *Fourteen Hours at Koh Tang*. Washington, D.C.: Office of Air Force History, 1985.

Dolle, Dennis B. *Operation Nickel Grass*. Maxwell AFB, Ala.: Air Command and Staff College, 1987.

The Dominican Republic Crisis of 1965: The Air Force Role. Maxwell AFB, Ala.: Aerospace Studies Institute, December 1966.

Harrington, Daniel F. *"The Air Force Can Deliver Anything!" A History of the Berlin Airlift*. Ramstein AB, Germany: U. S. Air Forces in Europe Office of History, May 1998.

Haulman, Daniel L. *The United States Air Force and Humanitarian Airlift Operations, 1947–1994*. Washington, D.C.: Air Force History and Museums Program, 1998.

Historical Handbook, 1941–1984. Scott AFB, Ill.: Military Airlift Command History Office, 1984.

Joint Military Operations Historical Collection. Washington, D.C.: Joint Chiefs of Staff, 1997.

Koura, Tony. *The Cambodia Airlift, 1974–1975*. Hickam AFB, Hawaii: Office of Pacific Air Forces History, 1976.

Launius, Roger D., and Coy F. Cross II. *MAC and the Legacy of the Berlin Airlift*. Scott AFB, Ill.: Military Airlift Command History Office, April 1989.

Little, Robert D. *Air Operations in the Lebanon Crisis—1958*. Maxwell AFB, Ala.: Air University Historical Liaison Office, 1960.

Mets, David R., ed. *Last Flight from Saigon*. Washington, D.C.: Office of Air Force History, 1985.

Operation Uphold Democracy: Initial Impressions, vol. 1. Fort Leavenworth, Kans.: Center for Army Lessons Learned, July 1995.

Operation Uphold Democracy: Joint After-Action Report (JAAR). Norfolk, Va.: U.S. Atlantic Command, June 1995.

Patchin, Kenneth L. *Flight To Israel: A Historical Documentary of Strategic Airlift to Israel*. Revised. Scott AFB, Ill.: Military Airlift Command Office of History, 1976.

Peterson, Wayne G., et al. *The Fall and Evacuation of Vietnam*. Hickam AFB, Hawaii: Office of Pacific Air Forces History, April 1978.

Rivard, David T. *An Analysis of Operation Urgent Fury*. Maxwell AFB, Ala.: Air Command and Staff College, 1985.

Steele, William M. *The Iranian Hostage Rescue Mission.* Fort McNair, Washington, D.C.: National War College, 1984.

Thomas, Charles S. *The Iranian Hostage Rescue Attempt.* Carlisle Barracks, Pa.: U.S. Army War College, 1987.

Tustin, Joseph P. *USAFE Humanitarian Missions, 1945–1962.* Ramstein AFB, Germany: U.S. Air Forces in Europe History Office, 1963.

Vien, Cao Van. *The Final Collapse.* Washington, D.C.: U.S. Army Center of Military History, 1983.

Willeford, Hugh B. *Airlift in Grenada.* Maxwell AFB, Ala.: Air Command and Staff College, 1988.

Yates, Lawrence A. *Power Pack: U.S. Intervention in the Dominican Republic, 1965–1966.* Fort Leavenworth, Kans.: Combat Studies Institute, U.S. Army Command and General Staff College, 1988.

Books

Ambrose, Stephen E. *Rise to Globalism, American Foreign Policy Since 1938.* New York: Penguin Books, 1991.

Beckwith, Charlie A. *Delta Force.* New York: Harcourt Brace Jovanovich, 1983.

Bolger, Daniel P. *Americans at War, 1975–1986: An Era of Violent Peace.* Novato, Calif.: Presidio Press, 1988.

Bowers, Ray L. *Tactical Airlift.* Washington, D.C.: Office of Air Force History, 1983.

Cantwell, Gerald T. *Citizen Airmen.* Washington, D.C.: Air Force History and Museums Program, 1997.

Clay, Lucius D. *Decision in Germany.* New York: Doubleday, 1950.

Colvin, Ian. The Rise and Fall of Moise Tshombe. London: Leslie Frewin, 1968.

Davis, Brian L. *Qaddafi, Terrorism, and the Origins of the U.S. Attack on Libya.* New York: Praeger, 1990.

Dougan, Clark, et al. *The Fall of the South.* Boston, Mass.: Boston Publishing Co., 1985.

Futrell, Robert Frank. *Ideas, Concepts, Doctrine: Basic Thinking in the United States Air Force,* vol. 1, 1907–1960, and vol. 2, 1961–1984. Maxwell AFB, Ala.: Air University Press, 1989.

Guilmartin, John F. *A Very Short War: The Mayaguez and the Battle of Koh Tang.* College Station, Tex.: Texas A&M Press, 1995.

Miller, Roger G. *To Save a City: The Berlin Airlift, 1948–1949.* Washington, D.C.: Air Force History and Museums Program, 1998.

Nalty, Bernard C., ed. *Winged Shield, Winged Sword: A History of the United States Air Force*, vol. 2, 1950–1997. Washington, D.C.: Air Force History and Museums Program, 1997.

Palmer, Bruce, Jr. *Intervention in the Caribbean: The Dominican Crisis of 1965.* Lexington, Ky.: The University Press of Kentucky, 1989.

Perusse, Roland I. *Haitian Democracy Restored, 1991–1995.* New York: University Press of America, 1995.

Powell, Colin L. *My American Journey.* New York: Random House, 1995.

Rowan, Roy. *The Four Days of the Mayaguez.* New York: W. W. Norton and Co., 1975.

el-Sadat, Anwar. *In Search of Identity.* New York: Harper & Row, 1977.

Schoonmaker, Herbert G. *Military Crisis Management: U.S. Intervention in the Dominican Republic, 1965.* New York: Greenwood Press, 1990.

Stanik, Joseph T. *"Swift and Effective Retribution": The U.S. Sixth Fleet and the Confrontation with Qaddafi.* Washington, D.C.: Naval Historical Center, 1996.

Tunner, William H. *Over the Hump.* Washington, D.C.: Office of Air Force History, 1985.

Venkus, Robert E. *Raid on Qaddafi: The Untold Story of History's Longest Fighter Mission by the Pilot Who Directed It.* New York: St. Martin's Press, 1992.

Wragg, David W. *Airlift: A History of Military Air Transport.* Novato, Calif.: Presidio Press, 1986.

Articles

"Africa: The Congo Massacre." *Time* 84 (December 4, 1964): 28–31.

Barela, Timothy P. "Calm Before the Storm." *Airman* 39 (October 1995): 2–9.

"The Congo: Killing Ground." *Newsweek* 64 (December 7, 1964): 47–48.

"Countering the Communists." *Time* 111 (June 5, 1978): 26–30.

Covello, Art. "Destination Zaire." *The Air Reservist* 30 (July 1978): 23.

"Curbing Saddam's Military Adventures." *Defense Issues* 11 (1996): 1–4.

Dare, James A. "Dominican Diary." *US Naval Institute Proceedings* 91 (December 1965): 36–45.

Davis, James L. "Building a Bridge for Hope." *Mobility Forum* 2 (May–June 1993): 38–39.

Freeman, Waldo D., et al. "Operation Restore Hope: A USCENTCOM Perspective." *Military Review* 73 (September 1993): 61–72.

Fulghum, David A. "Massed Airborne Forces Aimed at Heart of Haiti." *Aviation Week & Space Technology* 141 (October 10, 1994): 71–72.

Fursdon, Edward. "Operation Deny Flight." *Army Quarterly and Defence Journal* 125 (January 1995): 15–19.

"Germany to Zaire with a 'Fair Force' Reserve Pilot." *The Officer* 54 (August 1978): 12.

"Inside Kolwezi: Toll of Terror." *Time* 111 (June 5, 1978): 32–34, 36.

Kitfield, James. "Restoring Hope." *Government Executive* 25 (February 1993): 20–33.

Launius, Roger D. "The Berlin Airlift: Constructive Air Power." *Air Power History* 36 (Spring 1989): 9–22.

———. "The Berlin Airlift: Refining the Air Transport Function, 1948–1949." *Airlift* 10 (Summer 1988): 10–17.

———. "Lessons Learned, Berlin Airlift." *Air Power History* 36 (Spring 1989): 23.

"Massacre in the Congo: Story of a Rescue Attempt." *U.S. News and World Report* 57 (December 7, 1964): 41–43.

"NATO Aircraft Strike Targets in Bosnia." *Airman* 39 (October 1995): 10.

"NATO Airlift Deficiencies Seen in Zaire Evacuation." *Aviation Week* 108 (May 29, 1978): 22.

"New Threat to Bosnia Talks." *Jane's Defence Weekly* 24 (September 23, 1995): 3.

Ofcansky, Thomas. "Chaos in the Congo." *Airman* 27 (August 1983): 13–16.

———. "Congo Airlift, 1960–1964." *Airlift* 5 (Summer 1983): 22–25.

Owen, Robert C. "The Balkans Air Campaign Study: Part 1." *Airpower Journal* 11 (Summer 1997): 4–24.

Ramos, Francisco J. "The United Nations and the Congo Crisis." *Military Review* 45 (November 1965): 50–57.

Rogers, Marc. "NATO Begins to Assess Air Strike Damage As Peace in Bosnia Nears." *Jane's Defence Weekly* 24 (November 11, 1995): 19.

"Reservists in Crises." *Air Reservist* 17 (July 1995): 4–7.

"The Shaba Tigers Return." *Time* 111 (May 29, 1978): 28–30.

"Special Study of Operation VITTLES." *Aviation Operations Magazine* 11 (April 1949).

"United States Cooperates with Belgium in Rescue of Hostages from the Congo." *Department of State Bulletin* 51 (December 14, 1964): 838–48.

Viccellio, Henry. "The Composite Air Strike Force, 1958." *Air University Quarterly Review* 11 (Summer 1959): 3–17.

Watkins, Tarleton H. "Operation New Tape: The Congo Airlift." *Air University Quarterly Review* 13 (Summer 1961): 18–33.

Wyllie, James. "Saddam's Prospects." *Jane's Intelligence Review* 8 (November 1996): 504–505.

Yuen-Gi Yee. "Bridge to Berlin." *Airman* 28 (May 1984): 43–48.

Contributors

William J. Allen, presently Chief Historian, 37th Training Wing, Lackland AFB, Texas, was a historian at the Air Force Historical Research Agency, Maxwell AFB, Alabama, from 1996 through 1998. He earned a Bachelor of Science degree in history from Troy State University at Montgomery, Alabama, in 1998. Mr. Allen joined the Air Force in 1975 and worked as an administrative specialist until retraining as a historian in April 1987. As a wing historian, in 1991–92 he served in Operation DESERT STORM at Masirah Island, Oman, and Kuwait City. Subsequently, he deployed to Haiti for Operation UPHOLD DEMOCRACY in 1994 and to Southwest Asia for Operation SOUTHERN WATCH in 1995. During eleven years as an enlisted historian, Sergeant Allen wrote twenty-seven unit histories and six special studies, earning awards for Twenty-Second Air Force Historian of the Year in 1988 and 1989; Air Force Historical Program of the Year in 1992; Air Force Special Study of the Year in 1992; Pacific Air Forces Special Study of the Year in 1993; Air Combat Command Historical Publication of the Year in 1995; and the Air Force Historian's Special Achievement Award in 1996. He retired in June 1996 from active duty after over twenty-one years of service.

MSgt. David A. Byrd is assigned to the Archives Branch of the Air Force Historical Research Agency at Maxwell AFB, Alabama. He also has served as historian for the Ballistic Missile Office, Rome Laboratory, and the 354th Fighter Wing. In 1995, he deployed in support of Operation PROVIDE COMFORT. Sergeant Byrd holds a Bachelor of Arts degree in history from Utica College of Syracuse University. He has authored numerous studies and papers since joining the Air Force history program, including *Rail Based Missiles from Atlas to Peacekeeper* and *Forty Years of Research and Development at Griffiss AFB*, plus an award-winning study of Operation PROVIDE COMFORT Combined Task Force actions following the 1994 Blackhawk helicopter shootdown.

Judy G. Endicott is a historian in the Research Division of the Air Force Historical Research Agency, Maxwell AFB, Alabama. She holds a bachelor's and a master's degree in history from Pittsburg State University, Pittsburg, Kansas. Ms. Endicott initially began working at AFHRA as an archivist in 1969, six years later becoming the Chief of Circulation and Deputy Archives Division Chief. She was promoted in 1984, becoming a historian and Deputy Chief of the Organizational History Branch. The USAF expert in Lineage and Honors History, Ms. Endicott is the editor of two recent on-line publications on lineage of Air Force organizations and units. The publications are *Active Air Force Wings as of 1 October 1995* and *USAF Active Flying, Space, and Missile Squadrons as of 1 October 1995*.

Daniel L. Haulman is a historian in the Research Division at the Air Force Historical Research Agency, Maxwell AFB, Alabama. He holds a Bachelor of Arts from the University of Southwestern Louisiana and a master's degree from the University of New Orleans. After teaching high school social studies for five years, he earned his PhD in history from Auburn University, Alabama, in 1983. Dr. Haulman first began working at AFHRA as an archivist in 1982. The next year, he became a technical information specialist, then in 1985, he was promoted to a historian position. He is the author of two books, *The United States Air Force and Humanitarian Airlift Operations, 1947–1994* and *Air Force Aerial Victory Credits: World War I, World War II, Korea, and Vietnam*. His other publications include three USAF pamphlets: *The High Road to Tokyo Bay; Hitting Home: The Air Offensive Against Japan;* and *Wings of Hope: The U.S. Air Force and Humanitarian Airlift Operations*. He has written six articles and presented papers at seven historical conferences.

Edward T. Russell is a historian in the Research Division of the Air Force Historical Research Agency, Maxwell AFB, Alabama. He holds a bachelor's degree from Huntingdon College, Montgomery, Alabama, and a master's degree from Troy State University, Troy, Alabama. He has done postgraduate work at Auburn University of Montgomery and the University of

Alabama. He taught in the public school system and as an adjunct at local universities. In 1972, he began working at AFHRA as a technical information specialist; ten years later he moved to the Research Division as a historian. He coauthored a textbook entitled *Minorities in American History*, compiled the *Research Guide to the Published Project CHECO Reports*, and revised *The Organization and Lineage of the United States Air Force*. He also is the author of *Leaping the Atlantic Wall: Army Air Forces Campaigns in Western Europe, 1942–1945* and coauthor of *Africa to the Alps: The Army Air Forces in the Mediterranean Theater*, both commemorative pamphlets published by the Air Force History and Museum Program.

Frederick J. Shaw Jr. is currently Chief of the Research Division, Air Force Historical Research Agency, Maxwell AFB, Alabama. After receiving a PhD in history from the University of Florida in 1976, Dr. Shaw worked as historian at the Strategic Air Command Office of History, specializing in ballistic missiles and budgeting. He moved to AFHRA in 1986 and assumed his present position two years later. He has authored monographs on the development of the mobile and Peacekeeper ICBMs and also coedited *The Cold War and Beyond: Chronology of the United States Air Force, 1947–1997*.

A. Timothy Warnock is Chief, Organizational History Branch, Air Force Historical Research Agency, Maxwell AFB, Alabama. He holds three degrees—a bachelor's, a master's, and a PhD—from the University of Georgia. He taught at Georgia Southern College, Statesboro; the Air War College, Maxwell AFB, Alabama; and Auburn University's Maxwell Graduate Program prior to joining the AFHRA as a historian in 1980. In 1991, he was appointed to his present position. Dr. Warnock is the author of the book, *USAF Combat Medals, Streamers, and Campaigns* and two World War II commemorative pamphlets: *The Battle Against the U-Boat in the American Theater* and *Air Power versus U-boats: Confronting Hitler's Submarine Menace in the European Theater*. He has written several articles and professional papers. He is also coeditor of *The Cold War and Beyond: Chronology of the United States Air Force, 1947–1997*.

Index

Accra, Ghana: 25
Acheson, Dean: 38
Adams, Paul D.: 49
Adana, Turkey: 13–15, 17–18, 20, 181, 187. *See also* Incirlik
Addis Ababa, Ethiopia: 213
Adoula, Cyrille: 27, 53–54
Adriatic Sea: 222, 228
Aerospace Rescue and Recovery Service (ARRS): xxv, 126–27
Africa: 24–32, 43, 60–61, 78, 117–24, 136, 187, 216
African: 116, 120, 122, 145
  troops: xxiv, 55, 120, 123
Agadir, Morocco: 117
Agidjan, Ivory Coast: 117
Agra, India: 47
Aidid, Mohammed Farah: 215
Air America: 90–91
Airborne Warning and Control System (AWACS): xxvii, 138, 160, 162, 164–65, 174, 194, 232
Air Combat Command: 191, 232
Aircraft
  Commercial
    Boeing 707: 47
    Boeing 747: 127
    DC–8: 98–99, 102
    L–1011: 170
    UH–1: 90–91
    World Airways 727: 85
  Foreign
    AN–12: 50
    C–160 Transail: 118, 206
    F–5: 160
    IL–28: xx, 35–36
    IL–76 Candid: 149, 153–54
    MiG–21: 75
    MiG–23: 149, 154
    MiG–25 Foxbat: 184, 192
    MIG–29: 184
  U.S. Air Force
    Airlifters
      C–5 Galaxy: xxii–xxiii, 78, 80–81, 86, 114, 118–20, 123, 125–26, 139, 141–42, 161, 170–72, 175, 181, 184, 200–201, 205, 213, 216–18, 234–35
      C–9 Nightingale: 141, 201, 230
      C–17 Globemaster III: 142, 206–7, 218
      C–47: xvii, 3–4, 8, 50, 70
        VC–47: 49
      C–54 Skymaster: xviii, 4, 6–8
      C–74 Globemaster: 6, 8
      C–82 Packet: 8

C-97 Stratofreighter: 8, 70
C-119: xix, 14, 50
C-123: xviii, 70, 96
C-124 Globemaster II: xviii–xix, 8, 13–14, 19–20, 24–32, 37, 45, 65, 67, 69
C-130 Hercules: xviii–xix, xxi–xxii, xxiv, 14, 16, 19–20, 24–27, 29, 45–47, 49–51, 57–59, 61, 65–67, 70–72, 88–92, 96–99, 102, 111, 117–19, 121, 129, 131, 133, 138–39, 141–43, 172, 175–77, 180, 182, 184, 198–202, 204–8, 210, 212, 214, 218, 224, 232–35
   AC-130: xxv, 91, 101, 107, 110, 114, 138–40, 143, 176–77, 216, 232
   EC-130: xxiv, 101, 103, 112, 129, 132–33, 141
   HC-130: 103, 111, 126, 176
   MC-130: 128–29, 131–33, 138–39, 176–77
C-133: 32, 37
C-135 Stratolifter: xix, 28–29, 32, 37, 45
   EC-135: 66, 70, 194
C-141 Starlifter: xxiii–xxiv, 32, 78, 80–81, 88–90, 92, 99, 108, 114, 117–20, 122–23, 125–27, 131, 139, 141–42, 161, 170–76, 181, 184, 201–2, 204–7, 210, 213, 216–18, 224, 231–32, 234–35
U-10: 70

Bombers
  B-1: xxiv
  B-29: 7
  B-47: 37, 39
  B-52: 37–39, 185, 194
  B-57: 15, 17–18, 20–21

Fighters
  F-4: 80, 91, 101, 107, 110, 114
    F-4G Wild Weasel: 192
  F-15: 138, 160, 174, 185, 194
  F-16: 184–85, 191, 193, 224–25
  F-84: 37
  F-86: 17–18, 20
  F-100 Super Sabre: 15–21, 37, 69
  F-101: 40
  F-102: 40
  F-104: 69
  F-105: 37
  F-106: 40
  F-111 Aardvark: xxv, 107, 149–55
    EF-111 Raven: 150–52, 154, 174
  F-117 Nighthawk: 176, 194, 227

Helicopters
  CH-53 Knife: 91, 100–101, 103, 108, 112
  HH-53 Super Jolly Green Giant: 91, 99–101, 103, 108, 111, 126
  MH-53J: 176
  MH-60: 176

Reconnaissance
  RB-47: 38
  RB-66: 15, 17, 19, 34, 37, 69
  RF-4: 101
  RF-101: 15, 17, 20, 34, 69

INDEX

    U-2: 34, 37-38
    WB-66: 15, 17, 19
  Tankers
    KB-50: xix, 16-17, 37
    KC-10 Extender: xxiii, xxv, 81, 141, 151, 160-64, 174, 184, 213, 216, 218, 232
    KC-135 Stratotanker: xxiii, xxv, 81, 91, 101, 111, 141, 151, 160, 162-64, 174, 213-14, 216, 232
  Other
    A-7: 91, 101, 107-111, 113-14
    A-10: 140, 224
    A-37: 90
    E-2: 161
    E-3: 137, 141, 160-62, 164-65, 174, 185, 187, 194, 232
    OV-10 Bronco: 101, 110-11, 113
 U.S. Army
  UH-60 Black Hawk: 185
 U.S. Navy
  A-6 Intruder: 154, 161, 165-66
  A-7: 153
  EA-6B Prowler: 146, 150, 253, 193
  F/A-18: 153, 161
  F-14: 146
  P-3: 164
  R5D: 7
  RH-53: 129, 132-33
 U.S. Marine Corps
  CH-46: 90
  CH-53 Sea Stallion: 90, 99-100
Air Defense Command: 69
Air Expeditionary Force (AEF): xxix, 11, 21, 73, 193
Air Force (numbered)
  Third: 186
  Seventh: 89, 99, 107
  Ninth: 68
  Twelfth: 137
  Seventeenth: 200
  Nineteenth: xvii-xviii, 12, 16, 65
  Twenty-First: 77-78, 120, 125, 137, 144
  Twenty-Second: 77, 120, 161
  Twenty-Third: xxv, 171
Air Force Reserve (AFRES): xxiv, 39-40, 72, 120, 142, 199-200, 204, 216
  Reservists: 41, 121, 174
Air Force Special Operations Command: 134, 232
Airlift control element (ALCE): 117, 120-22, 161, 175, 204, 234-35
Airlift Support Unit: 25, 31, 46-47, 49, 65, 67
Airlift Task Force (ALTF): 65-66
Air Materiel Command: 9
Air Mobility Command (AMC): 206, 212, 214, 216-17, 232, 235
Air National Guard (ANG): 70, 73, 141-42, 199-201, 204, 216
Airways and Air Communications System: 7
Akashi, Yasushi: 223-24
Albertville, Democratic Republic of the Congo: 53

Algeria: 60
Allied Air Forces Southern Europe: 221, 228
Ambala, India: 47
American: xxi–xxii, 54–56, 58–61, 64, 77, 79–81, 85–89, 91, 96, 100, 104–5, 107–17, 120, 123, 125–27, 131, 133, 139, 141, 146–48, 154, 157, 159, 165, 172, 180–82, 185–86, 192, 194, 200–201, 208, 215–17, 221–22, 224–26
    forces: 17, 84–85, 96, 154, 217
    Foreign Service: 127
    intelligence: 34, 112
    troops: 121, 123, 181
Ancona, Italy: 204, 206–7
Anders Jr., Loyd J.: 91
Andersen AFB, Guam: 90, 92, 185
Anderson Jr., Rudolf: 34, 38
Andrews AFB, Maryland: 230
Andrus, James: 186
Antalya, Turkey: 187
Arab: 76–77, 79–80, 145
Arab-Israeli conflict: 78
Arabian Sea: 159, 164
Aristide, Jean-Bertrand: 229–30, 234–35
Arkansas: 89, 92, 232
Ascension Island: 57, 59–60
Ashy, Joseph W.: 221
Athens, Greece: 46, 126–27, 147
Atlantic Ocean: 57, 77, 119, 168, 213, 216, 230, 232
Austin, Hudson: 136, 138, 140
Austin, Randall W.: 108–9
Austria: 14, 20, 27
Aviano AB, Italy: 198, 222, 227–28
Avord, France: 120
Azores: 17, 77–79, 127, 213

Bab al-Aziziyah, Tripoli, Libya: 149, 152–53
Baghdad, Iraq: 182, 192, 194
Bahrain: 20, 193
Baidoa, Somalia: 210
Baledogle, Somalia: 214
Bandar Abbas, Iran: 164–65
Barbados: 136, 139, 141–42, 231
Bardera, Somalia: 210
Barksdale AFB, Louisiana: 174, 232
Barrakpore, India: 47
Batman, Turkey: 180
Beirut, Lebanon: 13–14, 19–20, 147
Beledweyne, Somalia: 210
Belen Huen, Somalia: 210
Belgian: 25, 31–32, 55–56, 58–59, 116–20, 123
    commandos: 58
    forces: 57, 120
    paratroops: 57–58
    soldiers: xxi, 57, 120
    troops: xxiv, 57, 59, 118, 120

INDEX

Belgium: xix, xxi, xxiii–xxiv, 57, 59–60, 116–17, 119, 212
Belgrade, Yugoslavia: 226
Benghazi, Libya: 149–50, 154
Berlin, Germany: xvii, 2–8, 10, 33, 37, 97–98, 148
Berlin Airlift: 2, 4, 6, 8–10, 25, 29–32, 102, 201
Berringer, Lynn T.: 151
Bihac, Bosnia: 203, 220, 226
Birdair: 96–99, 102
Bitburg AB, Germany: 222
Bjelimici, Bosnia: 203
Boeing: 47, 127, 163
Bomb
    BLU–82: 111, 113
    GBU–10: 153
    Mark 20 Rockeye Cluster: 165
    Paveways: 153
    Snakeye: 154
Bosnia: xxviii, 102, 187–88, 194, 198, 200–201, 206–7, 220, 222, 224–27
Bosnian civil war: 202, 205, 227–28
Bosnian Serb: 198–200, 202, 205, 220, 223–27. *See also* Serbs
    forces: 203, 205
Bosnian-Croatian: 226
Boutros-Ghali, Boutros: 214, 223–25
Bradley armored vehicles: 216
Brazil: 71
Brazzaville, Congo: 25, 30–31, 53–54
Breker, Craig A.: 202
Bridge of the Americas, Panama: 172
Bridgeton, SS: 161
Brindisi, Italy: 222
British: 5, 17, 19, 51, 55, 60, 148, 182, 208
    Commonwealth: 136
    soldiers: 205
Brussels, Belgium: 117–19
Burns, John J.: 99, 101, 107–12
Burtonwood, England: 6
Bush, George H. W.: xxvi, 158, 170–72, 177, 185, 189, 191–92, 212, 230

Cairo West, Egypt: 213, 216
Cairo, Egypt: 30, 56
Calcutta, India: 45–46
California: 34, 45, 92, 200
Cambodia: 87, 95–99, 102, 104, 106, 114, 144
Cambodian: xxii, 96–107, 111, 113–14
    (Khmer) air force: 96
    Communists: 96
    forces: 114
    government: 109, 112
    soldiers: 109
Canada: 44, 207, 212
Cannon, John K.: 4
Cap Haitien, Haiti: 231
Caribbean: 4, 9, 136, 141, 144, 172, 232
    countries: 230

257

    forces: 141
    states: 141
Caribbean Sea: 64, 136, 138
Carlton, Paul K.: 56–58, 77
Carriacou Island, Grenada: 140
Carter, James (Jimmy) E.: xxiv, 117, 127–28, 133, 145, 157, 168, 234
Castro, Fidel: 33–34
Cedras, Raoul: 230–35
Celle, West Germany: 5–6
Central Intelligence Agency (CIA): 33, 128
Chambers, James E.: 200
Chamoun, Camille: 13, 19
Charleston AFB, South Carolina: 28, 67, 141, 171, 173–75, 206, 232
Chateauroux AS, France: 24–28, 31, 45
Chehab, Fouad: 19
China: xx–xxi, 4, 43, 60, 95–96, 106
Chinese: 33, 44, 51
    forces: xxi, 49
    troops: 44
Christopher, Warren M.: 214
civilian airlines: 103, 166
civilian-contract aircrews: 102
civilian-contract airlift: xxii
Clark AB, Philippines: 88–89, 92, 161
Clay, Lucius D.: 2
Clinton, William J.: 185, 194, 199–200, 215, 217, 229, 234
Coard, Bernard: 136, 140
Cold War: xvii–xix, xxii, xxvi, xxix, 2, 8, 10, 12, 32, 43, 116, 187, 208, 212, 217, 228
Colmar, France: 117, 120
Commander in Chief Atlantic: 39
Communism: xix, 198
Communist: xxii, 2, 7–8, 10, 33, 44, 60, 85, 88, 90, 92, 95–96, 104, 112, 114, 116, 120, 138
    China: 54
    Cuba: xxii
    forces: xviii, xxii, 85, 106
    government: xxiv
    invasion: xviii
    Khmer Rouge: xxii, 87, 96, 98–100, 102–5, 111, 113
    military forces: 85
    Party: 219
    rebels: xxi
Composite Air Strike Force (CASF): xviii–xxi, 11–12, 15, 20
    Bravo: 13, 18
Congo: xix, xxi, xxiii–xxv, 24–25, 27–32, 53–55, 57, 59–60, 115, 117, 121
Congo River: 25, 53
Congolese: 55–56, 58
    army: 24, 27, 55, 57–58
    civil war: 27
    government: 24
    loyalists: 55
    Parliament: 27, 53

soldiers: 25
troops: 56
Congress: xxv, 32, 98, 117, 144, 171, 217. *See also* United States Congress
Continental Air Command: 72–73
Continental Air Defense Command (CONAD): 37, 40
Corsica, France: 117–18, 120–21
Cosand, Kathleen R.: 121
Crete: 79
Croatia: 198, 201, 204–5, 220, 226–27
Crowe Jr., William J.: 165
Cuba: xx, 33–34, 36–39, 41, 64, 69, 116, 136–39, 141, 174, 230, 235
Cuban: xx, xxii, 33–37, 40, 136, 138, 141, 144, 174–75
   Communism: 64
   forces: 143
   military: xxv
   troops: 123–24, 140
Cubi Point, Philippines: 108
Cyprus: 28, 78

Da Nang, South Vietnam: 84–85, 87, 99, 103
Dakar, Senegal: 25, 117, 119–20, 122
Dean, John Gunther: 99–100
Defense Attaché Office (DAO): 84–86, 89–91
Defense Intelligence Agency: 108
Delashaw, Robert L.: 65–66
Delaware: 119, 141, 234
Delligatti, Robert S.: 89
Department of Defense (DOD): xxiii–xxv, 44–46, 92, 125, 136, 141, 143
Desert One: 129, 131–33
Dhahran AB, Saudi Arabia: 193, 195
Diego Garcia: 161, 164
Dihok (Dahuk), Iraq: 181
Diyarbakir, Turkey: 180–81
Djibouti: 210, 213
Dobrynin, Anatoly: 39
Dominican: xxii, 64, 66, 70, 72–73
   forces: 72
   government: xxii
Dominican Republic: xxii, 64–66, 68–69, 71–72
Donaldson AFB, South Carolina: 13
Dover AFB, Delaware: 141, 234
Drury, Richard T.: 89
Duke Field, Florida: 176
Dum Dum, Calcutta, India: 45, 47
Dyess AFB, Texas: 174, 232

Edwards AFB, California: 34
Eglin AFB, Florida: 70, 92, 174
Egypt: xxiii, 25, 56, 60, 75–79, 81, 133, 213
Egyptian forces: 76, 81
Eisenhower, Dwight D.: 13, 24, 32–33
England: xxv, 78, 148, 151–52, 160, 216, 222. *See also* Great Britain and United Kingdom

English: 31, 151, 154
Erding, Germany: 14
Ethiopia: 27, 29, 210, 213
Europe: xxi, 2, 4, 7, 13–14, 17, 24, 30–31, 54–55, 57, 117–18, 120, 123, 127, 181, 199, 201, 208, 210, 216, 226, 228
European: xix, xxi, 24, 54, 56, 78, 115, 118, 120, 123, 148, 151, 220
    Allies: 154
    force: 40
    troops: 123
Evreux-Fauville AB, France: 24, 27, 30–31, 46–47, 57, 59

Falconara AB, Ancona, Italy: 204
Farris, Kelton M.: 77
Fassberg, West Germany: 5
5th Allied Tactical Air Force: 221, 227
Florida: 34, 37–40, 138, 176, 216, 230, 232
Fogleman, Ronald R.: 186, 195, 212
Ford, Gerald R.: xxii, 85, 88, 90, 96, 98, 105–7, 109, 113–14
Forgan, David W.: 151
Fort Bragg, North Carolina: 65, 171, 174
Fort Drum, New York: 216, 231, 235
Fort Stewart, Georgia: 216
France: xxiii–xxiv, 2, 13, 24, 27, 45–46, 51, 57, 59, 116–17, 119–20, 148, 205–7, 212, 222, 226–27
French: 6, 31–32, 116–18, 120, 123, 182, 198, 200, 206, 208, 222, 224–25
    embassy: 153
    forces: 120, 191
    Foreign Legion: 118
    soldiers: 120
    troops: xxiv, 118, 120
Furstenfeldbruck, West Germany: 14

Gabon: 120
Galbraith, J. Kenneth: 44, 46, 49
Gatow, West Berlin, Germany: 5–6
Gaylor, Noel A. M.: 85, 88, 99, 107
Gbenye, Christophe: 53, 55–58
Geneva, Switzerland: 117
Georgia: 138, 175, 216, 232
German: 7, 200–201
    soldiers: 205
Germany: 2–3, 5–6, 8, 10, 14–15, 19, 78, 119, 125, 148, 180–81, 201, 205, 207, 222, 227
Ghana: 27
Global Positioning System (GPS): 200, 218
Golan Heights: 75–76
Goldwater-Nichols Department of Defense Reorganization Act of 1986: xxv, 144, 159, 161, 166
Gorazde, Bosnia: 200, 203, 220, 224–26
Gradwell, Burgess: 57
Grand Anse, Grenada: 139–40
Grantley Adams International Airport, Barbados: 139

INDEX

Great Britain: 2, 4, 10, 13, 27, 57, 59, 136, 148, 191, 205–7, 226. *See also* England and United Kingdom
Great Falls AFB, Montana: 7
Greece: 14, 20, 46, 78, 126, 216
Greek: 28, 79
Greenland: 78
Grenada: 136–44
   army: 138
   government: xxv
   troops: 140
Grenville, Grenada: 137–38
Griffiss AFB, New York: 216, 234–35
Grozny: 38
Guam: xxvii, 90, 92, 185
Guantanamo U.S. Naval Base, Cuba: 37, 38, 230, 235
Gulf of Oman: 129
Gulf of Sidra: 146, 154
Gulf of Thailand: 107–9, 111

Haiti: xxviii, 64, 229–31, 234–35
Haitian: 229–30
   airports: 234
   armed forces: 230
Halvorsen, Gail S.: 7
Hammarskjold, Dag: 27
Handy, John W.: 213, 216
Harriman, W. Averill: 49
Hawaii: 4, 87
Henry, Patrick M.: 198
Heyser, Richard S.: 34
Himalayas: 4, 44
   region: xx, 50
Hispaniola: 64
Holloway, James L.: 17
Homestead AFB, Florida: 37, 232
Hong Kong, China: 105
Howard AFB, Panama: 72, 171–72, 177
Hoyt, Michael: 55–56, 58
Hunter AAF, Savannah, Georgia: 175, 216
Hurlburt Field, Florida: 176
Hussein, Saddam: xxvii, 180, 184–86, 188–89, 194

Incirlik AB, Turkey: xix, 13, 126–27, 180, 181. *See also* Adana
India: xx, 4, 27, 43–47, 49, 51
India-China border: 44, 47
Indian: 44–47, 49–51
   army: 46, 49, 51
     brigades: 49
   border: 44
   government: xx, 45, 47, 50
   officials: 44
   troops: 46, 49
Indian Air Force (IAF): 46–47, 49–51

Indian Ocean: 161, 214
Indonesia: 98
Indus River Valley: 50
Inter-American Peace Force (IAPF): 71–72
International Red Cross: 56, 120, 202, 223
Iran: xxiv, xxvi–xxvii, 46, 125–29, 144, 158, 165–66, 180
Iran Ajr: 164
Iran-Iraq War: 157–58
Iranian: xxiv, 126, 128, 131, 133–34, 136, 145, 159, 161, 165–66
    government: 127
Iraq: xxvi–xxvii, 76, 166, 180–86, 188–95
Iraqi: xxvii, 180–81, 183–85, 190–94
    air force: 191
    army: 181, 185
    forces: 184–85
    government: 13, 180
    troops: 180, 185, 187
Irbil, Iraq: 185–86
Israel: xxiii, 20, 25, 75–81, 157
Israeli: 76, 80
    armed forces: 78
    government: 77
Italy: 78, 119, 127, 148, 182, 222, 227
Ivory Coast: 120
Izetbegovic, Alija: 220

Jamaica: 136, 141, 231
Jamerson, James L.: 180–82
James Connally AFB, Texas: 69
Johnson, Lyndon B.: 32, 57, 60, 64, 71
Johnston, Robert B.: 212
Joint Chiefs of Staff (JCS): xxiii, 20, 37–38, 64, 121–22, 125–28, 144, 161, 165, 171, 214, 234
Jordan: 17, 19–20, 193

Kadena AB, Okinawa: 108
Kamina, Zaire: 57–59, 117, 119, 121
Kampong Seila, Cambodia: 96
Kano, Nigeria: 25, 28, 30
Karadzic, Radovan: 220, 226
Kasavubu, Joseph: 24, 27, 53–55
Kashmir, India: 44
Katanga Province, Democratic Republic of the Congo: 27–28, 55, 115–17. *See also* Shaba Province
Kelly AFB, Texas: 6
Kelso, Frank B.: 148, 150
Kennedy, John F.: xix, 32, 34, 37–38, 44
    administration: xxi
Kennedy, Robert F.: 37–39
Kenya: 56, 210, 214
Khobar Towers, Dhahran AB, Saudi Arabia: 195
Khomeini, Ayatollah Ruhollah: 125–27
Khrushchev, Nikita: xix, xx, 33–34, 38–39

Kinshasa, Zaire: 119–22. *See also* Leopoldville
Kismayu, Somalia: 210, 214
Kleine Brogel AB, Belgium: 57
Koh Tang, Cambodia: 107–14
Kolwezi, Zaire: 116, 118–19
Kompong Som, Cambodia: 107, 111, 113
Kurdish: xxvii, 180–82, 184, 186, 188, 194
Kurds: xxvii, 180–81, 184–86, 194
Kuwait: xxvii, 76, 180, 184–86, 188, 190, 192–93
Kuwaiti: 161, 190
   forces: 191
   government: xxvii, 159

Ladakh, India: 44, 49–51
Lajes, Azores: 15, 17, 77–81, 127, 213
Langley AFB, Virginia: 15–17
Laughlin AFB, Texas: 34
Lawson AAF, Fort Stewart, Georgia: 175
Lebanon: xix–xx, 11, 13–15, 17, 20–21, 144
Leh, India: 49–51
LeMay, Curtis E.: 2, 4
Leopoldville, Democratic Republic of the Congo: 25, 28, 30–31, 53, 55–56, 58–59.
   See also Kinshasa
Liberia: 27, 117, 119
Libreville, Gabon: 117
Libya: xxv, 27, 78, 145–49, 151–53
Libyan: 146, 148–50, 152–55
   airspace: 79
   Arab army: 146
   Arab monarchy: 145
Little Rock AFB, Arkansas: 232
Lod Airport, Tel Aviv, Israel: 78–80
Lome, Togo: 117
Lorence, Paul: 154
Lubumbashi, Zaire: 117, 119–21
Lumumba, Patrice: 24, 27, 53–58

MacDill AFB, Florida: 34, 37, 232–35
Macedonia: 220
Maglaj, Bosnia: 203
Malta: 78–79, 153
Manzariyeh, Iran: 129–30, 133
Marcos, Ferdinand: 89
Martin, Graham A.: 85, 87–88, 90
Maryland: 230
Marxist: xix, 117
   government: 124
   rebels: xxiii
Masirah, Oman: 129, 131–33
Massachusetts: 200
Masterson, Kleber S.: 66
Mayaguez, SS: xxii, 105–14
McCoy AFB, Florida: 34, 37

McCurdy, Garvin: 89
McDonald, Wesley L.: 136
McGuire AFB, New Jersey: 232, 234
McNamara, Robert S.: xx, 41, 57
McNickel, Marvin L.: 68–69
McPeak, Merrill A.: 186
Mediterranean: 28, 78, 140
Mediterranean Sea: 30, 79, 137, 151, 154, 213, 216, 222
Mehrabad Airport, Tehran, Iran: 125–27
Meir, Golda: 80
Mekong River: 96
Merritt, Francis E.: 25
Metcalf III, Joseph: 136–37, 139
Meyer, Richard L.: 137
Miami, Florida: 64, 72, 169, 177
Michler, Earl E.: 89
Middle East: xxvii, 12–13, 17, 80, 157
Middle East Forces: 159–61, 165
Military Air Transport Service (MATS): xviii, 4, 7, 9, 13–14, 20, 24–32, 37–38, 40, 45, 65, 67–68, 72–73
Military Airlift Command (MAC): xxiii, xxv, 77–81, 92, 96, 98–99, 102, 108, 117–23, 121–22, 125–27, 140–41, 144, 160–61, 170–72, 174, 176
Milosevic, Slobodan: 220, 226
Missiles: 36–39, 76, 79–80, 146, 153–54, 191, 193, 226
    air-to-air: 36
    antiradiation: 192
    antitank: 76, 131
    attack: 38
    cruise: 185, 194
    intercontinental ballistic (ICBM): xx, xxiv, 37
    intermediate-range ballistic (IRBM): xx, 34–35
    M72 LAW (light antitank weapon): 131
    medium-range ballistic (MRBM): xx, 34–35
    Peacekeeper ICBM: xxiv
    SA-5: 146
    Silkworm: 161
    sites: xx, 37–38, 192
    surface-to-air (SAM): 36, 75, 153, 160, 185, 203, 225, 227
    surface-to-surface: 165–66
    Tomahawk: 192
Mladic, Ratko: 220, 226
Mobutu, Joseph: 27, 55
Mogadishu, Somalia: 210, 212, 214–17
Mombasa, Kenya: 210, 214, 216
Montana: 7
Montgomery, Thomas: 214–15
Morocco: 27, 76, 120–21
Moron AB, Spain: 57, 61, 213
Moslem: 78, 198, 200, 202–3, 205, 220, 225
    rebels: 13
    regime: xxiv
Murat Sidi Bilal Training Camp, Tripoli, Libya: 149

INDEX

Myrtle Beach AFB, South Carolina: 15–16, 69, 71

Nairobi, Kenya: 57
Nasser, Gamal Abdel: 56, 75
nation building: xxii, xxvi, xxviii, 215, 217
National Security Council: 20, 128, 149
National Security Decision Directive 138: 146
Neak Luong, Cambodia: 96
Nehru, Jawaharlal: 44, 49
Netherlands, The: 205, 226
New Delhi, India: 44–45, 51
New Jersey: 119, 232, 234
New York: 16, 127, 216, 231, 234
Nidal, Abu: 146
Nigeria: 27, 212
Nixon, Richard M.: 77, 85
Nol, Lon: 95, 98–99
Noriega, Manuel: xxvi, 168–69, 171–72, 177
North Atlantic Treaty Organization (NATO): xviii, xxviii, 8, 10, 81, 116, 118, 204–8, 220–28
   forces: 151
North Carolina: xxii, 16, 61, 65, 117, 139, 171, 174, 177–78, 232
Northeast Frontier Agency, India: 44
North Vietnam: xxi, 88. *See also* Vietnam and South Vietnam
   Communist government: 84
North Vietnamese: 85, 89, 95
   Army: 85, 88, 90
   forces: 87
   troops: xxi, 95
North, Gary L.: 184
Nuclear: 34, 37, 189, 194
   confrontation: xxvi
   deterrent: xvii–xxix
   facility: 185, 192
   forces: xviii, xx, xxvi
   stalemate: xxvi
   strike: 38
   war: xvii, xix–xx, 37, 41
   weapons: xvii, xx, 33, 41

O'Grady, Scott: 225, 227
Oakley, Robert B.: 212, 217
Oberpfaffenhofen, West Germany: 6
Oddur, Somalia: 210
Okinawa: 108, 114
Oklahoma: 70, 160
Olenga, Nicholas: 53, 55–56
Operation
   BABYLIFT: 86
   BLADE JEWEL: 171
   BLUE BAT: xix, 13, 20–21
   BLUE BLADE: 12
   DECISIVE ENDEAVOR: 227

DELIBERATE FORCE: xxviii, 225–28
DENY FLIGHT: xxviii, 188, 194, 203, 220–28
DESERT SHIELD: xxvii, 178
DESERT STORM: xxvii, 189, 191, 212–13, 217
DESERT STRIKE: 185, 194
DRAGON ROUGE: xxi, 57, 59–61, 117, 123
EAGLE CLAW: 128
EAGLE PULL: 99, 101, 103–4
EARNEST WILL: xxvi, 159–60, 162–64, 166
ELDORADO CANYON: xxv, 149, 151
FREQUENT WIND: 90–93
FULL STRIKE: 61
HATRACK: 20
IMPRESSIVE LIFT: 211
JOINT ENDEAVOR: 226
JUST CAUSE: xxvi, 171–72, 174, 177–78
LONG SKIP: xxi, 43, 45, 51
NEW ARRIVALS: 92
NEW LIFE: 92
NEW TAPE: xix, xxi, 24–32
NICKEL GRASS: xxiii, 77, 81
NIMROD DANCER: 170
NORTHERN WATCH: 186, 194
PACIFIC HAVEN: 185
PLAINFARE: 2
POWER PACK: 64–67, 69, 72–73
PRAYING MANTIS: 163
PRAYER BOOK: 171
PRESS AHEAD: 71
PROVIDE COMFORT: xxvii, 180–82, 184, 186–88, 194, 200
PROVIDE PROMISE: xxviii, 102, 198–207, 220, 222, 224
PROVIDE RELIEF: 210, 212, 214
PROVIDE SANTA: 201
QUICK LIFT: 205, 226
QUICK TRANSIT: 185
RED FOX: 66
RESTORE HOPE: 212–18
SAFARI: 24
SECOND CHANCE: 201
SHARP GUARD: 220
SKY WATCH: 220
SOUTHERN WATCH: xxvii, 184, 186, 188–95, 213
SUNDANCE: 20
UPHOLD DEMOCRACY: xxviii, 229–30, 235
URGENT FURY: xxv, 136–37, 139, 141, 143–44
VIGILANT SENTINEL: 193
VIGILANT WARRIOR: 185, 191, 193
VITTLES: xviii, 2–10, 102, 201
ZAIRE I: xxiii, 118, 121–24
ZAIRE II: xxiii, 120–24
Organization of American States (OAS): 71, 230
Organization of Eastern Caribbean States (OECS): 136
Pacific Ocean: 9, 90, 92, 168, 214

Pacific
    Command: 85, 99, 107–8, 159
    Fleet: 159
    Theater Airlift: 89
Pakistan: 43, 210–11
    soldiers: 215
Palam Airport, New Dehli, India: 46–47, 49
Pale, Bosnia: 205, 224
Palmer Jr., Bruce: 68, 70, 72
Panama: xxvi, 72, 168, 170–75, 177–78, 236
    Canal: xxvi, 64, 172, 178
        Treaty: 168
        Zone: 168
    City: 171–72
Panamanian: xxvi, 169, 177
    Defense Force (PDF): 168, 172, 176–77
    government: 170–71
    National Guard: 168
Paris, France: 118, 226
Patterson, Robert B.: 137
Paulis, Democratic Republic of the Congo: 55–56, 58–59
Pearls, Grenada: 136–39, 142–43
Persian Gulf: xxvi–xxvii, 157–61, 164, 191, 194
Philippines: 40, 89–90, 92, 99, 107, 114
Phnom Penh, Cambodia: xxii, 87, 95–99, 101–4, 106
    Pochentong Airport: 96, 98–99, 102–3
Point Salines, Grenada: 136–39, 141–43
Pope AFB, North Carolina: xxii, 16, 61, 65–67, 71–72, 173–75, 232–34
Port-au-Prince, Haiti: 230–31, 234–35
    International Airport: 230–31
Portugal: 27, 78, 81, 151
Portuguese: 32
Powell, Colin L.: 214, 217
PRIME BEEF (Base Engineer Emergency Force): 21
Puerto Rico: 64, 66, 138, 141, 232, 235

Qadhafi, Muammar: 145–49, 155

Ramey AFB, Puerto Rico: 66–69, 71
Ramstein AB, Germany: 17, 200, 202, 204
Rapid Deployment Joint Task Force (RDJTF): xxiv–xxv. *See also* United States Central Command
Rapid Reaction Force: 29, 205, 226
Reagan, Ronald W.: xxiv–xxvi, 136, 145–49, 155, 158–59, 165
Red Sea: 213, 216
Rhein-Main AB, Germany: 5, 13, 45, 198, 200–204, 207
Ribas-Dominicci, Fernando: 154
Rio Hato Airfield, Panama: 172, 175–76
Riyadh, Saudi Arabia: 162, 193
Riyadh Royal Saudi Air Force (RSAF) Base: 159–60
Roberts Field, Monrovia, Liberia: 117, 119, 121
Robins AFB, Georgia: 232
Rogers, Bernard W.: 148

Rome: 146, 148
Roosevelt Roads NAS, Puerto Rico: 138–39, 232, 235
Royal Air Force
    Alconbury, UK: 200
    Fairford, UK: 151, 164
    Lakenheath, UK: 149
    Mildenhall, UK: 151
    Upper Heyford, UK: 150
    Woodbridge, UK: 126
Ryan, Michael E.: 221, 225–26

Sadat, Anwar: 75–76
Sahand: 165
Sahara Desert: 25, 29–31
Saigon, South Vietnam: 84–92, 96, 98–99, 103
Saigon River: 88
Salaban: 165
Sams Jr., John B.: 216
San Isidro Airport, Dominican Republic: 66–73
Santa Cruz, Brazil: 71
Santo Domingo, Dominican Republic: xxii, 64, 66, 68–71, 73
Sarajevo: 198–208, 220, 223–26
    Airport: 201–2, 207
Saudi Arabia: 20, 76, 159–60, 162, 166, 193, 213
Saudi Arabian forces: 191, 193
Scandinavia: 27
Schwartz Jr., William H.: 25
Schwarzkopf, H. Norman: 137, 139, 144, 212
Scoon, Paul: 136, 138, 141
Scotland: 78
Seko, Mobutu Sese: 115–17
Senegal: 120–21
Serbia: 198, 226
Serbian: xxviii, 205, 220
    military forces: 227
Serbs: 198, 220, 224–26. *See also* Bosnian Serb
Seymour Johnson AFB, North Carolina: 65–66, 174, 232
Shaba Province, Zaire: 116–17, 124. *See also* Katanga Province
Shaikh Isa AB, Bahrain: 193
Shalikashvili, John M.: 181
Shaw AFB, South Carolina: 15–16, 34, 70, 160
Sicily: 79
Sidi Bilal, Libya: 152–53
Sidi Slimane, Morocco: 25
Sihanouk, Norodom: 95–96
Sinai: 75, 80–81
Sirsenk Airfield, Iraq: 182
Slovenia: 198, 220
Smith, Joseph : 2–3
Smith, Leighton W.: 221, 225
Solenzara, France: 117
Somalia: xxvii, 210–18
Souda Bay, Greece: 213

Soumialot, Gaston: 53–55, 58
South Carolina: 15, 34, 67, 69–70, 119, 141, 160, 171, 173, 206, 232
South China Sea: 91
South Vietnam: xxii, 84–85, 88, 93, 95–96, 98, 103–4, 106, 117. *See also* North Vietnam and Vietnam
South Vietnamese: xxi, 85, 87–88, 90
   army: 86
   government: 88, 112
   marines: 89
   military forces: 91
   troops: 95
Southeast Asia: xxi–xxiii, 61, 113–14, 144, 149, 177
Southwest Asia: xxiv, xxix, 160, 185
Soviet: xix–xx, 8, 32–39, 41, 50, 64, 75–76, 80, 123, 134, 144, 149, 152–53, 157–58
   ambassador: 39
   blockade: xvii
   expansionism: xvii
   forces: 2, 7
   strategy: xix
Soviet Union: xvii–xix, xxvi, xxix, 2, 12, 24, 33–34, 37–39, 54, 60, 75, 77, 116, 123, 136, 159, 198. *See also* Union of Soviet Socialist Republics
Spain: 31, 57, 61, 78, 119, 148, 206, 213, 216
Special Air Warfare Center: 70
Split, Croatia: 204–5, 226
Srebrenica, Bosnia: 200, 203, 205, 220, 225, 227
St. George's, Grenada: 136–40
Stalin, Joseph: 2, 8
Stanleyville, Democratic Republic of the Congo: 25, 55–59
Steinle, Paul C.: 25, 31
Stevenson, Craig D.: 184
Stewart AFB, New York: 16
Stockholm, Sweden: 28
Strait of Gibraltar: 79, 151
Strait of Hormuz: 159
Strategic Air Command (SAC): xxv–xxvii, 4, 7, 30, 37–39, 67, 69, 138, 144, 151, 160, 163–64, 171–72, 174
Strickler, Marshall H.: 25
Subic Bay, Philippines: 92
Suez Canal: 76, 80
Sweden: 27, 212
Swedish troops: 25, 28
Symington, Stuart: 8–9
Syria: xxiii, 75, 77–78, 148
Syrian
   forces: 76
   front: 80

Tactical Air Command (TAC): xviii, xix–xx, 20, 34, 37–40, 65–66, 70–73, 160, 162, 171, 174, 191
Tan Son Nhut, South Vietnam: 84, 86, 88–91
Tanks: 216
   M–48: 80
   M–60: 80

T-55: 76
T-62: 76
Tanker Airlift Control Center: 213, 216
Task Force
   Alpha: 14-15
   Atlantic: 171-72
   Bayonet: 172
   Bravo: 14
   Charlie: 14-15
   Delta: 19
   Echo: 19
   160: 165
   Pacific: 172
   Semper Fi: 172, 177
Tegel, West Berlin, Germany: 5-6
Tehran, Iran: xxiv, 46, 126-27, 129-30
Tel Aviv, Israel: 81
Tempelhof Airport, West Berlin, Germany: 3, 5-6
Tesanj, Bosnia: 203
Texas: 4, 34, 69-70, 174, 201, 232
Thailand: 91, 96, 98-99, 101-2, 105, 107, 109, 112, 114
Thatcher, Margaret: 148
Thurman, Maxwell R.: 171
Timberlake, Clare H.: 31
Tinker AFB, Oklahoma: 160
Tocumen Military Airfield, Panama: 172, 175-76
Togo: 120-21
Torrejon AB, Spain: 123
Torrijos International Airport, Panama: 168, 172, 175-76
Travis AFB, California: 45, 200
Traynor, Dennis: 86
Tri-wall aerial delivery system (TRIADS): 200, 207
Tripoli, Libya: xxv, 149-50, 153
   Airport: 149, 152-53
Truman, Harry S: xvii, 2
Tshombe, Moise: 24, 27, 54-58, 60, 115
Tunis, Tunisia: 30
Tunisia: 27, 30, 76, 146, 212
Tunner, William H.: 4, 6-10
Turkey: xix, 13-15, 19-20, 38-40, 78, 126, 180-88, 222
Turkish: 182
   government: 127, 184, 186
Turks: 28, 184, 186
Tuzla, Bosnia: 200, 220

Udbina, Croatia: 224-25
Uganda: 27, 54
Undorf, Robert W.: 110-11
Union of Soviet Socialist Republics: 41, 126. *See also* Soviet Union
United Kingdom: 44, 205, 222. *See also* England and Great Britain
United Nations (UN): xxvii-xxviii, 24, 26-28, 32, 53, 106, 148, 181-84, 189-92, 194-95, 198, 200-208, 210, 212, 214-15, 217, 220, 224-28, 230
   force: 27-28, 205, 214, 223, 225

INDEX

soldiers: 205
troops: xix, xxvii–xxviii, 31–32, 53, 210–11, 215, 222
United Nations Security Council: 24, 27, 180, 220, 223
    Resolution 688: 189
    Resolution 814: 214
    Resolution 816: 220
United States: xvii–xxviii, 2, 4, 6–8, 10, 12–13, 15, 32–33, 36–41, 43–46, 49, 50–51, 55, 57, 60, 64, 66, 71–73, 76–78, 81, 84–85, 87–88, 90, 92–93, 95, 97–99, 101–2, 106–7, 111–14, 116–18, 120–21, 123–28, 132–33, 136, 138–46, 148, 154, 159–61, 164–66, 168–72, 177, 180–82, 184–86, 190, 193, 198–99, 201, 206–8, 210, 212–17, 222, 225, 227–31, 235–36
    ambassador: xxii, 31, 85, 99, 148, 212
    forces: xxii–xxiii, xxvii, 17, 19, 64, 68, 71, 73, 92, 108, 114, 140–41, 144, 168, 170, 177, 191, 193–94, 212, 214, 217, 229, 235
    government: xvii, xxi–xxii, 84, 99, 101, 155
    military: xxii–xxiii, xxvi
    servicemen: 148
    troops: xxvii, 71–72, 83, 95, 138, 214–16
United States Air Force (USAF): xvii–xxiii, xxv–xxix, 4–6, 10–13, 15, 17, 24, 31–32, 37, 39, 41, 44–45, 47, 50, 58, 66–67, 70–73, 78, 80–81, 86, 88, 90–91, 93, 96, 98–103, 107–9, 111–12, 117, 120–21, 123–24, 128, 134, 137–44, 148–49, 154–55, 159–61, 164–66, 172, 175–77, 180, 182, 186–87, 189, 191–95, 198–208, 210, 212, 217, 222, 225, 227–32, 235–36
    ELF-ONE: 160, 162–63, 166
    forces: 51, 151, 160
    Squadron
        2d Aeromedical Evacuation: 202
        40th Aerospace Rescue and Recovery: 91, 100, 108
        7th Airborne Command and Control: 101
        963d Airborne Warning and Control: 162
        964th Airborne Warning and Control: 162
        965th Airborne Warning and Control: 162
        37th Airlift: 198, 202, 204, 207
        38th Airlift: 204
        312th Airlift: 201
        429th Air Reconnaissance: 17
        15th Air Transport: 45
        498th Bomb: 15
        42d Electronic Warfare: 150
        353d Fighter: 20
        512th Fighter: 224
        526th Fighter: 224
        331st Fighter-Interceptor: 69
        2d Mobile Communications: 47
        353d Tactical Fighter: 69
        776th Troop Carrier: 57
        777th Troop Carrier: 57
    Group
        1st Aeromedical Evacuation: 71
        105th Airlift: 201
        352d Special Operations: 200
        919th Special Operations: 176

11th Strategic: 151, 160
507th Tactical Control: 70
60th Troop Carrier: 3
61st Troop Carrier: 3

Wing
    7th: 232, 235
    23d: 204, 232
    1st Air Commando: 70
    552d Airborne Warning and Control: 160, 162
    62d Airlift: 202
    86th Airlift: 204
    314th Airlift: 16, 89, 232
    315th Airlift: 202
    317th Airlift: 199
    349th Airlift: 201
    435th Airlift: 198, 200, 202, 204
    436th Airlift: 234
    437th Airlift: 202, 206
    4505th Air Refueling: 16
    137th Air Transport: 70
    1501st Air Transport: 45
    1602d Air Transport: 25–28, 45
    1611th Air Transport: 45
    36th Fighter: 222
    86th Fighter-Interceptor: 17
    60th Military Airlift: 99
    436th Military Airlift: 119
    437th Military Airlift: 118
    438th Military Airlift: 119
    1st Special Operations: 176–77
    56th Special Operations: 91, 100, 108
    306th Strategic: 151
    307th Strategic: 101
    4080th Strategic: 34
    55th Strategic Reconnaissance: 38
    317th Tactical Airlift: 175
    374th Tactical Airlift: 88–89, 96
    345th Tactical Bombardment: 15
    48th Tactical Fighter: 149–50
    354th Tactical Fighter: 15–17, 20, 69, 71
    388th Tactical Fighter: 101
    432d Tactical Fighter: 101
    363d Tactical Reconnaissance: 15, 18, 36, 34, 69
    60th Troop Carrier: 14
    63d Troop Carrier: 13–14
    312th Troop Carrier: 16
    317th Troop Carrier: 14, 45–46
    463d Troop Carrier: 16, 57, 59, 61, 65, 68, 72
    464th Troop Carrier: 67

Division
    832d: 21

INDEX

322d Air: 14–15, 19–20, 24, 28, 31–32, 45, 47, 49–51, 61
    Detachment 1: 57
United States Air Forces in Europe (USAFE): 2–4, 8–9, 13, 18, 20, 24, 27–32, 45–47, 49, 61, 117, 149, 187, 198, 202, 216
United States Army (USA): xxii, xxiv–xxv, 7, 14, 17–18, 20, 37–38, 40, 44, 64–65, 67, 69, 71, 123, 128, 134, 138, 170, 172, 177, 183, 191, 212, 230–31, 234
    airborne troops: 140
    forces: 137, 191
    Rangers: 130–31, 138–40, 143, 172, 175–76
    soldiers: 235
    Special Forces: 177
    troops: xxv–xxvi, xxviii, 13, 139, 141
    units: 234
    XVII Airborne Corps: 173
    XVIII Airborne Corps: 171
    82d Airborne Division: xxii, 64–65, 67, 117, 139, 143, 172–73, 175, 230
    832d Airborne Division: 21
    15th Field Hospital: 71
    193d Infantry Brigade: 172
    5th Infantry Division: 170
    7th Infantry Division: 170, 172
    24th Mechanized Infantry Division: 137
    10th Mountain Division: 231, 235
    75th Ranger Regiment: 175
United States Atlantic Command (USACOM): 68, 126, 136, 143, 230–31, 234–35
United States Central Command (CENTCOM): xxv, 159–61, 166, 187–88, 191
United States Congress: 85. *See also* Congress
United States Department of State: 31, 38, 46, 123, 125–27
United States European Command (USEUCOM): 9, 148, 161, 187–88, 198
United States Marine Corps (USMC): xxiii, xxv, 13, 17, 19, 37, 40, 64, 66, 85, 87, 90–91, 99, 100–101, 103, 108–10, 112, 114, 126–27, 134, 137–40, 143, 150, 170, 172, 183, 191, 212
    forces: 137
    Marines: 13, 37, 64, 100, 108–9, 111–13, 139–40, 170, 177–78, 212
        2d Expeditionary: 170
        31st Marine Amphibious: 99
United States Navy (USN): xxv, 7, 39, 64, 91, 103, 106, 108–9, 111–12, 128, 134, 140, 146, 148–49, 152–54, 161, 164–66, 181, 183, 185, 191–94, 212, 222
    SEALs: 138, 140, 165
    Special Forces: 177
    Naval
        air strike: xxv
        blockade: xx
        escort: xxvii
        forces: 137, 146, 159
        units: xxvi
    Second Fleet: 136
    Sixth Fleet: 13, 17, 146, 148, 150
    Seventh Fleet: 91
    USS
        America: 152, 154
        Boxer: 66
        Coral Sea: 108, 111, 114, 152, 154

Harold E. Holt: 108
Henry B. Wilson: 108
Independence: 140
Midway: 91
Nimitz: 129, 131–34
Okinawa: 99, 102–3
Pueblo: 106
Samuel B. Roberts: 165
Vincennes: 166
United States Southern Command (USSOUTHCOM): 71, 171
United States Special Operations Command: xxiv, 134, 165
U Thant: 27, 56
U-Tapao Royal Thai Naval Airfield, Thailand: 96, 98–99, 108

Vandenberg, Hoyt S.: 4
Viccellio, Henry: 17, 47
Vicenza, Italy: 221, 228
Vienna, Austria: 27, 146, 148
Vietnam: xxii, xxiv, 84–85, 92–93, 95, 144. *See also* North Vietnam and South Vietnam
Vietnam War: xxii, 171
Vietnamese: 85–88, 90–93
Virginia: 15
Vung Tau, South Vietnam: 85–86, 88–89

Wajir, Kenya: 210
Wake Island: 90, 92
Walters, Vernon: 148
Washington, D.C.: 38–39, 70, 188
Watkins, Tarleton H.: 24
Webb AFB, Texas: 69
Weinberger, Caspar W.: 159, 161, 217
Welch, William L.: 65–66
Wessin y Wessin, Elias: 72
Westbrook III, Sam W.: 149, 151
Wheelus AB, Libya: 25, 28, 30, 47
Wiesbaden, Germany: 2, 5, 47
Willi Tide, SS: 165
Wilson, Woodrow: 109, 168
World War II: xviii, 2, 4, 10, 25, 47, 176, 227
Wright, Robert L.: 224–25
Wright-Patterson AFB, Ohio: 207, 226

Yemen: 210, 213
York, Robert H.: 65
Yugoslavia: xxviii, 198, 219–20, 223, 226

Zaafaraniyah Nuclear Fabrication Facility, Iraq: 192
Zagreb, Croatia: 198
Zaire: xxiii–xxiv, 115–24
Zepa, Bosnia: 200, 203, 205, 220, 225, 227

www.ingramcontent.com/pod-product-compliance
Lightning Source LLC
Chambersburg PA
CBHW081915170426
43200CB00014B/2730